AFGHAN

Politics, Economics and Society

Revolution, Resistance, Intervention

Bhabani Sen Gupta

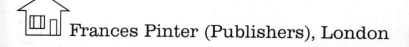 Frances Pinter (Publishers), London

© Bhabani Sen Gupta 1986

First published in Great Britain in 1986 by
Frances Pinter (Publishers) Limited
25 Floral Street, London WC2E 9DS

British Library Cataloguing in Publication Data

Sen Gupta, Bhabani
  Afghanistan: politics, economics and society.
  —(Marxist regime)
  1. Afghanistan—Social conditions
  I. Title   II. Series
  958 '1044   HN670.6.A8

  ISBN 0-86187-390-4
  ISBN 0-86187-391-2 Pbk

Typeset by Joshua Associates Limited, Oxford
Printed by SRP Limited, Exeter

Editor's Preface

'Of all the Marxist revolutions in the Third World, the Afghan revolution has been most conspicuously from above.' This book, which is unique in many respects, contains a detailed analysis of that revolution and its internal and external dynamics. It is also a timely and important contribution to overall analysis of Marxist regimes. The study of Marxist regimes has for many years been equated with the study of communist political systems. There were several historical and methodological reasons for this.

For many years it was not difficult to distinguish the eight regimes in Eastern Europe and four in Asia which resoundingly claimed adherence to the tenets of Marxism and more particularly to their Soviet interpretation—Marxism–Leninism. These regimes, variously called 'People's Republic', 'People's Democratic Republic', or 'Democratic Republic', claimed to have derived their inspiration from the Soviet Union to which, indeed, in the overwhelming number of cases they owed their establishment.

To many scholars and analysts these regimes represented a multiplication of and geographical extension of the 'Soviet model' and consequently of the Soviet sphere of influence. Although there were clearly substantial similarities between the Soviet Union and the people's democracies, especially in the initial phases of their development, these were often overstressed at the expense of noticing the differences between these political systems.

It took a few years for scholars to realize that generalizing the particular, i.e. applying the Soviet experience to other states ruled by elites which claimed to be guided by 'scientific socialism', was not good enough. The relative simplicity of the assumption of a cohesive communist bloc was questioned after the expulsion of Yugoslavia from the Communist Information Bureau in 1948 and in particular after the workers' riots in Poznań in 1956 and the Hungarian revolution of the same year. By the mid-1960s, the totalitarian model of communist politics, which until then had been very much in force, began to crumble. As some of these regimes articulated demands for a distinctive path of socialist development, many specialists studying these systems began to notice that the cohesiveness of the communist bloc was less apparent than had been claimed before.

Also by the mid-1960s, in the newly independent African states 'democratic' multi-party states were turning into one-party states or military dictatorships, thus questioning the inherent superiority of liberal democracy, capitalism and the values that went with it. Scholars now began to ponder on the simple contrast between multi-party democracy and a one-party totalitarian rule that had satisfied an earlier generation.

More importantly, however, by the beginning of that decade Cuba had a revolution without Soviet help, a revolution which subsequently became to many political elites in the Third World not only an inspiration but a clear military, political and ideological example to follow. Apart from its romantic appeal, to many nationalist movements the Cuban revolution also demonstrated a novel way of conducting and winning a nationalist, anti-imperialist war and accepting Marxism as the state ideology without a vanguard communist party. The Cuban precedent was subsequently followed in one respect or another by scores of regimes in the Third World who used the adoption of 'scientific socialism' tied to the tradition of Marxist thought as a form of mobilization, legitimation or association with the prestigious symbols and powerful high-status regimes such as the Soviet Union, China, Cuba and Vietnam.

Despite all these changes the study of Marxist regimes remains in its infancy and continues to be hampered by constant and not always pertinent comparison with the Soviet Union, thus somewhat blurring the important underlying common theme—the 'scientific theory' of the laws of development of human society and human history. This doctrine is claimed by the leadership of these regimes to consist of the discovery of objective causal relationships; it is used to analyse the contradictions which arise between goals and actuality in the pursuit of a common destiny. Thus the political elites of these countries have been and continue to be influenced in both their ideology and their political practice by Marxism more than any other current of social thought and political practice.

The growth in the number and global significance, as well as the ideological political and economic impact, of Marxist regimes has presented scholars and students with an increasing challenge. In meeting this challenge, social scientists on both sides of the political divide have put forward a dazzling profusion of terms, models, programmes and varieties of interpretation. It is against the background of this profusion that the present comprehensive series on Marxist regimes is offered.

This collection of monographs is envisaged as a series of multi-disciplinary textbooks on the governments, politics, economics and society of these countries. Each of the monographs was prepared by a specialist on the country concerned. Thus, over fifty scholars from all over the world have contributed monographs which were based on first-hand knowledge. The geographical diversity of the authors, combined with the fact that as a group they represent many disciplines of social science, gives their individual analyses and the series as a whole an additional dimension.

Each of the scholars who contributed to this series was asked to analyse such topics as the political culture, the governmental structure, the ruling party, other mass organizations, party-state relations, the policy process, the economy, domestic and foreign relations together with any features peculiar to the country under discussion.

This series does not aim at assigning authenticity or authority to any single one of the political systems included in it. It shows that depending on a variety of historical, cultural, ethnic and political factors, the pursuit of goals derived from the tenets of Marxism has produced different political forms at different times and in different places. It also illustrates the rich diversity among these societies, where attempts to achieve a synthesis between goals derived from Marxism on the one hand, and national realities on the other, have often meant distinctive approaches and solutions to the problems of social, political and economic development.

University College *Bogdan Szajkowski*
Cardiff

Contents

List of Maps

List of Tables

Preface

This book has not been easy to write. The Afghan revolution and the Soviet military intervention have polarized East and West in a grim confrontation of will and might. One of its first casualties is objectivity. There is a terrible dearth of reliable credible information, and almost every image is coloured. The problem is minimal for those who have partisan views, maximal for those who would like to be fair and objective. I have taken information from both polarized sources. Where necessary I have shown the discrepancies in the Notes.

This volume is different in format from most of the others in this series. The Marxist regime in Afghanistan is far from stabilized. It is at best a regime-in-the-making amidst blood and tears of millions of Afghans. The Soviet invasion or intervention—I have used the latter expression which I believe is justified under international law—cannot be separated from the Afghan revolution nor from the Marxist regime in Kabul. The resistance, with its external supports and internal–external ramifications, is also an integral fact of the revolution.

This volume is more about the story of the Afghan revolution and its weak offspring, the Marxist regime in Kabul, than a comprehensive profile of a Marxist government in charge of the destiny of a Third World nation.

In writing this volume, I have drawn upon the knowledge and expertise of many students of Afghanistan and international communism. I have also relied often on my own observations, conversations and investigations in Kabul, Pakistan, Moscow and Washington DC. I have gained from my participation in an international conference on Afghanistan held in February 1985 at Columbia, North Carolina, under the auspices of the Department of International Relations of the University of North Carolina.

The untimely death of my wife delayed the writing of the manuscript by a year. I am grateful to the General Editor of the Series, Bogdan Szajkowski, for giving me the time to complete it.

I must thank the Director of the Centre for Policy Research, New

Delhi, Dr V. A. Pai Panandikar, for giving me research and secretarial facilities for writing this volume; the information and cultural affairs ministry of the Afghan government and the Afghan embassy in New Delhi for making available a lot of official reports; an Indian friend in the United States (who does not wish to be identified) for sending me a number of the latest books on Afghanistan; and Mr M. C. Roy for helping with secretarial work.

Centre for Policy Research,   *Bhabani Sen Gupta*
Diplomatic Enclave
New Delhi, India
1 July 1985

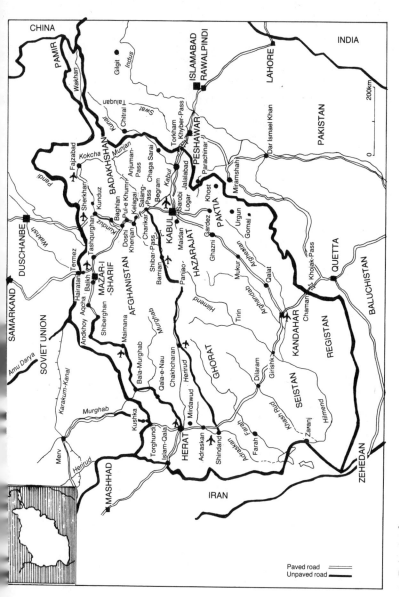

1. Principal towns

Source: Adapted from Albert A. Stahel and Paul Bucherer, *Afghanistan: 5 Jahre Widerstand und Kleinkried*, Frauenfeld, Switzerland, Huber & Co., 1984

Paved road
Unpaved road

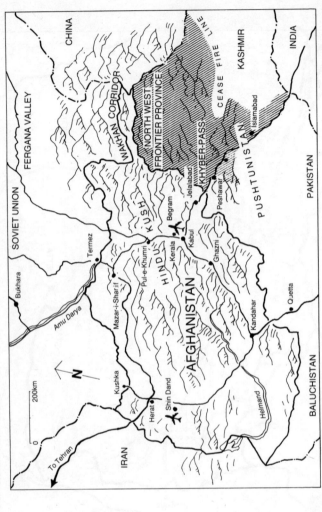

2. Physical features

Basic Data

Official name	Democratic Republic of Afghanistan
Location	Central Asia, bounded by USSR (N), Iran (W), Pakistan (E & S), China (NE). Landlocked.
Population	14.2 million
Population density	58 inhabitants per square mile
Population growth (% p.a.)	1.9 (average, CIA, 1984)
Population distribution	84.6% rural (UNFPA, 1980)
Life expectancy	42.0 (male), 43.4 (female) (UNFPA, 1975–80)
Infant death rate (per 1,000)	217 (official estimates, 1972–73)
Ethnic groups	60.5% Pushtuns; 30.7% Tajiks; 5% Uzbeks; Mongolian and others. (All citizens are Afghans.)
Capital	Kabul, 800,000
Major cities	Kandahar, 191,405; Herat, 150,497; Mazar-i-Sharif, 110,367; Jalalabad, 57,824; Kunduz, 57,112; Baghlan, 49,240; Maymana, 40,212; Pul-i-Khomri, 32,695 and Ghazni, 31,985
Land area	249,933 square miles, of which 22% is arable land, 0.8% under permanent crops, 10% permanent pasture, 75% other
Land boundaries	3,424 miles
Official languages	Pushtun and Persian. Persian is the chief language of government and business. Since 1978, minority languages have been given official recognition and are now officially patronized.
State and government	The Democratic Republic of Afghanistan, proclaimed after the Marxist 'revolution' of 27 April 1978, is a state in which the People's Democratic Party of Afghanistan (PDPA), the communist party, governs as the leading element in a coalition of 'democratic'

forces, that is, political forces that are opposed to feudalism, capitalism and imperialism. DRA signed a defence treaty of peace, friendship and co-operation with the USSR in December 1978. Afghanistan has been in a state of intense and widespread civil war since 1978, which was highly accelerated following the Soviet military intervention of 27 December 1979 and became internationalized, with the Islamic insurgents receiving help from Pakistan, the United States, Saudi Arabia, China and several other countries.

In 1985 (at the time of going to press) government authority is vested in a 57-member Revolutionary Council which has a 7-member Presidium. Both are headed by Babrak Karmal, who is also Commander-in-Chief of the Armed Forces. His installation followed the deposition of Hafizullah Amin on 27 December 1979.

Karmal has been trying to build an institutionalized mass base for the PDPA regime. A National Fatherland Front was created in 1981 with PDPA representatives, and national and tribal groups. A National Assembly was held in 1984 after 'elections' to local assemblies. Opposed to the PDPA regime are a number of *mujahidin* groups, who have failed to form a grand alliance.

Membership of international organizations	UN and most of its specialized agencies; Asian Development Bank (ADB)
Foreign relations	Diplomatic relations with some 29 countries; representatives of 26 countries residing in Kabul
Political structure Constitution	After the coup of 27 April 1978 (the Saur Revolution), the 1977 Constitution was abolished. Both Taraki and Amin promised new constitutions but were removed from power before any drafts had been prepared by special commissions which they had

appointed. On 21 April 1980 the Revolutionary Council ratified the Basic Principles of the Democratic Republic of Afghanistan. These are to remain valid until the ratification of the Constitution by a Loya Jirgah (National Assembly).

Highest legislative body	7-member Presidium
Highest executive body	57-member Revolutionary Council
Prime Minister	Soltan Ali Kishtmand
President	Babrak Karmal
Ruling party	People's Democratic Party of Afghanistan (PDPA)
Secretary General of the PDPA	Babrak Karmal
Party membership	Officially 90,000 in over 2,000 primary party organizations. These figures are almost certainly inflated. More realistic estimates give the PDPA membership around 11,000.
Exports	US$670 m. (1982)
Imports	US$880 m. (1982)
Main exports	natural gas (20% of US$ value), fruit, nuts, karakul pelts, raw cotton, carpets, wool
Main imports	sugar, tea, petroleum products, tyres, textiles, vehicles and machinery, pharmaceuticals, fertilizers
Destination of exports	USSR, 59.3%; Pakistan, 8.7%; India 6.1%; West Germany, 5.9% (1982)
Source of imports	USSR, 60%; Japan, 12.2%; Hong Kong, 4.3%; India, 2.7% (1982)
Main trading partners	USSR, Japan, Pakistan
Foreign debt	recent data n.a.
Armed forces	
Total active armed forces	46,000 (actual strength disputed)
Military service	two years (1984)
Army personnel	40,000
Organization	3 armoured divisions; 11 infantry divisions; 2 mountain infantry brigades; 1 artillery brigade; 3 commando regiments
Major equipment inventory (1984)	350 medium tanks; 100 light tanks; 400 APCs; 900 guns/howitzers; 100 mortars; 50 rocket launchers; 350 towed AA guns; 20 SP AA guns; 'Sagger', 'Snapper' ATGWs

Air Force personnel	6,000
Organization	1 light bomber squadron; 12 fighter/ground attack squadrons; 4 transport squadrons; 2 helicopter squadrons; 1 air defence division, 1 operational conversion unit
Major aircraft types (1984)	135 fighter/ground attack; 72 helicopters; 31 cargo-transports

Education and health

Schools and institutions (1984)	3,825 primary schools (enrolment 1,115,930); 447 secondary schools (124,488); 42 vocational schools (4,427) and 5 universities and higher institutions (enrolment 12,868)
Adult literacy	About 8%
Population per hospital bed	approx. 3,333 (WHO, 1981)
Physicians per population	0.74 per 10,000 (WHO, 1981)

Economy

GNP	US$19 bn. (UN, 1978)
GNP per capita	US$211 (UN, 1978)
GDP by %	agriculture and forestry, 69.1%; mining, manufacture and utilities, 13.8%; construction, 3.2%; commerce, 9.1%; transportation and communication, 3.5%; other 1.5% (UN, 1982)
Inflation	3% (UN, 1980)
State budget (expenditure)	US$117.3 m. (1980)
(revenue)	US$344.7 m. (1980)
Defence expenditure	US$326 m. (1981)
Monetary unit	100 puls = 1 afghani
Main crops	wheat, cotton, fruit, nuts
Other agricultural products	karakul pelts, wool, mutton
Industrial products	textiles, soap, furniture, shoes, carpets, fertilizers, cement
Natural resources	natural gas, crude oil, coal, copper, talc, sulphur, gems
Electric power generation	1,100m. kWh (1984)
Capacity	415,000 kWh
Atomic power plant	none

Natural gas production	2,595 bn. cu.m. (1975–76)
Labour profile	60.5% agriculture; 11.1% manufacturing; 1.3% construction and mining; 1.7% transport and communication; 3.5% commerce (1979)
Tourists	6,623 (1980)
Land tenure	2.4 acres per capita
Main religions	Muslim, 99% (of which 90% are Sunni and 10% Shia); small groups of Hindus, Jews, Parsees

Transport and communication

Roads	11,652 miles of all-weather and gravel road (1984)
Vehicles (registration 1982)	34,904 passenger vehicles; 30,800 trucks and buses (WMVD)
Railroads	Prior to Soviet military intervention, there were plans to build 1,127 route miles of rail-road during 1978–79
Civil aviation	41 airfields—35 usable, 11 with permanent-surface runways, 8 with runways over 8,000 ft. Total scheduled airline traffic: 163 passenger-kilometres (ICAO, 1980)
Radio	135,000 sets in use, or 82 per 1,000 population (1982)
Television	12,000 sets (1982)
Newspapers	13 dailies, with a combined circulation of 130,000, or 9.9 per 1,000 population (1983)
Telephones	23,680 sets in use, or 1.57 per 1,000 population (1980)

Population data

Median age	17.4 years (UNFPA, 1980)
Age distribution	0–14: 45.1%
	15–64: 52.3%
	65+: 2.6% (UNFPA, 1975–80)

Population Forecasting

The following data are projections produced by Poptran, University College Cardiff Population Centre, from United Nations Assessment Data published in 1982, and are reproducecd here to provide some basis of comparison with other countries covered by the Marxist Regimes Series.

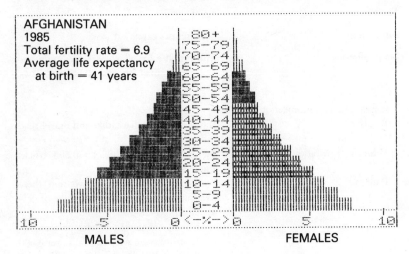

AFGHANISTAN
1985
Total fertility rate = 6.9
Average life expectancy
   at birth = 41 years

MALES   FEMALES

Projected Data for Afghanistan 1985

Total population ('000)	18,092
Males ('000)	9,258
Females ('000)	8,834
Total fertility rate	6.90
Life expectancy (male)	40.0 years
Life expectancy (female)	41.0 years
Crude birth rate	48.4
Crude death rate	23:1
Annual growth rate	2.53%
Under 15s	44.92%
Over 65s	2.44%
Women aged 15–49	22.20%
Doubling time	28 years
Population density	28 per sq. km.
Urban population	18.0%

Glossary

Angar	'Burning Embers' (newspaper)
Aqsa	secret police
aqsaqal	village elders
arbab	village headman
Dari	variation on the Persian language
des	a Nuristani community
ghulam bachha	servant boys
hakim	Islamic judge
Hazaras	racially pure Afghan group
Hezb-i-Inquelabi-i-Meli	central committee of the National Revolutionary Party
Jamaat-i-Islami	Islamic Council
Jamaat-i-Ulama	council of religion
Jawanam-i-Musulman	Muslim Youth
jihad	religious war
jirgah	conference
jirib	measure of land (0.25 hectares)
Kalashas	Nuristani Islamic communities
Khalq	'Mass' political party
Khalq	Khalq party newspaper
loya jirgah	assembly of tribal leaders
madrasa	college of Islamic sciences
Mahr	dowry
mujahidin	guerrilla
Nida-yi-Khalq	'Voice of the People' (newspaper)
Olelamar	secular leader ruling with the authority of Allah
Parcham	'Flag' political party
Parcham	Parcham party newspaper
Pathans	people of the North-West Frontier Province
Pravda	Russian newspaper
Pushtun	dominant ethnic group in Afghanistan
ruhani	Sufi spiritual leaders
Sarandoy	military police force
Saur	April (revolution)
Setem-i-Meli	'National Opposition' (Maoist) faction
spetsnaz	special purpose commando units
Tajiks	second largest ethnic group in Afghanistan

Tass	Soviet news agency
ulemas	Muslim scholar, jurist
Watan	'Homeland' (newspaper)

Abbreviations

ADB	Asian Development Bank
ANLF	Afghan National Liberation Front
CIA	Central Intelligence Agency
CPI	Communist Party of India
CPI-M	Communist Party of India—Marxist
CPSU	Communist Party of the Soviet Union
DPPA	Democratic Party of the People of Afghanistan (Khalq)
DRA	Democratic Republic of Afghanistan
GOA	Government of Afghanistan
JIA	Islamic Society of Afghanistan
MRD	Movement for the Restoration of Democracy
NLF	National Liberation Front
NWFP	North-West Frontier Province
PCT	Parti Congolais du Travail (Congolese Labour Party)
PDPA	People's Democratic Party of Afghanistan
PDRY	People's Democratic Republic of Yemen
PKI	Indonesian Communist Party
RGA	Royal Government of Afghanistan
RTV	Refugee Tented Villages
SDI	Strategic Defence Initiative
USAID	United States' overseas aid programme

1 History and Political Traditions: The Monarchy

Of all Marxist regimes in the world, Afghanistan stands out with a uniqueness of its own. Within twenty months of the Saur or April revolution of 1978, a 'limited contingent' of Soviet troops, variedly estimated between 85,000 and 110,000, intervened in Afghanistan to defend the fledgling Marxist regime from internal collapse and external military-political-religious pressures. The Soviet military intervention instantly transported Afghanistan to the volatile dynamics of Soviet–American antagonism. For the five years of the 1980s, Afghanistan has remained a major bone of contention in the second cold war. The Marxist regime has continued to be under the protection of Soviet arms. It has been fighting an internal war with several anti-regime armed guerrilla forces. These forces have been receiving arms and materials as well as training from the United States, Iran, China, Egypt and Saudi Arabia. The Marxist regime claims that Americans and others impart military training to Afghan *mujahidin* at more than one hundred bases which ring the city of Peshawar in the North-west Frontier province of Pakistan, and that the great bulk of military supplies reach the rebels through Pakistan territory. While the internal war, the two interventions, the Soviet military presence, and the arid hostility of the cold war confuse and blur the personality of the Marxist regime, a search for a comprehensive political settlement of the Afghan problem has been zigzagging for more than three years under United Nations auspices. With firm Soviet commitment of arms and financial aid, the Marxist regime appears to be slowly gaining ground. Its defenders and its opponents agree that time is in its favour over a long haul. It has been trying to construct a National Democratic state along the non-capitalist model of economic and social development. Its survival is not in doubt. If it can stand on its own feet and bring about relatively rapid socio-economic transformation of Afghanistan, the impact of the political experiment may well be felt on a number of backward Islamic countries in South and South-west Asia.

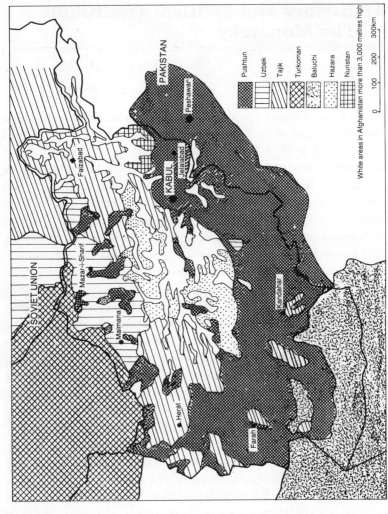

3. Ethnic distribution

In the middle of 1985, as this book is being written, everything about Afghanistan is controversial. Facts, myths and fantasies derived from two divergent sources—one American-Pakistan, the other Soviet-Afghanistan—cut across almost every image one may put together of the Marxist regime, its present state of health, its future prospects. American perceptions of the PDPA as a communist party differ vitally from those of the PDPA leaders as well as the image-makers of Moscow. The two warring sides even present two different pictures of Afghan history, its society, population, cultural and economic structures and institutions. The events preceding the Afghan revolution are also interpreted differently in the two camps; the events that have followed the revolution totally lack shared terms of reference.

Afghanistan is a landlocked country roughly the size of Texas. Arid, economically backward, it has a strategic location at the conjunction of Central Asia, the Persian Gulf and the subcontinent. To the north, it shares the southern frontiers of the USSR, to the south-west, it has common borders with Iran, while its eastern frontiers, disputed for the last thirty-seven years, but traditionally demarcated by the Durand Line, are with Pakistan. Afghanistan has also a narrow border with China in the remote reaches of the Hindu Kush in the north-east.

The first-ever census, taken in 1979, placed the total population of Afghanistan at 15.5 million. The Afghans are a gaggle of ethnic nationalities. They speak twenty languages, though most of them understand two—Pushtun or Pashto, and Dari, which is a special variation of Persian. The Pushtun are the dominant nationality or tribe. They are kinsmen of the Pathans of the North-west Frontier province of Pakistan, as the Baloch and Brahuis are kinsmen of Pakistani Baluchistan. Similarly, to the north, the Tajiks, who make up the second largest nationality of Afghanistan, have their kinsmen in the Soviet Central Asian republic of Uzbekistan. To the west, the Afghan-Iran border divides as many as six nationalities—Baloch, Brahui, Turkmen, Fariswan, Aimaq and Siailbash. Only the central mountains of Afghanistan nurse a tribe or nationality that is purely and completely Afghan—the Hazaras. Afghanistan is exposed to several cross-national ethnic pressures, a political-geographic factor that has come sharply into focus since the revolution of 1978, both for internal and external reasons.

The diversity of the population of Afghanistan has persauded some scholars to emphasize the country's 'regionalism'. As one scholar puts it, 'There is no doubt that throughout history the existing geographical and cultural regionalism has been a major obstacle toward the social, economic, and political integration of the country.'[1] Geography has also precluded close integration.[2] One-third of Afghanistan is high mountains. Roadbuilding in these areas is six times as costly as in the flatlands. Few rivers are navigable even to small craft. The climate is arid, with a wide annual range of temperature reaching 48.8°C (120°F) in summer in the south-west, and falling to −26°C (−15°F) in the winter in the Hindu Kush mountains. There is very little rain except between January and April.

Afghanistan's total land area is 652,090 sq. km. In most parts of the country, from 50 to 75 per cent of the agricultural land—14 million hectares are cultivable, but only 5.34 million hectares are irrigated—is not used owing to insufficient precipitation and inadequate irrigation facilities.

It is estimated that of the total area of the country only 7.8 million hectares comprising 12% of the total area is under cultivation. Of this area only 5.3 million hectares or 9% have irrigation facilities, but due to lack of water only 2.5 million hectares or 4% of the total area of the country is used regularly every year. Moreover, only 4.78% of the total area of the country, mostly in the south and east, is under forests. Much of the uncultivated countryside, however, provides summer grazing land for large herds of sheep, goats, and camels, all of which are important sources of income.[3]

Afghanistan's most convenient access to the sea lies through Pakistan, or alternatively on the road and rail container route through the Soviet Union. A network of asphalted highways connecting the main towns has been built with Soviet and American help; 1,060 km. of new road were planned to be constructed by 1984. All-weather highways link Kabul with Kandahar and Herat in the south and east, Jalalabad in the west and Mazar-i-Sharif and the Oxus, on which there is water traffic. A feasibility study for the country's first railway, linking Kabul to Pakistan and Iran, was completed in 1977. Work cannot begin until peace and amity is restored between Afghanistan and its two Islamic neighbours.

The generation of men and women that has grown up in the world since World War II has little knowledge of how Afghanistan dominated relations between two empires—the British in the south and the Russian in the north—for well over a hundred years, spanning three centuries. 'Modern Afghanistan', wrote Lord Curzon, 'is indeed a purely accidental geographical unit, which has been carved out of the heart of Central Asia by the sword of conquerers or the genius of individual statesmen.'[4] Geography placed the central Asian kingdom precariously between the competition and conflicts of two swelling imperial themes. Associated with the modern history of Afghanistan are the names of the great empire builders of Britain—Gladstone and Disraeli, Dufferin, Lansdowne, Lytton, Ripon, Kitchener, Grey, Curzon and Churchill.

The Great Game of nineteenth-century geopolitics was played by British imperial power expanding northward from the Indian subcontinent and Russian imperial power pushing southward through Central Asia. Britannia ruled the seas. But the Jewel of the Crown—India—was most vulnerable from the historical invasion routes in the north-west; across these routes lay Afghanistan. The British were determined to secure these invasion routes from Russia; they were also anxious to avoid a war with the Tsar over Afghanistan. The two imperial powers never did actually collide over Afghanistan. However, a clash did occur between Afghans and Russians in March 1885 at Pul-i-Khatum, near Panjdeh, along the Afghan frontier. The Afghan force had to retire with heavy losses, leaving Panjdeh to the Russians. A British-Indian force, stationed nearby, did not stir, but did, in fact, retreat to a safer spot. Gladstone, then Prime Minister, spat fire, obtained from a roused House of Commons a vote of credit of £6,500,000 to meet the situation created by Russian victory at Panjdeh. The British public cried out for war. British bellicosity was matched by Russian. However, diplomatic negotiations led to the establishment of the north-western frontier of Afghanistan. The British made major concessions; the Russian frontier now extended to the very threshold of Afghanistan. The ruler of Afghanistan approved of the transaction; but the Afghans began to nurse serious doubts as to whether they could ever expect Britain to defend Afghanistan in a war with Russia.[5] The nation of Afghanistan was thus delineated by the clash of two empires. But to live in peace with Russia became a cardinal principle of Afghanistan's external relations.

It was the British rather than the Russians who wanted to annex Afghanistan to their empire. More than a hundred years ago, in the 1870s, the Russians wanted Britain to concede Afghanistan as a buffer state between the two empires. The British refused. The term 'buffer state' did not enter the vocabulary of protracted Anglo–Russian diplomatic negotiations, though other concepts such as 'neutral zone' and 'neutral territory' did. In the agreement of 1873, Afghanistan was not recognized as a buffer state because Russia conceded that it was beyond its sphere of influence. Even in the convention of 1907, which came into force without the consent of the ruler of Afghanistan, and which generated Afghan fears that the two imperial powers might one day partition the country between themselves, Afghanistan was not given the status of a buffer state. It retained its 'independence' within the British sphere of influence; Britain promised not to interfere in its internal affairs, or to tamper with its territorial integrity. Russia was given the right to have only 'local contacts' with Afghans across the border. For substantial business with Afghanistan, the Tsar had to use the good offices of Britain.[6]

Fearing an expansion of Russian influence to Afghanistan, the British invaded the country twice as pre-emptive measures, but both expeditions failed, and the British forces had to retreat. The 'fearful' tribesmen who had turned back the mighty British from their rugged land became the subject of legend. Kipling, poet of the British Indian empire, warned his countrymen:

> When you're wounded an' left on Afghanistan's plains,
> An' the women come out to cut up your remains,
> Just roll to your rifle an' blow out your brains,
> An' go to your Gawd like a soldier.

Afghanistan only succeeded to some extent in easing out of the British sphere of influence after World War I. The process began with the coming of Amanullah to the throne in Kabul, with his declaration that Afghanistan was no one's puppet, but a fully independent sovereign state. His demand that this status for Afghanistan be formally recognized by the British Government and the Viceroy of India was rejected by both. But support came immediately from a newly-born state: the Soviet Union. Lenin recognized Afghanistan as a sovereign independent state and received a friendly communication from Amanullah. In less than a month the British declared war on Afghanistan. Nearly 35,000 British troops, equipped with aircraft, heavy artillery and armoured cars, were opposed by a rabble of 50,000 Afghan soldiers. Even then victory eluded the British. The shortest of the three Afghan wars did not last more than thirty days. The armistice, signed on 3 June 1919, led to a peace treaty on 8 August, but in neither did the British formally recognize Afghanistan as a sovereign state. Afghanistan, however, signed a treaty of friendship with the Soviet Union on 28 February 1921. Lenin, in a letter to Amanullah, observed that the treaty gave 'formal consolidation to the friendship and mutual sympathy between Afghanistan and Russia which have grown and strengthened in the past two years.' 'Both countries', Lenin added, 'prize their independence and freedom for themselves and for all nations of the East . . . There are no issues between Afghanistan and Russia likely to lead to differences, or even cast a shadow on Russo–Afghan friendship.'[7] Following the agreement with the USSR, Afghanistan concluded treaties with Turkey, Iran, France and Italy. These treaties finally led to an Anglo–Afghan Treaty in which Britain renounced control of Kabul's external relations.

The treaty with the Soviet Union helped Amanullah to establish Afghanistan's independence, but Afghan–Soviet relations were never fully trouble-free. Before the 1921 treaty was concluded, Amanullah, taking advantage of the civil war and intervention in the newly-born Soviet state, had joined Turkey in an effort to create a Pan-Islamic state in Central Asia. Friction between Afghanistan and the Soviet Union had reached a critical point in the spring of 1920 when Afghan troops moved into the Merv–Kushk area. In return, the Soviets encouraged the Jamshidi tribe to raid Afghan settlements. The 1921 treaty was signed after the Soviet forces had brought the civil war under control and had retaken lost territories in Central Asia. The 1921 treaty did not remove all friction between Moscow and Kabul, despite the friendly rhetoric of Lenin. The Afghans resented the Soviet policy of assimilation in Bukhara and Khiva, and renewed their agitation in those areas. In July 1922 the Soviets handed to the Afghan minister in Moscow a list of demands including an end to Afghan raids in Turkistan. In December 1925, the Afghans accused the Soviets of invading their territory north-east of the Panjdeh district near the Oxus river.[8] However, the two countries concluded a non-aggression treaty in 1926. Peace prevailed. But Amanullah did not give up his claims to a patch of territory south of the Oxus.[9]

In 1929, Amir Amanullah fell from power because of intensified opposition in Afghanistan to his drive for reform and modernization. (The British had a hand in the Amir's fall.) Neither Britain nor the Soviets recognized a short-lived government set up by the rebel leader, Amir Habibullah. After Habibullah was deposed and executed on 15 October 1929, Nadir Khan became King of Afghanistan. He tried to reduce Soviet influence in Afghanistan but at the same time concluded several treaties with the USSR, including the neutrality treaty of 1926, renegotiated in 1931, a postal accord in 1932 and an agreement to appoint officials to study frontier disputes, also in 1932;[10] and a trade agreement. During Nadir Khan's rule, Soviet–Afghan relations improved considerably, even if they were not entirely free of strain. Nadir followed a policy of non-intervention in Soviet Central Asia, and refused to allow northern Afghanistan to be used to promote anti-Soviet, Pan-Islamic, and Pan-Turkic activities.

Under the next Afghan monarch, Muhammed Zahir Shah, who ruled Afghanistan for forty years from 1933 to 1973, Kabul's relations with the Soviet Union improved considerably. Muhammed Zahir Shah renewed the Soviet–Afghan Mutual Assistance pact concluded in 1931, and signed a new trade agreement in 1936. Russian exports to Afghanistan had doubled in volume between 1928 and 1933; now, under the renewed mutual assistance deal, the Soviets began to supply technologies and experts to Afghanistan to help Kabul build a textile industry. When Afghanistan signed an alliance in July 1937 with Iraq, Iran and Turkey, the Saadabad Pact, as it was called, was welcomed by the Soviet Union as an extension of the collective security system Moscow was then championing.[11] In 1936 Afghanistan began to receive arms from the Soviet Union.

Afghanistan improved its relations with Germany in the 1930s and in October 1936 concluded a protocol with Germany under which German arms were to be supplied to Kabul. Afghanistan maintained its friendly relations with Germany through World War II. This was not liked by Britain and the USSR but neither wanted to take punitive action against Afghanistan.

In the post-World War II period, Afghanistan first tried to keep balanced relations with the Soviet Union and the United States, which now replaced Britain as the leading Western power. This balanced relationship policy was pursued from 1946 to 1953. Then came a ten-year period when Afghanistan tilted towards the Soviet Union in view of a sharp deterioration in its relations with Pakistan. After 1963 Afghanistan appeared to be trying to normalize its relationship with all its neighbours, including Pakistan. In the post-war period the countries with which Afghanistan interacted most were the USSR, the United States, and Pakistan, with India as a somewhat distant fourth.[12]

In the period 1946–53 Afghanistan tried to maintain this balanced relationship with the Soviet Union and the United States, engaging both in its economic and infrastructural development. It refused to join the chain of anti-Soviet alliances forged under American initiative; a military alliance between Kabul and Washington was forbidden under the Soviet–Afghan treaty of 1931 which was still in force. Immediately after World War II, however, the Afghan monarch appeared to be looking up to the United States both as a protector of its independence from a Soviet threat (the imminent withdrawal of British imperial power from the Indian subcontinent left Afghanistan without its traditional policy of balancing Russian influence with British) and as provider of development assistance. The Afghan Prime Minister, Shah Mahmud Khan, son of King Zahir Shah, declared in 1946 that he was

convinced that America's championship of the small nations guarantees my country's security against agression. America's attitude is our salvation. For the first time in our history we are free of the threat of great powers' using our mountain passes as pathways of empire. Now we can concentrate our talents and resources on bettering the living conditions of our people.[13]

American response was initially lukewarm. The situation, however, changed in the late 1940s after the promulgation of the Truman Doctrine which brought Turkey and Greece under American protection. The United States began with a modest aid programme in Afghanistan. Between 1949 and 1979, American economic aid to

Afghanistan totalled about $500m.[14] American aid failed to make much of an impact on Afghanistan because it was small in size, the interest rate was heavy and the loans carried short-term maturities.[15]

But military aid was another matter. In the vacuum left by Britain's withdrawal from the Indian subcontinent in 1947, the Afghan ruling family envisaged creating an American military connection as crucial defense against Soviet power. Despite its prodigious security assistance efforts elsewhere, the Truman Administration remained unimpressed—either with Afghanistan's strategic importance or with the efficacy of American military aid containing Soviet expansion in that theater. A Pentagon study in 1949 concluded that Afghanistan's 'geographic location coupled with the realization by Afghan leaders of Soviet capabilities presages Soviet control of the country whenever the international situation so dictates'. Two years later, an NSC assessment of Afghanistan's situation was equally resigned: 'The Kremlin apparently does not consider Afghanistan's meager assets to be worthy of serious attention . . . (but] there is little doubt that Afghanistan could be conquered . . .' The analysis did note that 'In the event of an invasion, it is possible that certain elements . . . would continue to resist.'[16]

The South-Asian state with which the United States wished to build a close political-military relationship was Pakistan. Pakistan appeared to be far more attractive to Americans than Afghanistan or even Iran in the late forties as the key nation that could make the United States a key lever in the stability and security of the Persian Gulf–South Asian region, and in this major policy decision the United States was strongly influenced by the British foreign office. Afghanistan had a long-standing claim to the Pushtun-speaking areas of Pakistan which bordered it. In 1949 the Afghan ruler denounced the frontier agreements with the departed British, and demanded that the Pushtun-speaking areas in Pakistan be given independence as a sovereign state of Pushtunistan. In response, Pakistan closed the border, on which Afghanistan depended heavily for imports. Thus ensued a verbal war of attrition between the two Muslim neighbours. The United States, coveting Pakistan's participation in a chain of military alliances ringing the Soviet Union, could not but turn down Afghan requests for military aid. 'To repeated Afghan entreaties for military aid, US officials cited a tempering of the "Pushtunistan" issue as a crucial precondition.'[17]

In 1954, the United States concluded a military treaty with Pakistan, and the latter joined the chain of interlocking alliances forged by Washington to contain Soviet influence. A year earlier, King Zahir Shah had appointed his first cousin, Mohammed Daoud Khan, an ardent protagonist of Pushtunistan, to the office of prime minister. That year, 1953, was also the year of the death of Stalin; by 1954 the Soviet Union had entered a new era in foreign and domestic policies with Nikita Khrushchev as leader of the CPSU.

As the British withdrew from the Indian subcontinent and the two conflict-locked sovereign states of India and Pakistan were born, Afghanistan proceeded to improve and stabilize its relations with the Soviet Union. A boundary agreement was concluded in 1948. It was followed in 1950 with a four-year trade agreement. The Soviet–Afghan treaty of 1931 was extended. In 1954 the Soviets voiced support for Pushtunistan, thus trying to draw Afghanistan toward its influence as the United States brought Pakistan into its own. The Soviets began to extend economic aid to Afghanistan, which had the distinction of becoming the first country with which the Soviets started experimenting with their post-Stalin Third World diplomacy. Khrushchev visited Afghanistan in December 1955, shortly after his and Bulganin's highly successful visit to India. In that year Daoud convened a *Loya Jirgah* (an assembly of tribal leaders) which approved his concept of a security treaty with the Soviet Union. A big programme of Soviet development started with a $100m. credit for road building, developing industries and irrigation and the construction of a modern airport at Kabul; this was followed by a credit of $80m. to build a highway from the Soviet border through the city of Herat to the commercial centre of Kandahar close to the border with Pakistan in the south. This project was financed by long-term, low-interest credit which the Afghans were to pay back with exports of their agricultural produce which, at that time, consisted of grain, fruit, nuts and cotton. The Soviets also extended credits, once again long-term, low interest, as well as technical aid to explore for petroleum reserves near Sherghan in north-west Afghanistan, just south of the Russian border, to develop Afghanistan's rich reserves of natural gas, and minerals like iron, copper, lead and coal. As large-scale comprehensive economic and trade relations flowered and Afghanistan began to figure in Soviet scholarly writings as a model relationship between two countries with different social and political systems, the Soviets approved the first delivery of Russian and East European weapons to Kabul. In a long span of twenty-five years, up to the historic watershed of December 1979, Afghanistan received from the USSR $2.5b. in economic and military aid. The Soviets trained 6,000 Afghan university students and 4,000 Afghan soldiers of officer rank.

Years later, Khrushchev recorded his Afghan diplomacy with a considerable hint of satisfaction:

I went there [to Afghanistan] with Bulganin . . . on our way back from India [in 1955]. We were invited by the King of Afghanistan to stop over in Kabul . . .. It was . . . clear that America was courting Afghanistan . . .. The Americans were undertaking all kinds of projects at their own expense, building roads, giving credit loans, and so on. But . . . the Americans hardly bother to put a fig leaf over their self-centered, militaristic motives. . ..

It's my strong feeling that the capital we invested in Afghanistan hasn't been wasted. We have earned the Afghans' trust and friendship, and it hasn't fallen into the Americans' trap; it hasn't been caught on the hook baited with American money.[18]

Daoud came to be known as the 'red prince', but Afghanistan remained a non-aligned country, leaning, in foreign policy matters, toward India rather than the Soviet Union. Daoud's rhetoric was assertively nationalist:

Our whole life, our whole existence, revolved round one single focal point— freedom. Should we ever get the feeling that our freedom is in the slightest danger, from whatever quarter, then we should prefer to live on dry bread, or even starve, sooner than accept help that would restrict our freedom.[19]

In the first decade of Daoud's prime ministership, 1953–63, a funda-mental contradiction tore across Afghanistan's political economy. The economic infrastructure developed considerably, but it was unmatched by political development. King Zahir Shah had tried in the late forties and early fifties to introduce elections to the people of Afghanistan. A 'liberal parliament' was formed in 1952 through 'relatively free elec-tions [by Afghan standards]'[20] and the result was the election of fifty leftist candidates in a House of 120, and several newspapers sprang up suddenly, flaunting titles that unnerved the King and his royal kinsmen—*Nida-yi-Khalq* (Voice of the People), *Watan* (Homeland), *Angar* (Burning Embers). Fearing a coming assault on the status quo, the King suppressed the 'liberal parliament' before the second election, which was due in 1952, crushed the newspapers and arrested the leftist leaders. The ferment created by the 'liberal parliament', however, continued. Daoud came to power in 1953, riding on the crest of this ferment. In a decade he built a close political, economic and military relationship with the Soviet Union, whose influence was now felt on urban, educated youth and on the officer corps in the army. Daoud, an enlightened, forward-looking man, realized that something had to be done to bridge the growing chasm between economic and infra-structural development and political stagnation. He wrote a series of letters to the King, proposing a sweeping programme of reforms, including the granting of a constitution and elections to a national assembly. The King did not respond and relations between the two became strained. At this time, Daoud's passionate support for Pushtunistan led to exchanges of fire across the Afghan–Pakistan border. Pakistan closed the border, which immediately affected Afghanistan's transit trade with India. Daoud tendered his resignation as Prime Minister and for ten years waited in the sidelines of Afghan politics, becoming a rallying point for urban leftist intellectuals.[21]

King Zahir Shah appointed Muhammed Yusef as Prime Minister but determined to take personal charge of the state. Although he eased Daoud out of office, he was impressed by some of the dismissed Premier's premonitions. It appeared that he would be moving towards the establishment of a constitutional monarchy. A partly elected and partly nominated *loya jirgah* was convened to approve a constitution which the King promulgated in October 1964. Two elections were held under this constitution, in 1965 and in 1969; the third, scheduled for August/September 1973, was never held. Several vital provisions of the constitution were never implemented; for instance, political parties were forbidden, and provincial and municipal councils not created. However, the Press Law of 1965 made way for a relatively open political life. This was manifested in the appearance of a number of leftist newspapers. And, more significantly, in the founding in 1965 of the Khalq party, the first Marxist party in Afghanistan.

The full name of the political party was the People's Democratic

Party of Afghanistan (PDPA). Twenty years later, at a function celebrating the twentieth anniversary of the party, Babrak Karmal, now President of the People's Democratic Government of Afghanistan, recalled, 'Twenty years ago, while working in semi-underground conditions, I proclaimed at the midnight hours from a simple rostrum covered with a red cloth the first congress of our party. It was attended by 27 delegates, elected a central committee of seven members . . .'[22] There is some dispute as to whether Babrak Karmal or Noor Mohammad Taraki was the number one leader of the PDPA. In one of its earliest political formulations, PDPA, also popularly known as Khalq, announced that it would work to remove 'the boundless agonies of the oppressed people of Afghanistan', and linked itself to the Bolshevik revolution and the Communist Party of the Soviet Union (CPSU) in the world-wide 'struggle between international socialism and international capitalism.'[23]

Predictably, the ruling family and the 300,000 mullahs of Afghanistan were alarmed. Twenty members of the upper house of the Afghan parliament asked for an official investigation of the activities of Khalq. The party organ, *Khalq*, defending the PDPA from these accusations, declared that it was not opposed to the tenets of Islam, it recognized that Afghanistan 'in its present state of development' needed the monarchy, and that it was for full implementation of the fundamental rights enshrined in the constitution. However, the PDPA continued to advocate land reforms and nationalization of certain types of properties and businesses, and was regarded by the monarchy as violating the fundamentals of Islam. The newspaper *Khalq* was banned in May 1966.[24] In late 1977, the PDPA split into two. The original Khalq group continued to be led by Taraki; the other group, Parcham, broke away, led by Karmal. A third group of Marxists formed a pro-China faction—a splinter group of Parcham, it was known as Setem-i-Meli—Against National Oppression. Its manifesto called for 'Maoist-type mobilization, and a localization of power in the countryside, i.e. for a combination of Maoism and ethnocentrism.'[25]

While the *Khalq* had been suppressed, the organ of the Karmal faction, *Parcham*, continued to be published until July 1969. This led the Taraki group to see the Karmal group as being close to royalty and the Taraki group derisively called it the 'Royal Communist Party'. The

Parcham faction claimed to be closer to the Soviet Union, but Moscow sought to maintain an equal level of contact with both. Neither was regarded as a communist party meriting invitation to CPSU congresses or even relations with the Soviet party.

Zahir Shah was caught between the forces of the status quo and the forces of change and he lost a sense of political direction. Daoud, who had been waiting for his chance to return to the helm of power, and who had built up contacts with leftist elements in the political factions as well as in the army, now took an extraordinarily bold step. In an almost bloodless coup, on 17 July 1973, Daoud not only recaptured power, but also abolished the monarchy and proclaimed a republic. He drew support from a large number of young reform-orientated army officers who had had military training in the Soviet Union but were nationalist in their political fervour. The political career of Afghanistan entered an altogether new phase.

In the last decade of the Afghan monarchy, the United States conducted a reappraisal of the prospects for and the need for influence-building in Afghanistan, and came to the conclusion that the landlocked country was not of great importance to the United States nor was the United States in a position to dislodge the Soviet Union from the vantage point it had achieved since the early fifties. Robert G. Neumann, who was United States ambassador to Afghanistan from 1966 to 1973, has recorded that John Foster Dulles had turned down Afghan requests for military aid because of the 'location and poor communications' of Afghanistan, which would require the United States to undertake 'an enormous logistics effort', risking an escalation of the cold war with the USSR.[26] Neumann's successor, Theodore L. Eliot, jnr., gave two additional reasons for the conclusion reached by Dulles. The first was the close relations the United States had built up with Pakistan. The second was that 'sending military equipment to Afghanistan would so alarm the Soviets that they would make some kind of move against Afghanistan.'[27]

Neumann prepared a policy review for the State Department in June 1971. In this review he said,

For the United States, Afghanistan has at the present limited direct interest; it is not an important trading partner; it is not an access route for US trade with others; it is not presently . . . a source of oil or scarce strategic metals; . . . there are no treaty ties or defense commitments; and Afghanistan does not provide us with significant defense, intelligence, or scientific facilities . . . .. However, Afghanistan has important interests for us which have in large part derived from its strategic location between Central Asia and the Indian subcontinent.

[Neumann added,] The United States has long understood that Afghanistan has had litle choice but to have close relations with the USSR. Among the factors are: the long border, the slowly developing desire to transform the economy and the concomitant need for massive economic assistance; the decision to have a modern military force; and the intermittent preoccupation with its quarrels with Pakistan. The Soviets responded to these opportunities and since 1953 they have assiduously exploited the situation and developed a strong position here with considerable and growing influence and leverage.

Neumann listed additional factors that worked in favour of the Soviet Union in Afghanistan. The Soviets were Kabul's largest trade partner. Kabul owed a large debt to Moscow. Soviet agents had infiltrated the Afghan Government. Afghanistan was dependent on Soviet arms. The Soviets exercised strong influence over the Afghan education system, especially higher education, and operated a large exchange programme for military and civilian students as well as the rest of the Soviet propaganda apparatus existing in Afghanistan. The result of all this was that 'although the RGA (Royal Government of Afghanistan) may not do everything the Soviets wish it to do, it is rare that the RGA does what the Soviets strongly wish it *not* to do.'

2 Afghanistan as a Republic

The Republic of Afghanistan proclaimed by Daoud on 17 July 1973, with himself declared its Founder, President and Prime Minister, became, five years later, the victim of its own political contradictions. Perhaps it was a grave mistake on Daoud's part to abolish the monarchy, for more than a century the one unifying factor in a land divided by geography and ethnicity. A first cousin of the King, Daoud could easily have proclaimed himself his successor. Daoud's second major mistake stemmed from his essentially authoritarian imperatives. He toppled the monarchy with the declared objective of stopping King Zahir Shah's apparent moves to improve relations with the United States and lower Afghanistan's commitment to Pushtunistan. But Daoud ended up with a pact with the Shah of Iran which was seen by others as a move to reduce Soviet influence in the Northern Tier and an understanding with Pakistan's volatile President, Zulfikar Ali Bhutto, to run down the Pushtunistan movement. Known as the Red Prince, Daoud came to power with the support, if not the active help, of leftist-orientated army officers and Parcham, but soon moved to reduce, and if possible eliminate, Marxist influence in the fledgling republic. Having aroused hopes that Afghanistan would now have a genuine representative government, Daoud determined to constitute a *loya jirgah* that would be only partly elected. As Louis Dupree put it,

The nation waited for the president to appoint a new cabinet, and most observers hoped that he would bring in new blood, including some moderate leftists. But at this crucial turning point—in the opinion of this author [that is, Dupree], the crucial turning point—Mohammad Daoud reverted to the behaviour of an old tribal khan. He appointed friends, sons of friends, sycophants, and even collateral members of the deposed royal family.[1]

Instead of introducing true democracy in Afghanistan, Daoud made it into a single-party state: the National Revolutionary Party, and he himself nominated the members of its central committee.

As already noted, King Zahir Shah's flirtation with the concept of a constitutional monarchy created a political–intellectual ferment in Kabul and other cities. The Marxists made fiery speeches in parliament which were then printed in their newspapers. They organized street rallies and demonstrations, some of which resulted in bloodshed. Parliament passed legislation legalizing political parties, but the King refused to sign it. Robert G. Neumann, who was American ambassador in Kabul, saw the situation in 1972 as the King's 'crisis of survival'. Wrote Neumann in a policy review for the State Department,

For the king and leadership groups, survival is the first objective with all other goals considered secondary. The result is an excessively cautious governing style which invariably seeks to balance off external and internal forces perceived as threatening the regime's power. Domestically new power groups increasingly press for progress. . . . Barring progressive decisions or very good luck, the survival of the present Government for more than another year is problematical.[2]

Neumann proved prophetic. Zahir Shah fell within thirteen months and, with him, the Afghan monarchy too.

There was a clause in the constitution which Zahir Shah gave his people which forbade any member of the royal family from becoming Afghanistan's prime minister. This clause might have been intentionally drafted to keep the ambitious and powerful Daoud from returning to the prime ministership. In his decade of hibernation, Daoud developed close relations with leftist army officers as well as with leaders of the Parcham faction of Marxists led by Babrak Karmal. Having been one-time commander of the central-forces garrison, with the rank of a lieutenant-general, Daoud had some clout with the Afghan military. He discussed his political plans with various opponents of the Zahir Shah regime, including army officers considered to be pro-Soviet and leaders of both Marxist factions, Parcham and Khalq.[3]

King Zahir Shah went to Italy in July 1973. While he was taking mud baths at Ischia on 17 July, army units supporting Daoud took over strategic points in Kabul. There was hardly any organized resistance. In a nearly bloodless coup that lasted a few hours, Daoud captured power, and immediately announced on the radio the establishment of a 'republican system, consistent with the true spirit of Islam'.[4]

Daoud promised to introduce 'basic reforms' and 'real democracy to serve a majority of the people'. The 'pseudo-democracy' of Zahir Shah, he told the people of Afghanistan, was a 'corrupt system' that rested 'on personal and class interests, intrigues and demagogy.' The reforms Daoud actually introduced proved to be half-way measures, sharpening discontent in most political groups. As already noted, he set up a new parliament that was only partially elected. He appointed a cabinet which disappointed his well-wishers. Finding the cabinet useless, Daoud turned to an inner cabinet consisting of the Vice-President, Sayyid Abdullah, the Defence Minister, General Ghulam Haider Rasuli, the Interior Minister, Abdul Qader-Nuristani, and his own brother, Mohammad Naim. Six ministers resigned in protest when Daoud personally selected all members of the central committee of the National Revolutionary Party (Hezb-i-Inqelab-i-Meli). Even when they withdrew their resignations at the request of Daoud, it was clear that his regime lacked a solid and coherent political foundation.[5]

Babrak Karmal's Parcham group extended its support to Daoud when the latter proclaimed the republic. Daoud began with what appeared to be a large measure of co-operation from Parcham. Several leftists were given important government positions, including one in his cabinet. Two army officers known to be Parcham men—Major Abdul Qader and Mohammad Aslam Watanjar—were posted to strategic positions. About 160 ardent youth cadres of Parcham were sent out to the rural areas to mobilize support for the republic. But they were effectively neutralized by the provincial elite. Most of them returned to Kabul utterly disillusioned, and some adequately corrupted and made cynical by rural realities.

Nevertheless, the American ambassador in Kabul, Theodore Eliot, jun., perceived Daoud's regime to be under the considerable control of Parcham. 'In the first months following the coup', Eliot wrote later,

there were reports that Babrak Karmal and his principal lieutenants . . . formed a kind of subcommittee of the GOA [Government of Afghanistan] Central Committee, which passed on all senior appointments in the GOA. During the same period, there were reported defections from . . . Khalq . . . to the Parchamists, who clearly appeared to be coming out on top.[6]

Within two years Daoud tried to reduce the influence of the left. The leftist member of the cabinet was dismissed—Major Qader lost his command. Several other Parcham officials were either dismissed or sent abroad on diplomatic assignments. Eliot saw, in 1975, a significant change in Daoud's relationship with the left. According to him,

there has been no explicit voicing of anti-left sentiment . . . While Daoud's domestic 'platform' might be described 'populist' and includes calls for land reform and educational parity, he publicly eschews socialism and carries the banner of unreconstructed Islam during all his public speeches. Those leftist officials who have been fired have never had their ideological beliefs thrown up as a reason for dismissal, but only their corruption or inefficiency . . .

We believe it most likely that Daoud, having used the left to gain power, is now methodically trying to whittle it down. . . . He is sniping away at some of the left's strength without leaving himself open to charges of discrimination against it . . .

In looking toward its future the Afghan left must contend with an entrenched autocrat who does not brook competition . . .[7]

In foreign policy, Daoud gave an appearance of distancing Afghanistan somewhat from the Soviet Union without being actually able or willing to do so. The Soviets gave no evidence of being annoyed or concerned by his foreign policy moves. On the contrary, they were pleased with Daoud's support for the Brezhnev concept of Asian collective security—they gave Afghanistan $437m. in economic aid in 1975; while, in the following year, a new Afghan–Soviet trade treaty envisaged a 65 per cent increase in two-way trade by 1980. The *Wall Street Journal* perceived Soviet influence in Afghanistan in September 1977 to be greater than that of any other power.[8] This was confirmed by three American diplomats who had served in Kabul in the 1960s and 1970s. Ambassador Neumann said that the fall of Daoud had little to do with his foreign policy; whatever changes he might have brought about did not alter the fact that the Soviets were stronger in Afghanistan than any other external power. Daoud was 'unfailingly careful' not to hurt Soviet interests. In the United Nations, Afghanistan always voted with the Soviet Union or the Non-Aligned Group. Within Afghanistan, no Western activity was allowed in the northern part, even if it was only economic activity. Westerners had no access to projects built by the Soviets, even when built in collaboration with Kabul. Soviet economic data were not disclosed to Western correspondents or diplomats.

Ambassador Eliot agreed with Neumann's assessment. He told an American author that Daoud's foreign policy did not cause any anxiety in Moscow and was not a factor in the latter's downfall. This was also the view of Eliot's political counsellor, Bruce Flatin.

All three Americans also insist that the US government for years had made it clear to the Soviets that the United States understood Soviet security interests in Afghanistan and had no thought of disturbing the peaceful relations between the USSR and Afghanistan. As Ambassador Neumann put it, 'The United States never tried to weaken the Soviet-Afghan relationship. We recognized that the Soviet Union had a vital interest in Afghanistan, while the United States did not. Any attempt on our part to replace the Soviet Union would have been a no-win situation. There was no point in our picking a quarrel with the Soviets over Afghanistan. No American interest would have been served by such a policy.'[9]

Daoud paid his last visit to Moscow in April 1977, about a year before his overthrow. *Pravda* reported that his talks with Brezhnev had taken place 'in an atmosphere of friendship, trust and mutual under-standing'; the two neighbours were 'filled with resolve to further consolidate their relationship of friendship and good-neighbour coop-eration.'[10] A month later, the Soviet leadership sent Daoud a cable that was warm in appreciating the results of his visit.

The Soviets had no apparent reason to feel unhappy about Daoud's foreign policy, but they had little reason to be pleased with Daoud's flirtations with the Shah of Iran, and his sudden determination to improve relations with conservative Islamic countries like Saudi Arabia and the UAE. For a year and more of his presidency, Daoud kept close to the USSR and increased his support to the Pushtunistan movement, so much so that in 1975 Pakistan's Bhutto accused him of training 15,000 Pushtuns and Balochs in Afghanistan for infiltration into the two Pakistani provinces of the North-west Frontier and Baluchistan. In 1976, after Jimmy Carter had entered the White House, American diplomacy became somewhat active in Afghanistan. The National Security Council, headed by Zbigniew K. Brzezinski, devised the concept of regional influence and identified the Shah of Iran as the first of that newly labelled cluster of heads of state with which the United States could do a lot of business. The Shah of Iran was anxious to play a greater role in the intermeshing regions of the Persian Gulf and South

Asia; Afghanistan provided the link between the two even more than Pakistan. The Carter administration encouraged the Shah to take over a large share of the American burden of policing the strategic region of the Gulf.

After the 1971 war between Pakistan on the one hand and the Bangladesh liberation army and India on the other, as a result of which Bangladesh emerged as a sovereign nation in what had hitherto been the eastern wing of Pakistan or East Pakistan, the Shah of Iran embarked on an influence-building role in South Asia. His role began with Pakistan. The Shah committed his military forces to the preservation of Pakistan's territorial integrity and extended to Bhutto considerable military help in putting down the Baloch uprising of 1974–75. The Shah then proceeded to improve relations with India; he and Mrs Indira Gandhi, then Prime Minister of India, exchanged visits in 1974, and Indo–Iranian relations rapidly acquired a certain strategic dimension. The Shah simultaneously sought to build bridges of friendship with Afghanistan. He wanted the Persian Gulf and South Asian regions to be less polarized between the two superpowers, and wanted countries like Saudi Arabia, Pakistan, Afghanistan and India to draw a little distant from their respective superpower friend or patron. At the superpower level, the Soviet Union was trying to persuade the Shah to be less dependent on the United States, while the United States pleaded with India and Afghanistan to be 'genuinely non-aligned' between Washington and Moscow. The instrument the Shah used to make his regional influence foreign policy a success was financial aid. He committed to India credits worth $1b., to Pakistan $750 m., and to Afghanistan $50 m. between 1973 and 1975. The Shah's foreign policy perspective and objectives were put forward with considerable lucidity at an international seminar in Tehran in February 1975 by Amir Tahiri, then editor of the *Kahyan International*, who had close links with the palace and the Iranian foreign office:

Iran is anxious to prevent the polarization of the political situation in the region. During the past ten years Iran has reaped great benefits from correct and mutually profitable relations with both the United States and the USSR. I would thus wish to see the present balanced situation continue for at least another decade during which, as Iranian decision-makers assert, Iran would become strong enough to hold its own against all eventualities. Iran is unhappy about the reactionary stance of several Arab regimes in the peninsula and wary of hotbed radicalism in both Iraq and South Yemen. But it believes that any open attempt to challenge the status quo would immediately lead to polarization. In a polarized political setup Iran itself would be forced to stand and be counted on this or that side. And this, according to Iranian policy-makers, would not be advantageous, to say the least . . ..

The same dislike of polarization has been manifest in Iran's policy towards Afghanistan. The Daoud coup was described by Tehran press as a triumph for Russia. But Iranian policy-makers did not take the same view and Iran was one of the first countries to recognize the new republican regime in Kabul. Later, Iran began patiently cultivating the new regime's friendship and *succeeded in helping Daoud take his distance from the USSR*. By the end of 1974 Irano–Afghan relations were better than they had ever been since the emergence of Afghanistan as an independent state.[11] [Emphasis added.]

Ambassador Eliot was advising Daoud to cultivate closer ties with Iran and countries of the Middle East. Washington also asked Iran, Saudi Arabia, Kuwait and Japan to give more economic assistance to Afghanistan. Eliot told an American author that he tried to persuade Daoud to be 'truly non-aligned' and to realize that support for Pushtunistan made him excessively dependent on the Soviet Union. He tried to improve relations between Afghanistan and Pakistan, and was not entirely unsuccessful.[12] Daoud halted Afghan mass media attacks on Pakistan and, in 1977, was said to be close to reaching an understanding with Bhutto on the basis of which he could 'expel' the Pushtun and Baloch partisans who had fled to Afghanistan and were allegedly being trained by the Afghan army.

An American specialist on Afghanistan claimed that in 1974 the Shah of Iran promised to provide Afghanistan with $2 b. in economic aid over ten years, of which $50 m. was actually given in that year. The Shah pressed Daoud to build a railroad linking Kabul to the nearest railhead in Iran. This project, if completed, would have significantly reduced Afghanistan's trade dependencies on the Soviet Union.[13]

In the last two years of his reign, and of his republic's life, Daoud did appear to be cautiously but systematically asserting Afghanistan's independence and 'genuine non-alignment'. He was sending his soldiers to Egypt, India and the United States in larger numbers than before. At Havana, Daoud worked closely with the centrist group in the Non-Aligned Movement rather than associate himself with the pro-Soviet cluster led by Cuba and Vietnam. In 1978 he paid official visits to India, Pakistan, Egypt, Libya, Turkey and Yugoslavia. The Shah of Iran announced a planned trip to Kabul in June, and Daoud himself said he would be visiting President Carter in Washington before the end of the year. In March 1978 Afghanistan and China concluded a trade protocol which provided for increased trade between the two, and a credit of 100 m. yuan for Kabul. Just a few days before he was overthrown, Daoud paid another official visit to Saudi Arabia.

If the Soviets took a dim view of Daoud's flirtations with the Shah of Iran, the President of Pakistan, and the royalty of Saudi Arabia, there is nothing on record to confirm it. On the contrary, as already noted, the Soviets continued to befriend Afghanistan and Moscow's rhetoric did not betray visible irritation with Daoud's tentative search for 'genuine non-alignment'. However, changes that occurred in world politics in the second half of the seventies could not but have their impact on Afghanistan. Vietnam, followed by Angola and Mozambique, rapidly built an image of the United States as a declining power. Correspondingly, the world saw the Soviet Union as an emergent global superpower, capable of intervening, and willing to intervene, with arms, weapons and economic aid, and, as in southern Africa, effectively using Cuban troops on behalf of national liberation movements in the Third World. Jimmy Carter's attempt to move away from the foreign policy of the Nixon and Ford administrations, of which the principal architect had been Henry K. Kissinger, introduced an increasing instability in the American–Soviet relationship. This instability weakened several Third World regimes, especially those regimes that were overly dependent on the United States. The Carter administration's foreign policy further unsettled the balance of power prevailing between the superpowers as well as in several Third World regions. Highly volatile regional forces were released in the Third World, especially in the Persian Gulf, the Middle East and southern Africa. The aspirations for power of several regional states clashed or meshed with one another in confused tangles. World politics entered a period of great and prolonged disorder.

In the geopolitical region in which Afghanistan is located, profound political change took place in 1977–8. In India, Mrs Indira Ghandi's Emergency regime ended in February 1977 with her, and her party's, first-ever defeat in a national election; installed in power in Delhi was a new regime of the Janata (People's) party, a hurriedly contrived merger of several opposition groups which had been polarized from the ruling Congress party during the seventeen-month-long Emergency. The leaders of the new regime talked of 'genuine non-alignment', although Prime Minister Morarji Desai visited Moscow before going to Washington and showed himself as particular as his predecessor, Indira Ghandi, in preserving India's Soviet connection. In the summer of 1977, the Pakistani military overthrew the representative regime of Zulfikar Ali Bhutto, and General Zia-ul Haq, whom Bhutto had promoted to the office of army chief over the head of several senior officers, assumed power as head of a martial law regime. In Iran, the Shah and his American patrons had no idea even in 1978 that the most important Western outpost in the Persian Gulf–Middle Eastern region would not last another year. It is one of the profound ironies of our times that when the president's men in Washington were diligently building up Mohammad Reza Shah Pahlavi as an effective 'regional influence' they were actually trying to prop up a straw regime headed by a straw man!

In the humble universe of South Asian communism, two significant developments took place in 1977. In India and in Afghanistan warring communist factions came together in response to changing realities in the two countries' respective domestic politics. In Afghanistan, Parcham and Khalq reunited in July to oppose the regime of Daoud Khan. Thus was reborn the PDPA, with Nur Mohammed Taraki and Babrak Karmal as its first two front-rank leaders. In India, the Communist Party of India (CPI), which had supported Indira Ghandi's Emergency regime, and the Communist Party of India (Marxist)—or CPI-M—which had opposed it, determined in their respective congresses to build a unity-in-action between themselves after thirteen years of bitter conflict and competition since the split of the united CPI in 1964. The CPSU played a part in both cases. Reports indicated that the two Afghan Marxist groups had reunited under Moscow's pressure. The truth probably was that the Marxists themselves realized the need to combine forces to be able to defeat Daoud's plans to eliminate their influence in Afghan politics, and the CPSU encouraged them to re-unite.[14] In the case of the two Indian communist factions, the initiatives definitely came from their own leaders. Moscow welcomed the change in the CPI's tactical line in view of the fact that a self-confessed coalition of conservative and pro-Western parties had captured power in Delhi.[15]

In the elections in India in 1977–8, the CPI-M emerged as the dominant political force in the two neighbouring eastern states of West Bengal and Tripura, and formed Left-Front governments in both, in coalition with other, smaller leftist groups including the CPI. The fortunes of the Marxists in Afghanistan took a quantum leap in April 1978 for which neither they nor the Soviets were prepared. In the last three years of his rule, Daoud had alienated both Parcham and Khalq factions of Marxists, and the alienation had reached out to army officers of leftist, pro-Soviet persuasions. Daoud had singularly failed to construct a political base for his regime. The National Revolutionary Party existed only in name; it commanded the loyalty or credibility neither of the urban middle class nor of the tribal chiefs. Moderniza-tion, despite its slow pace, had changed social formations in Afghani-stan, especially in those provinces which had enjoyed relatively stabler relations with the central administration. Louis Dupree noted con-siderable economic vigour and diversity in Afghanistan in 1976–77, and a 'remarkable improvement in Afghanistan's economic status'.[16]

Before the newly-formed PDPA could build its organization as a strong rallying point of the urban middle class, even before it could come to grips with political and social change in Afghanistan, and certainly before it could sort out the power equations between its two long-feuding, suddenly reunited partners, it found itself catapulted to power in a revolution whose actual leadership, crucial direction, decision-making apparatus, and class character were all highly controversial, and remain still to be documented with complete cre-dibility. From the primary and secondary material available, two con-clusions may be drawn with a high degree of confidence. First, the Afghan communists realized that their time was coming fast: in the struggle for power that would ensue after the death of Daoud, who was then 68, if they could not capture power, their opponents would wipe them out. Secondly, as the leadership of the united party was with the Khalq, it was the Khalq leaders, especially Taraki and Amin, who were mainly responsible for the turn of events in the last fortnight of April 1978.

PDPA was an illegal party. It had to operate secretly. Hafizullah Amin was leader of the left wing in Khalq. He was given the crucial and adventurous task of building party cells in the armed forces, the police and the palace guards. Parcham had penetrated the Government. Although Daoud had dismissed the Parcham heavyweights whom he had placed in strategic positions when founding the republic, there were many Parcham cadres in the Government which could be used for vital information. The Marxists were undoubtedly helped by the incredible inefficiency and inertia of the civil servants, the police and even the armed forces; nobody seemed to care for Daoud.[17] Daoud's Interior Minister, Abdul Qadtr-Nuristani, had begun to crack down on left-wing radicals. A prominent leader of the Parcham faction, Mir Akbar Khyber, was assassinated in Kabul on 17 April. This incident set off a chain reaction that Daoud's Government could not handle. PDPA brought its followers to the streets to protest the murder; for the first time since he had returned to power in 1973, Daoud had to face large public demonstrations against him. On 19 April some 15,000 Afghans paraded the streets of Kabul and marched towards the American embassy shouting anti-American slogans.

Daoud was presumably shocked to discover the strength that the communists had acquired, and he determined to crush them. In the next few days, Taraki, Amin, Karmal and several other leaders of the PDPA were arrested. The policemen who took Taraki away in the night of 25/26 April injured his wife when she offered resistance, but did not care to search his personal papers. Amin was placed under house arrest for several hours. No one prevented him from contacting his friends, and when he passed instructions to party cadres in the army through his sons, they were not stopped from leaving the house. According to accounts of the revolutionary coup published by the Taraki regime, Amin sent instructions to twenty Army and Air Force officers, asking them to act. He appointed Colonel Aslam Watanjar as Commander of Revolutionary Ground Forces, and Colonel Abdul Qader as leader of the Revolutionary Air Force.[18] Amin gave detailed

directions on the Army and Air Force units that were to seize key
government installations, including the airport and the broadcasting
station. Their ultimate target was the presidential palace, defended by
elite guards whom Amin expected to offer resistance. On the night of
26 April, Amin, Karmal and others were taken to jail. The fate of the
revolution hung on the action of the leftist officers of the Army and the
Air Force.[19]

Around 8 o'clock in the morning of 27 April, the rebel Fourth
Armoured Division began to move towards Kabul from its base at Puli
Charkhi, south of the city. Led by Watanjar, it met with no resistance
until it reached the heart of the government district on its way to key
buildings and the presidential palace. Qader's Air Force men seized the
airport. Rebel tanks surrounded the presidential palace in which the
Cabinet was in session to determine the fate of the arrested leftist
leaders.

Thursday 27 April was a half-holiday for government employees.
Friday is the weekly holiday for Afghans. In Dupree's account of the
revolutionary coup,

at noon, just as the fighting intensified, Kabul offices emptied into the streets.
Despite the danger, people queued up for buses—even in the firefight zone!
Taxis honked for tanks to move over, and wove in and out as the fighting
continued. At some corners, traffic policemen motioned the tanks to pull
over to the curb.[20]

After taking the Air Force headquarters at Begram, forty miles north
of Kabul, Qader ordered air strikes on the palace. Planes fired rockets
and 20-mm. shells and dropped several bombs on the President's
house. The Republican Guards offered resistance and many of them
were killed. Rebels took the interior ministry and released Taraki,
Karmal and other arrested communist leaders. Daoud's Defence
Minister rushed from one Army unit to another trying to mobilize the
troops to fight the rebels, but received no more than token response.
Meanwhile, the Fourth Armoured Division, which was now joined by
rebel infantry units, moved into the modern part of Kabul and gained
control of key roads and intersections. The ministries of communication, foreign affairs and other government buildings fell to the rebels
without significant resistance.

Earlier in the day, Daoud had ordered loyal units at Shindand Air Force base, 500 miles to the west, to rush to his defence. They arrived early in the afternoon, before the rebels had attacked the presidential palace, but they had fuel for only ten minutes flying time, found no way to refuel and returned to their base without joining action. In the late afternoon, rebel tanks broke into the palace courtyard and the surviving guards offered no resistance. Inside the palace, Daoud and some thirty members of his family were gathered in a conference room. There was some fighting. Daoud was either killed by the rebels or else shot himself. Many members of the presidential family, including his brother Muhammad Naim, were killed.[21]

At 7.05 in the evening, Colonel Qader announced on Radio Afghanistan that 'for the first time in the history of Afghanistan an end has been put to the sultanate of the Mohannadzais. All power has passed to the hands of the masses.' Qader said that the Military Revolutionary Council headed by himself would exercise power for the time being. Three days later, it was announced that power was being exercised by a Revolutionary Council consisting of civilian as well as military personnel, with Taraki as leader.

The Afghan revolution, then, was a one-day affair, unlike any other communist revolution or take-over in history. It was also the least expensive in terms of human lives: casualties were definitely below the figure of two thousand. The timing and the manner of the revolution suggest that it was in fact thrust upon the communists. They did not appear to have planned it in any detail, though they might have been working towards it. Decisive action was taken by the armed forces rather than the party. However, within three days, the party had taken over leadership of the revolutionary regime or, more precisely, the Khalq faction in the party to which both Taraki and Amin belonged. However, during the take-over and for several months thereafter, Khalq and Parcham worked together. Taraki later said that the arrests of the leftist leaders had precipitated the revolution. 'The direct action of the comrades from the army was not planned a long time in advance', he disclosed. Only after the PDPA leaders had been taken into custody was the order given to army cadres to act.

There is some controversy as to whether the Soviets had anything to do with the Afghan revolution. Cyrus Vance, who was Secretary of

State in the Carter administration when the revolution took place, said in his memoirs, 'We had no evidence of Soviet complicity in the coup.'[22] However, ambassador Eliot believes that with 3,000 Soviet advisers present in Afghanistan, it was highly probable that Moscow knew about the revolution, even if it had no part in its planning and execution. (Soviet combat units took no part in the military operations.)[23]

The Afghan revolution was described by Americans and others as a coup, or even a palace or an army coup rather than a revolution. The communist movement in Afghanistan was weak. It was not even listed in the *Yearbook on International Communist Affairs* until 1978. *Marxist Governments: A World Survey*, edited by Bogdan Szajkowski of the University College, Cardiff, Great Britain, published in 1981, did not include the PDPA regime in Afghanistan. The country's political system did not permit the existence of a legal and open communist party. Parcham and Khalq were factions composed of urban Marxist intellectuals and middle classes, mostly confined to Kabul. Neither had much of a rural or even provincial base before the revolution. The Afghan revolution was therefore very different from the revolutionary take-over in the People's Republic of South Yemen, founded in November 1967, and three years later rechristened the People's Democratic Republic of Yemen (PDRY). No national liberation movement led by the communists existed in Afghanistan; neither Khalq nor Parcham had a peasant base. The street action of April 1978 did not take on the aspects of an insurrection. Although the turnout of 15,000 people frightened the Daoud Government, the mass action might have withered after the arrest of the Marxist leaders. If the military units under the command of Marxist officers had not intervened with an impressive display of force, the Afghan revolution would not have taken place.

It was, however, not a military take-over. The military officers acted on instructions from Hafizullah Amin, who, this writer was told by authoritative sources in Kabul, issued his 'orders' on behalf of the PDPA, not on behalf of himself.[24] Watanjar and Qader were committed members of Khalq. On 27 April, Qader's radio broadcast named himself as chief of the Revolutionary Military Council that would rule Afghanistan 'on behalf of the masses'; it did not mention the party. But Hafizullah Amin broadcast several 'victory bulletins' from the ministry of communication after it had been taken by the revolutionary units of the army. For three days there was an intense debate amongst the Marxist leaders as to who should compose the new government, on the relative role of the party and the army in the new, revolutionary dispensation. It was unanimously decided that the party would rule Afghanistan, and that the army would be subordinate to the party. On this issue there was no difference between Taraki and Amin on the one hand and Babrak Karmal on the other. The Red Officers in the army were 'against Bonapartism'. Afghanistan, therefore, was not a case of military communism and cannot be bracketed with Ethiopia.[25]

The dramatic and surprising success of the Afghan revolution betrays the fundamental weakness of modernizing regimes in the Third World not based on sound and developing political systems linked to the masses. In the next chapter we take a close look at Afghanistan's political economy—the nature of the state—at the time of the Saur (April) revolution.

3 The State that the Revolution Inherited

With all its disadvantages—no revolutionary base of its own, no experience of a long political struggle, the PDPA membership of no more than 5,000 (most, if not all of them, recruited from Kabul and the provincial towns)—what kind of a state did the Saur revolution inherit or seize on 27 April 1978? What was the state of Afghanistan's political economy? What was the social base of its ruling class in the republic founded by Daoud? What kind of relationships prevailed between the state, the tribe and the periphery? What was the character of the central bureaucracy, the provincial and rural power structure, the shape of local government? What impact had modernization had on Afghanistan's extremely dispersed socio-political structure and its largely tribal and very diverse population? What role did Islam play in the total life-style of the people of Afghanistan? An appreciation of the Afghan political economy in its entirety is necessary to identify what Roderick Aya has called the 'political crux' of the Afghan revolution, namely, 'an open-ended situation of violent struggle wherein one set of contenders attempts successfully or unsuccessfully to displace another from state power.'[1]

'Before the April Democratic Revolution', declares a publication of the Marxist regime in Kabul, 'the long domination of feudalistic and pre-feudalistic rule, combined with the influence of neo-colonialism, had made Afghanistan one of the 31 least developed and most back-ward countries of the world.' More than 91 per cent of its people were illiterate; only 29 per cent of school-age children (including 9 per cent of school-age girls) attended school. In education, Afghanistan ranked 127th among world nations, in public health 119th. Only one hospital bed was available for 5,000 people and one doctor for 13,000. The government spent 2 per cent of GNP on education and 0.65 on public health. 'Distribution of the per capita income was terribly unfair. More than 40 per cent of the population could not meet even the minimum social needs and lived in absolute poverty.' Although 85 per cent of people lived by an agrarian economy, agriculture's share of GNP was a mere 5.9 per cent. Only 19 per cent of the country's land was under irrigation, and only half of the irrigated land was actually cultivated. More than 40 per cent of the first-class arable land was in the hands of 4 per cent of the population—feudal landlords. Despite a reasonable balance of soil and water, only 10–20 per cent of water resources were utilized. Manufacturing industries contributed 21 per cent of GNP, but only 0.9 per cent of employment. Only fifteen productive plants employed 500 workers or more each. Mining, metallurgical and material processing industries were virtually non-existent. Energy consumption, at 47 kg. of coal per head, was one of the lowest in the world. Less than 0.2 m. tons of coal were extracted annually. Oil extraction and refining did not exist: Afghanistan had to import 4.28 m. tons of oil every year. Exploitation of firm deposits of 120 b. cu.m. of natural gas started in 1968, with Soviet help. But power generation in thirteen scattered power plants was only 776 m. kWh per year, and not more than 50 per cent of this could be distributed. Per capita electricity consumption was 60 kWh a year—also one of the lowest in the world.

The relative share of trade in the GNP was less than 15 per cent. Only 16 per cent of GDP came from exports, which was 13 per cent lower than average exports of the forty-two least developed countries in the world. Until 1968, the bulk of Afghanistan's exports consisted of agricultural and livestock products; after 1968, natural gas became the leading export earner. Per capita gross agricultural product hardly reached $27.0 in more than fifty to sixty decades of feudal and pre-feudal rule.

Permanent transition towards a relatively new life in Afghanistan started only 20 years before the April Democratic Revolution under the pressure of the new economic conditions of the world after the Second World War, emergence of a world-wide socialist system and expansion of the revolutionary struggle of the Afghan people against reactionary-dominated ruling societies. Slow movement started in the shape of half-ripened actions for the democratization of social life, the growth of the role of the State in socio-economic development and the formulation of five-year development plans. The five-year development plans, drawn up and implemented with the assistance of the Soviet Union, had a progressive effect, despite the serious limitations due to the policies of the ruling governments.

In 1971, a World Bank mission wrote of the pervasive disillusionment about the past and pessimism regarding the future in Afghanistan, as the Marxist regime's document recalled. 'It concluded that "such pessimism is justified as even in areas where development activities were undertaken, with heavy inputs of capital investment and foreign advice, returns have been dismally low."'[2]

Soviet scholars and commentators have described Afghanistan at the time of the April revolution in the same vein. 'A backward country, with a rigidly feudal way of life', wrote a Soviet scholar in a Moscow publication of 1980. The book quoted a French communist publication for the additional information that, with the exception of Kabul, 'the country has practically no electricity, no railroads, and very few highways. In a word, Dark Ages.'[3] Another Soviet publication noted in 1981,

Hard labour, disease, hunger, poverty and illiteracy were the lot of the overwhelming majority of the Afghan people. They suffered from corruption rampant among government officials, arbitrariness and violence . . .. The peasants, workers, intellectuals, artisans and petty traders, deprived of elementary human rights, had at the same time no opportunity to conduct any legal organized struggle for their rights, as political parties were officially banned.[4]

In an article in the journal *Asia and Africa Today* in 1980, a Soviet scholar remarked that the Nadir Shah dynasty had 'personified the most brutal form of class and national oppression of the working people and seriously impeded Afghanistan's economic, social and cultural development.'[5] 'Capitalism in Afghanistan developed in specific conditions', wrote an analyst in *New Times*, and echoed the same observations: 'The workers were ruthlessly exploited, working conditions were extremely hard. The employers paid them the minimum necessary to maintain their capacity to work but cared nothing for the needs of their families.'[6] Another Soviet specialist on Afghanistan found the country's condition in 1978 similar to that prevailing in the Soviet Central Asian republics at the time of the Bolshevik revolution.[7]

American political and social anthropologists who have specialized in Afghanistan speak of a far more complex political society than is visible in Soviet–Afghan Marxist analyses. In April 1978, Afghanistan was not an entirely tribal society. It looked tribal to those who saw it from Kabul or from Peshawar after the revolution, because the vast majority of the refugees clustered in that Pakistani city were Pushtuns who lived a tribal life. The non-Pushtun, non-nomadic peoples such as the Tajik, Hazarah, Fariswan and Uzbek were not organized tribally, in the same way as the Pushtuns. 'In cases where tribal ideology exists, as among the Pashai and Nuristani, its role in the political processes is considerably different. More important, even among the Pushtun, the role of the tribe as a unit of military and political mobilization is often assumed rather than demonstrated by research.'[8] In several provinces of Afghanistan, the anti-Saur revolution mobilization cut across tribal patterns.

There was no uniform popular attitude to central authority in Afghanistan when the communists captured state power. When Nadir Shah founded the Musahiban dynasty in 1929, after crushing the reformist regime of Amir Amanullah, he formed an alliance of traditional religious leaders and rural khans which formed the core of the social base of the ruling class in Afghanistan right up to 1978.

Sharing power with the traditional religious and secular leaders, the Musahiban rulers were able to consolidate a measure of central authority in the country. However, they were fully aware of the tenuous loyalties of the traditional powerbrokers, and they were determined to create new bases of support among the younger generation to ensure the future of the monarchy.[9]

This was carried out mainly by the creation of a modern Army and police force and, secondly, by expanding education and rationalizing the bureaucracy. The royal Army had consisted of sons of loyal Pushtun tribes and tribal chiefs and, on a much lower scale, sons of non-Pushtun tribal notables under a form of court patronage known as *ghulam bachha* ('slave boys' or 'servant boys'). Recruitment began to change in the latter 1950s, after the Government had received substantial military aid from the Soviet Union. The military academies were permitted to recruit officer cadets from all ethnic and linguistic groups and social strata. About the same time, educational facilities were rapidly expanded, especially in the urban areas, to cater to an enlarging middle class. At the time of the Saur revolution, nearly a million

Afghans were attending more than 4,000 schools and over 600,000 had completed some formal education.[10] In the 1960s many of the educated youth entered the bureaucracy. In the 1970s, foreign aid declined, and jobs became scarce. Thousands of educated young people were jobless, and many of them were drawn to the leftist groups either as cadres or as supporters. However, Daoud failed to bring about his desired 'revolution of national integration'. His modernizing actions only modernized traditional loyalties and cleavages. This became evident after the Saur revolution. The radical reforms introduced by the Marxist regime alienated the majority of educated youth who joined their elders to defend traditional values and institutions, and, more than anything, Islam.

In the modernizing period of the Musahiban rule, as well as during Daoud's republican leadership, three major political forces emerged in Afghanistan. The dominant force was the royal household and the traditional and new political elite; second in importance were the 'non-official, community-based traditional leaders who for the most part avoided contact with the authorities and were concerned with the welfare of their own communities above all else.' The third political force were the mostly urban, partly rural, educated elements who had entered the political process since the mid-fifties.[11]

Over the years, segments of the Afghan population learnt to co-operate with the central government. The Pushtuns, constituting about half of the total population, and long patronized by Daoud, had a dual relationship with Kabul. They were more identified than any other ethnic segment or nationality with the central authority. At the same time, the Pushtuns enjoyed a large measure of local autonomy which the central government allowed, partly as a tactical move of adoption and accommodation, partly under duress. Those non-Pushtun nationalities which had links with the central government harboured at the same time a latent hostility towards it and more acutely towards the dominant Pushtun group.

In such a political milieu, the bureaucracy could only be a vehicle for minimum administration, by no means for radical change—a fact that the Marxists did not appreciate before 1980. The civil and military bureaucracies had been designed solely to preserve the status quo. Both were weak institutions, as the PDPA discovered at great cost to the revolution. 'The provincial administration soon proved incapable of making major changes in the face of local opposition, and the military proved unable to put down this opposition when confronted with armed rebellion.'[12]

The Marxists inherited an administrative organization which had no experience in implementing large-scale unpopular reforms in rural regions. Purges and personnel changes following the coup weakened the rural administrative machinery. The Marxists' only realistic hope for the successful implementation of their reforms was that the rural dwellers would voluntarily accept them. But the government's inflammatory rhetoric and its arrogant distancing from Islam and the trappings of Islamic legitimacy, together with its headstrong approach to reform, doomed its efforts regardless of good intentions behind them.[13]

The arm of central government did not extend to the rural areas except in the limited sphere of tax collection and administration of justice through Islamic courts and judges. In many respects the villagers were left to run their own affairs as long as they paid taxes and allowed their sons to be conscripted for military service. Local officials were corrupt by compulsion as well as by tradition; their success depended on their ability to understand and manipulate the structure and organization of local politics and to get along with village elders. In the context of civil and criminal justice, the government symbolized Islam. Indeed, for the vast majority of the Afghan people, Islam conferred legitimacy on royalty as well as on the republican regime of Daoud.

The form of local-level politics was determined by economic realities. Political competition was confined to the khans, supported by their respective tenant clients.

Land was of key political importance, since (through the cultivation of rice as a cash crop) it provided wealth that could be used to subvert an enemy's followers, solidify alliances, bribe government officials, and allow one to live in a style necessary for acceptance among the Pushtun-dominated Afghan elite. Land was also important in determining the number of supporters a khan could mobilize in confrontation with his enemies because the number of tenants obligated to support him was in direct proportion to the size of his holdings. Because land was of such importance, most political confrontations concerned it in one way or another; political fortunes rose or fell in relation to success or failure in land disputes, and where land was at issue, each khan was the potential rival of all others. Some khans allied with one another when threatened by a common enemy, but the political factions formed by such alliances tended to be of short duration. In general khans were suspicious of one another and perceived themselves as relatively isolated in a sea of potential enemies.[14]

In most of Afghanistan two power structures were in existence at the time of the Saur revolution. One was the local government administration run through the institution of *arbab* or *qaryadar* (village headman). The *arbab* was elected by the adult males of a village, but had to be approved by the *hakim*, the Islamic judge, before he could represent the village to the local administration. More important than the institution of the *arbab* was the traditional institution of the community, based on kinship and headed by the *aqsaqal*, or village elders, who had to be relatively prosperous and respected by the community. Most village disputes were settled by the elders and few would go to the *hakim*.[15]

Land, as noted, was the source of power all over Afghanistan. Land hunger was widespread at the time of the Saur revolution, but most Afghan households had some land, and only about 25 per cent of households were landless. Over 70 per cent owned tiny plots of 1–2 hectares. Large landlords did not exist. In effect, 40–44 per cent of land was owned by 4–9 per cent of households, but the average size of the land was only 6+ hectares (see Tables 1 and 2, both based on the writings of Marxist scholars, one Soviet, the other Indian).

Much more serious than the land hunger was the burden of debts and mortgages that Afghans had to carry. In a survey of seventeen villages in eight provinces carried out in 1968–9, as many as 56.8 per cent of the families interviewed had debts averaging 16,316 afghanis, or $400.[16] In 57 per cent of the families, money had been borrowed to meet daily necessities, and in 30.5 per cent of cases to meet the costs of marriages and funerals. An interest rate of 50 per cent was common.[17] In the early seventies, a severe drought compelled large numbers of villagers to mortgage their land for loans; debts and mortages resulted in a heavy alienation of land. Villagers had to borrow because their income was too low to make both ends meet and also because their holdings were too small to generate the capital they needed to keep them under cultivation.[18]

Table 1. Size, ownership and distribution of privately-owned land in Afghanistan (Soviet figures)*

Size of holding (Ha.)	Families owning land		% of families deserving land†	Total land owned in category (Ha.)	% of all privately held land
	Number	%			
0	420,000– 670,000‡	0	25.9	0	0
0.1–1.0	470,000	39.0	29.0	520,000	26.0
1.0–2.0	450,000	37.5	27.7		
2.0–6.0	230,000	19.2	14.2	660,000	33.3
6.0+	51,600	4.3	3.2	800,000	40.00

Source: V. Glukhoded, 'Economy of Independent Afghanistan', *Social Sciences Today*, Moscow, 1981, pp. 241–2.

† Calculations are based on 420,000 families.

‡ Figures do not include 2.0–2.5 million pastoral nomads who are considered 'landless' and are entitled to land.

* The figures are recalculated on the basis of first-grade land.

Table 2. Size, ownership and distribution of privately-owned land in Afghanistan (Indian figures)*

Size of holding (Ha.)	Families owning land		Total land owned in category (Ha.)	% of all privately held land
	Number	%		
0	N.A.	N.A.	N.A.	N.A.
0.1–2.0	805,000	67.0	1,100,000	24.1
2.1–4.0	161,000	13.4	738,000	16.0
4.1–6.0	125,000	10.4	702,000	15.6
6.0+	109,000	9.0	2,000,000	44.4

Source: S. Mukherjee, *What is Happening in Afghanistan*, New Delhi, People's Publishing House, 1981, pp. 16–18.

* The figures reflect estimates of absolute landholdings.

Despite grinding poverty and the strong tribal and Islamic hold on the rural Afghan, his life in April 1978 was not entirely bereft of the influence of the modern world. Transportation, as noted, had opened up much of the countryside. The villages were not isolated from one another, and people moved from province to province on a wider scale than even in the fifties. Mobilization had become easier than before. There was hardly any village without a transistor radio, which brought the world into the huts of the Afghan villager. He could listen to broadcasts coming in from Pakistan, Moscow, the BBC and the Voice of America. The Marxists tried to make the best use of the radio but they were beaten in the propaganda war by external wavelengths for the simple reason that the villager could neither understand the language of the new revolutionary ideology nor was he in a mood to listen. He was more quickly and effectively moved by symbols than by the Marxist ideology which in 1978–9 was begging for an Afghan language that the Afghan villager could understand. Islam was the symbol that meant most to the Afghan, and the moment the agents of the Saur revolution chose to wage a propaganda war on Islam, they lost the sympathy of the majority of the village people as well as the urban middle class.

4   Revolution: the Khalq Phase

The People's Democratic Party of Afghanistan installed a revolutionary Marxist regime in Kabul on 27 April 1978. Considerable political distemper prevailed in the region surrounding Afghanistan. In Pakistan, the military ruler, General Zia-ul Haq, was under considerable domestic and international pressure to give up his resolve to hang Zulfikar Ali Bhutto who had been sentenced to death in a controversial trial, and was seeking the support of the conservative fundamentalist Jamaat-i-Islami in finding a political base for his regime. In Iran, the Shah could hear the first rumblings of a very different Islamic fundamentalist upheaval that would throw him and his regime out in less than a year. India was ruled by the Janata party whose foreign policy slogan was 'genuine non-alignment'. The Afghan revolution caused surprise in the neighbouring capitals but no visible concern. Initially, the PDPA regime was seen in India, as it was in the United States, more as a government of a radical shade of Afghan nationalism than as a pro-Soviet Marxist one.

The government that was announced on 28 April was a coalition of the PDPA's two factions, Khalq and Parcham. It also included the leader of a Maoist faction that was outside the party, namely, Setem-i-Meli or National Opposition. No non-Marxist political group was given a berth in the government. Eleven of the members of the Council of Ministers belonged to Khalq, ten to Parcham. This near-equality of representation was probably aimed at reassuring the CPSU which was closer to Parcham than to Khalq, for the Khalq was the dominant group in the party, and the real maker of the revolution. Of the ministers appointed, thirteen had been full or alternate members of the original central committee of the PDPA set up in 1965, with nine full and ten alternate members. Only three ministers belonged to the armed forces, even through the army had played a crucial role in over-powering the Daoud regime, and the Khalq had considerable following in the ranks of army officers. At least ten of the ministers had taken part in the 1965 and 1969 elections and five had been elected. None of the ministers had been known to have attended any international meeting of communists.[1] All but a few of the ministers began their political life in the liberal 'constitutional' period 1963–73. Five of the ministers had been jailed at least once for their political activity.

It was a youthful council of ministers. Only the head of the Government and the party, Noor Mohammed Taraki, was older (61). The other civilian ministers were between 40 and 50 years old. Ten cabinet ministers had been to the United States for advanced studies, two to Egypt, and one each to France and the German Federal Republic. Four had only received their education in Afghanistan. The three military men in the Cabinet had been trained in the Soviet Union. Almost all the ministers knew English, only four also knew Russian. By occupation, eleven cabinet members were in Government at the time of the revolution: three in the armed forces, two on the faculty of Kabul University, five in the civil service and one on the staff of Radio Kabul. Also, three of the ministers were 'unemployed writers', two doctors, two lawyers and two academics—all without jobs at the time of the revolution—and one a landlord. Eleven ministers belonged to the dominant Pushtun nationality, six were Persian-speaking Tajik, two Persian-speaking Hazara, and two Turkic-speaking Uzbek. All the ministers spoke Pushtu and Persian, the two dominant languages. The first revolutionary Cabinet and council of ministers, then, were fairly representative of the social and cultural realities of Afghanistan, though not of the political realities.[2]

The President and Prime Minister of the Democratic Republic of Afghanistan (DRA) was Taraki, who was also the General Secretary of the PDPA. Born in 1917, Taraki belonged to the Ghilzai tribe of the Pushtun nationality. Self-educated, he became a poet and a prolific writer of journalistic prose as well as fiction, with a sharp revolutionary political edge. While working in Bombay, in the 1930s, Taraki came under the influence of the Communist Party of India and became a Marxist. In the 1940s, Taraki worked for the Afghan government publication agencies in Kabul and was also involved in the student movement. In 1952, Taraki was appointed press attaché in the Afghan embassy in Washington, DC. After Daoud became Prime Minister in 1953, Taraki publicly denounced him as repressive and autocratic, and resigned his diplomatic job. But in less than two months, Taraki returned to Kabul as a self-proclaimed loyal citizen. His official biography states that soon after his arrival in Kabul, he telephoned Daoud to say, 'I am Nur Muhammad Taraki. I have just arrived. Shall I go home or to the prison?' For the next twenty-five years Taraki lived as a journalist and creative writer. He ran a translation service whose customers included the American embassy and USAID. In his novels he portrayed an Afghan society that was unjust and oppressive. Around him gathered a group of radical writers and intellectuals. By the early sixties, Taraki was a full-blown Marxist who was converting educated youth to a political line that saw the Soviet Union as the centre of world revolution. It was in Taraki's house that the PDPA was born in 1965, according to the Khalqi version of the party's history.[3]

Taraki was the 'Beloved Leader' of the Saur revolution; his 'Noble Student', Hafizullah Amin, was Deputy Prime Minister and number-two man in the Marxist Government. Amin was born in 1927 of Ghilzai parents near Paghman; like Taraki, he, too, was a Pushtun. Of peasant stock, Amin was born in an age when education spread to the provinces. A bright student, he continued his education at Kabul University and went to the Teachers' College of Columbia University with a scholarship. After his return to Kabul with a Master's degree, he became principal of a boarding high-school for rural Pushtun boys. He went back to Columbia University with a second scholarship in 1963. This was a time of political change in Afghanistan. Although political parties were not allowed, open political activity became possible. Amin became active in the Afghan Students Association in the United States, a fact that was used by Babrak Karmal and others after 1979 to accuse Amin of being a CIA agent. In the United States, Amin was known as an ardent supporter of the Pushtunistan movement, and in 1963 he was converted to Marxism at a students' meeting in Wisconsin. He returned to Kabul without completing his doctoral work and plunged into the Marxist politics of the PDPA as a firebrand leader and theoretician of the Khalq faction.

Amin was narrowly defeated in the 1965 election. Joining the faculty of Kabul University's Institute of Education, he devoted most of his time to building the party and converting Afghan youth to Marxist–Leninism. Over time, Amin became the strongman of Khalq, though he recognized the leadership of the elder Taraki. A man of dynamic leadership and burning ambition, Amin was able to recruit several devoted cadres in the Army and the Air Force, which, as we have seen, became crucial in the triumph of the Saur revolution.[4]

The third most important man in the PDPA Government was Babrak Karmal, who was destined to lead the second phase of the Saur revolution, that began in the last days of December 1979, along with the Soviet military intervention, to save the collapsing regime founded on 27 April 1978. Babrak was born in Kabul province, and brought up in Kabul city; his father was an army general. He was caught up in the students' movement in the early fifties, and proved himself, even in his early youth, to be a charismatic leader. He was imprisoned for a number of years under Daoud's first regime. In the sixties Babrak emerged as the undisputed leader of the Parcham faction of the PDPA. It was on his initiative that Parcham broke away from the PDPA in 1967; Babrak brought his faction back to the party in Daoud's republican regime.

A spellbinding orator, Babrak closely identified himself with those intellectuals who spoke Dari. Unlike Taraki and Amin, his followers were not confined to the Pushtuns. He had some followers among the young military officers, but his main political base was among urban intellectuals and students. In the early seventies, Babrak, who displayed a more realistic assessment of political forces in Afghanistan than did Taraki and Amin, realized that the 'democratic' opening of the sixties had spent itself. He threw in his lot with Daoud, and helped the 'Red Prince' to put an end to the monarchy and to found a republic. Daoud made use of the Parcham cadres and threw them out when he had finished with them. When Babrak joined Taraki and Amin to reunite the PDPA, he knew that he represented the minority faction in the party. Babrak therefore accepted the position of a deputy prime minister in the first Taraki Cabinet, but had the satisfaction of seeing Parcham represented in the council of ministers almost equally with Khalq. In the first months of the revolutionary regime, Babrak devoted himself to strengthening his own support base. He was shrewd enough to anticipate an imminent struggle for power.[5]

After proclaiming Afghanistan a Democratic Republic, the leaders of the revolution sought to reassure their countrymen as well as the outside world that they were not communists and that the Government was not Marxist. President Taraki declared at a news conference on 6 May, 'We are non-aligned and independent'. He denied that the PDPA was communist or Marxist, and he appealed to all the countries of the world, including the United States, for economic aid. Taraki said the new regime was reformist, constructive and tolerant of Islam. It was born of a revolution, not a coup, he affirmed. He denounced Daoud and the old monarchy in the strongest language, and said nothing of the new regime's Soviet connection.[6]

If this was a tactical move on the part of Taraki, it worked well for a few months in terms of external, especially American responses to his regime. But a bitter political struggle started among the leaders of the regime immediately after the revolution. Operating behind the Government was a thirty-five member revolutionary council, whose membership has never been fully disclosed.[7] It was in this revolutionary council that the strategic-tactical issues were fought out. Three political groups contended with one another from the very beginning. Amin pressed for a hard, leftist political line. Only an openly and uncompromisingly revolutionary line could polarize Afghanistan along the desired class lines, he argued. Amin did not overlook the intensity and size of the inevitable counter-revolution. His argument was that if the revolution lost its offensive and retreated before the counter-revolution, it would lose precious ground and stood the risk of being overpowered by the counter-revolution. Pitted against Amin's political line was the moderate gradualist line of Babrak Karmal. The revolution, Karmal argued, had founded a National Democratic state, not a Workers' state. The struggle in Afghanistan was for a national democracy, which meant the mobilization of the largest possible mass of people against the hardest class enemies: in Afghanistan's case, the ruling family and its political, social and economic allies, the big landlords where they did exist, and known and unknown agents of imperialism together with the imperialists in the world outside. Karmal argued for a cautious, moderate political line that would not alienate the traditional village leaders, and an Islamic policy which would be broadly acceptable to the religious leaders. Babrak also pleaded that during the first stage of the democratic revolution, Marxist terminologies and concepts should be carefully avoided, and the language of the regime should be strongly anti-imperialist and nationalist. Taraki, never much concerned with the applied side of ideology, and always romantic in his dispensation, sided with Amin. Karmal sought but failed to get the support of Abdul Qader, Defence Minister, and an eminent nationalist figure.[8]

Doctrinal contradictions haunted the PDPA from the time it was created. Its constitution, adopted in 1965, and unchanged through the seventies and eighties, unmistakably modelled the party on the CPSU.[9] Article 1 defined the character of the party:

The PDPA is the highest political organ and the vanguard of the working class and all labourers in Afghanistan. The PDPA, whose ideology is the practical experience of Marxism–Leninism, is founded on the voluntary union of the progressive and informed people of Afghanistan: the workers, peasants, artisans, and intellectuals of the country.

The structure of the party was based on the 'main principle and guideline' of 'democratic centralism' (Article 7). The highest party authority was the party congress, with its representatives to be elected by provincial conferences. The party was to be run by its central committee which would hold plenums if necessary between party congresses; the central committee would be run by its secretariat which would be responsible to the party's political bureau, to be elected by the central committee (Articles 14–22). The party would also have a central supervisory and control commission (Article 23).

Taraki and Amin were prompter to reveal the external affiliation and orientation of their regime than its domestic role. Whether or not the Soviets had anything to do with the Saur Revolution, they stood by it the moment it was proclaimed. Moscow was the first to extend diplomatic recognition. Within three weeks of the inauguration of the regime, Hafizullah Amin, who was also Minister for Foreign Affairs, went to Moscow where he declared that Afghanistan was 'linked by unbreakable ties of brotherly friendship and neighbourliness with its great neighbour, the Soviet Union'. 'The revolutionary government', Amin added, sought 'consolidation, widening and expanding of friendly relations' with the USSR.[10] Amin's role at the Non-Aligned summit at Havana was to place revolutionary Afghanistan firmly in the radical group that included Cuba, Vietnam and other countries of Marxist orientation.[11] Taraki, in an interview granted to an East

German newspaper in June, was even more categorical. The reporter asked, quoting from the manifesto of PDPA, 'The fight between international socialism and international imperialism that has been waged since the Great October Revolution is the basic conflict of contemporary history. Is this assessment in line with your ideology?' Amin replied, 'I think this analysis is correct. That is the way it is. One camp represented by the Soviet Union, the other by America.'[12]

The first few months of the PDPA regime went off relatively well. Taraki's emphasis on the non-Marxist character of the regime concealed for a short while the bitter political and personality clashes that marked the teething period of the new government. During this period, the regime's new nationality policy appeared to have made a positive impact on some of the non-Pushtun tribes or national groups. The policy now was to treat all nationalities as equal and to recognize Afghanistan as a multinational state. For the first time, the official media used the Uzbek, Turkoman, and Baloch languages, and the government allowed publication of the works of the great Uzbek poets.[13] Announcements that the government was framing radical policies on land reforms, rural debts, marriage laws and women's education indicated that these were the issues around which the political groups clashed in the first outwardly quiet months after the revolution. The struggle around political lines was fought with characteristic Afghan personality conflicts; under pressure of both, the Parcham faction suffered a humiliating defeat.

In July, Karmal and most other Parcham members of the government were exiled to ambassadorships, some to East European capitals. This, as Louis Dupree has pointed out, was the method Daoud had used to neutralize his political opponents.[14] Karmal was despatched to Prague, Nur Mohammad Nur to Washington, Abdul Wakli to London, Mahmud Baryalay (Babrak's brother) to Islamabad, and Dr Anahita Ratebzad to Belgrade. All of them had been cabinet ministers.[15] Then came the turn of the 'nationalist' faction that had turned down Karmal's overtures. In August an indefinite number of Afghans belonging to this group were put under arrest. Prominent among them were Major-General Qader—Army Chief of Staff—Lt.-Gen. Shapur Ahmadzai, and Dr Mir Ali Akbar, President of the Jamhuriat Hospital. All these three were charged with plotting to overthrow the government. Several other cabinet ministers and ministers of state were arrested in the following days, some were placed under house arrest. 'Confessions' extracted from these leaders of the revolution were broadcast over Kabul Radio and printed in the state-owned newspapers. Babrak Karmal was shown to be the ringleader of the plotters. Karmal, Qader, Nur, Kishtmand, Rafi and Anihita were expelled from the PDPA. In October, the Government ordered all the Parcham ambassadors to return to Afghanistan. None did. Karmal disappeared in the Soviet Union. According to Dupree, most of the arrested and expelled people belonged to Parcham, and wanted the party to adopt a slower pace of reform and to keep Afghanistan more convincingly non-aligned.[16]

Almost immediately after seizing power, the Taraki regime had dismissed a large number of Afghans holding important positions in the civil and development bureaucracies who were suspected of being anti-communist. Afghanistan was already short of trained and experienced personnel. The dismissal of a large number of men of training and experience severely weakened the administration, which was never very strong. The weakness was felt in no time throughout the country when the government sought to implement a series of radical reforms through the derelict administrative machinery. The dismissals also alienated many educated middle-class people from the regime. When these people returned to their homes in the provincial towns and villages they were easily drawn to the ranks of the rebels.

After getting rid of the Parcham and 'nationalist' elements in the government and party leadership, the Khalq faction, now in complete control of the regime, launched its controversial reforms. The thirty-point programme, which was called 'Basic Lines of Revolutionary Duties of the Government of the Democratic Republic of Afghanistan', had been announced on 9 May, less than two weeks after the revolution. Implementation began in July/August. The programme brought almost the entire fabric of Afghan society within reach of the reforms. The reforms were characterized as 'democratic': their purpose was to abolish and eliminate a feudal and pre-feudal social structure and make it fit for a non-capitalist development of Afghanistan.

The Articles of the Basic Lines programme were implemented in the form of Decrees issued under the authority of the revolutionary government. The first two Decrees, issued on 30 April and 1 May, announced the formation of the thirty-member Revolutionary Council and named twenty-one members selected by the Council to serve in the PDPA Cabinet. Decree No. 3 was issued on 14 May, abrogating the 1973 constitution framed by Daoud and establishing legal procedures to be followed until a new constitution could be drawn up. The Decree kept the existing legal system basically intact, but set up a military court to try those who had 'committed offenses against the revolution'. Then came three Decrees in June, announcing a new design for the national flag and a new emblem (solid red with golden symbols); depriving twenty-three members of the royal family of citizenship (they were living abroad and were not affected); and abolishing usury in the villages—the first reform that struck at the root of Afghan society. Decree No. 7, promulgated in October, conferred equal rights on men and women, regulated dowry and marriage expenses, and banned forced marriages. Finally, Decree No. 8, which came in November, introduced land reforms. It recognized private ownership of land, but set rigorous ceilings on holdings, encouraged the formation of co-operatives to facilitate the provision of credits to peasants and distribution of fertilizer, seed, and other agricultural inputs. There was no mention of collectivization.[17]

Some of the reforms were not conceptually new. The republican constitution provided for equal rights for men and women, and land reforms had been talked about since the heady days of Amir Amanullah. However, tradition had triumphed over conceptual enlightenment. Neither equal rights for women nor land reforms were ever enforced. Decrees Nos. 6, 7 and 8 provided the 'political crux' of the Saur revolution. Together, they mounted a frontal assault on the peasant problems of land mortgage and rural indebtedness caused by usurious practices, they limited bride price payments, gave women the freedom to choose their own marriage partners and provided for land reforms through confiscation and redistribution.

Even if land reforms and equal rights for women had been tried by previous Afghan regimes without success, as some American specialists on Afghanistan claim,[18] there is no doubt that the abolition of rural indebtedness and usury was entirely new in Afghanistan's history. Poverty and its twin brother indebtedness were widespread in the

Afghan villages, as we have already noted. A Soviet economist, Vladimir Glukhoded, has estimated that, based on the 1978–9 exchange rate of US$1.00 to about 30 afghanis (afs.), the debt burden of the Afghan peasants totalled a staggering figure of $1 bn! Glukhoded found that Decree No. 6 'considerably eased the burden of usurious debts lying on the landless and land-hungry peasants, repealed the payment of interest on debts, and deferred mortgage payments, etc. According to estimates, the peasants were relieved from paying debts to the sum of about 30 thousand million afghanis.'[19]

The aim of Decree No. 6 was to free 'millions of toiling peasants from the yoke of exploiters'.[20] Land which had been mortgaged before March 1974 by people who did not own more than two hectares of first-grade land or its equivalent was simply to be returned to them after any crops planted on it had been harvested. Land mortgaged after March 1974 had also to be restored to its original owner, but the owner had to repay a percentage of the first mortgage, to be fixed in accordance with the time that would have lapsed between the first mortgage and the date of the announcement of the Decree. Debts owed to 'landowners and usurers' by landless peasants were totally cancelled where these had been taken out before 1974. But differing portions of loans taken out in or after that year had to be repaid, up to a maximum of 90 per cent of loans transacted in 1979, that is, after the Decree had come into force. To implement the Decree, it was decided to set up in each sub-province a Committee for the Solution of Peasants' Problems with representatives of the ministries of agriculture, education and justice, and of the parties directly concerned, presided over by the sub-governor.[21]

Decree No. 7, entitled 'Democratic Rights of Women', was promulgated in October 1978. Afghanistan had a long tradition of efforts to improve the legal and social status of women.

Afghan history and folklore are replete with idealized accounts and legends of heroic women who provided guidance and inspiration to their menfolk in times of crisis. If the ideal personality type for Afghan men is the warrior-poet, a lauded personality type for Afghan women is the poet-heroine.[22]

Amir Amanullah attempted to institutionalize reforms for women. He pressed for the abolition of child marriages, forced marriages and for the assurance of widows' rights. His queen, Suraya, and his sister, Siraj ul-Banat, were the first Afghan women to speak out publicly for women's equality. The conservatives gained power after Amanullah's fall and the movement for women's rights suffered a prolonged setback. However, Daoud moved cautiously towards removing some of the disabilities of, and restrictions on, women during his prime ministership of 1953–63. His government, for instance, supported voluntary removal of the veil and an end to seclusion. Women were encouraged to join the national labour force. The 1964 constitution gave Afghan women the right to vote, and guaranteed women's 'dignity, compulsory education and freedom to work', which, of course, was never implemented. In the 1960s, Afghan women came out into the streets of Kabul to demonstrate for their rights. Further progress was made in the seventies, at least on the statute book, when the penal code and the civil law forbade child marriage, forced marriage and abandonment. The Government did not mean to enforce these laws, and there was always a stronger current of conservative opposition to women leaving their age-old traditional roles. By the time the Marxists took over, the female milieu in Afghanistan was a mixture of liberal trends and values fighting deep-rooted customs, traditions and prejudices, often couched in Islamic rhetoric against liberating women from their feudal shackles. As an American political anthropologist saw the situation:

Few Afghan women wished to destroy their respected status, but many began to ask for a more precise definition, in modern terms, of what constituted honourable behaviour on their part. After all, women had been asked to contribute to national development and enhance the image of a progressive Afghanistan. They had responded with distinction, functioning with poise and dignity, with no loss of honour to themselves or to their families, and with much credit to their nation. They had proved the correctness of the modernist contention that there is nothing inconsistent with Islam, or modesty, and full participation. But as they became increasingly aware of the importance of their roles, women began to examine their opportunities as individuals rather than stereotypes or national symbols. They longed to be released from the strictures of family consensus and given the right to deter-mine life-crises decisions as individuals. They began to articulate goals which conflicted with male-oriented ideals.[23]

The PDPA regime, then, was not attempting anything entirely new or extremely radical in promulgating Decree No. 7. It had been trying to mobilize women politically from the time it was first installed in April. An adult literacy campaign was launched with greater seriousness of purpose than in the past; seminars were held in Kabul and other cities. Taraki said that he believed that 'without the participation of the toiling women no great movement relating to the toiling masses has achieved victory, because women form half of the society.'[24] He told journalists from Poland that 'the People's state not only protects the women's movement but will also carry on intensive and effective struggles to equalize the rights of women with those of men. Afghan women from now on are free in the real sense of the word and have equal rights with men.'[25]

Entitled 'Dowry (*Mahr*) and Marriage Expenses', Decree No. 7 was promulgated with the objective of ensuring 'equal rights of women with men and in the field of civil law and for removing the unjust patriarchal feudalist relations between husband and wife for consolidation of further sincere family ties'. The clumsy phrasing showed that the Decree had been hastily drawn up. Its six Articles benefited men more than women.[26] Article 1 declared, 'No one shall engage a girl or give her in marriage in exchange for cash or commodities'. The immediate benefit went to fathers of marriageable girls, many of whom could not find the money to pay bride price and had to delay their daughters' marriages as a result. Article 2 ordained that 'No one shall compel the bridegroom or his guardians to give holiday presents to the girl or her family.' Article 3 decreed that 'The girl or her guardian shall not take cash or commodities in the name of dowry [*mahr*] in excess of ten dirham according to Shari'at, which is not more than 300 afs. on the basis of the bank rate of silver.' This provision, strictly implemented, would leave a woman with nothing to fall back upon if she were divorced, for Islam does not provide for alimony, and the Decree itself gave no protection to divorced women. Article No. 4 laid down that

Engagements and marriages shall take place with the full consent of the parties involved: (a) No one shall force marriage; (b) No one shall prevent the free marriage of a widow or force her into marriage because of family relationships or patriarchal ties; (c) No one shall prevent legal marriages on the pretext of engagement, forced engagement expenses, or using force.

Article 5 determined that 'Engagement and marriages for women under sixteen and men under eighteen are not permissible'. Finally, Article 6 provided punishment for violaters: '(1) Violaters shall be liable to imprisonment from six months to three years; (2) Cash or commodities accepted in violation of the provisions of this Decree shall be confiscated.'[27]

Decree No. 8—land reforms—was issued in December 1978. Land reform in Afghanistan had first been attempted by Amanullah in the 1920s by selling off large tracts of public land mostly to large proprietors, thereby favouring large ownerships.[28] In 1975, Daoud announced a land reform law, which was in the event barely implemented; if implemented it would have made the middle landowners stronger. At the time of the Saur revolution, considerable inequalities in land ownership prevailed in Afghanistan. There was considerable variation of ownership from region to region; relatively large holdings were common in the south and west. North of the Hindu Kush, large holdings existed side by side with very small ones.[29]

The land reforms Decree of the PDPA regime had two principal provisions. First, it laid down that in future no family could own more than 30 jiribs of first-grade land (4 jiribs make one hectare) or its equivalent; a family could retain larger areas of poorer land in inverse relation to the land's productivity. Holdings in excess of the ceilings specified were to be confiscated by the Land Reforms Department without compensation. (The Decree included elaborate coefficients on the basis of which poorer quality land could be converted into high-grade land.) The second main provision was that confiscated land was to be distributed free to 'deserving persons' in units of 5 jiribs of high-grade land, 6 jiribs of second-quality land, and so on up to a maximum of 50 jiribs of seventh-grade land.

The radical reforms promulgated by the PDPA Government in the latter half of 1978 were significantly in advance of the party's First Programme adopted in 1966. The 1966 document, originally published in the party's then official organ *Khalq* on 11 April of that year, was reprinted in the *Kabul New Times* of 7–10 January 1985 in the midst of the official celebration of the twentieth anniversary of the party. The First Programme of Action of the PDPA had also envisaged the founding of a National Democratic State as the first stage of an Afghan revolution. The National Democratic Government, it stipulated, would be set up by a 'national united front of all progressive, democratic and patriotic forces'; it would include, besides workers, peasants and all working people, the petty as well as the national bourgeoisie, all the forces that took part in 'the national and democratic struggle for national independence, for democratizing social life and for the triumph of anti-imperialist, anti-feudal democratic movement.' The programme said nothing specifically about women. It pledged the party to 'basic land reforms' with the participation of the peasants 'in the direct interest of the landless and petty landholders'. The thrust was anti-feudalistic. The party would cultivate the support of 'small and middle land holders' and would 'guarantee their interests' and work for 'the immediate emancipation' of small and middle peasants, tenant farmers and hired peasants 'from mortgage, loan, forced labour and other feudal burdens of urban and rural landlords and usurers.'

In building a National Democratic State, the PDPA Government announced a nationality policy that was not only politically novel but that also had great potential for making an impact on neighbouring Pakistan and Iran if it could be successfully implemented. In the Marxist–Leninist perception of the PDPA,

Afghanistan is a country whose society is composed of toiling peoples and nationalities who have different cultures and languages. They have lived together for centuries and have unitedly carried out anti-feudal and anti-colonial struggles with common feelings and sufferings. However, as a result of feudalist administration and pro-imperialist policies, the existence of oppression and exploitation, they have not only been deprived of the rights and freedoms, but all these reactionary policies have stood as a great barrier in the way to unity and social progress of the peoples and nationalities of Afghanistan.

The PDPA would therefore reorganize local administration in Afghanistan, taking into account the economic, linguistic and cultural condition of the different nationalities who would enjoy equal rights in the National Democratic State.[30] The PDPA regime not only announced its nationality policy immediately after it came into existence, but also mounted a vigorous propaganda campaign to explain its meaning and implications to the different linguistic groups. Kabul Radio introduced regular broadcasts in Dari, as we have already noted. The regime, then, declared itself against Pushtun domination of Afghan politics, without creating a mass support base either in the Pushtun areas or among the other large national groups.

Between July and December, and right through the summer of 1979, there was a drive to implement all the above reforms simultaneously. At the same time, there were drives against high prices and rampant corruption. Never before in Afghan history had there been such a ruthless attempt to push through so many basic reforms and fundamental changes in so short a period of time.[31] Taken together, they amounted to an unprecedented intervention in the political, economic, social and cultural life of the entire Afghan people. Some of the reforms were undertaken without scientific studies of the macro and micro aspects of the prevailing social and cultural realities. The PDPA had no organization in the provinces; its cadres, small in number, were mostly urban and middle class. The regime therefore had to depend helplessly on the provincial and sub-provincial bureaucracy to implement revolutionary reforms! The officials neither understood the language of the regime nor had much sympathy with its political ideology and objectives. In Afghanistan, as in all other traditional societies, the local officials had long-standing and strong links with the landlords, tribal chiefs and mullahs—the powerbrokers of ancient vintage—deeply entrenched in the rugged land lying between the rocky fingers of the Hindu Kush. The reforms alienated from the regime the entire ruling class in Afghanistan without creating for it supporting constituencies among the deprived and exploited sections of the population. It was not surprising, therefore, that there was resistance to the reforms, and that the resistance was strong and armed in the time-tested traditions of Afghanistan. The single strongest factor that enabled the resistance to snowball in 1978–9 was the regime's singular failure to come to terms with Islam.

5 Islam and the Saur Revolution

The First Action Programme of the PDPA, adopted in 1966, did not mention Islam at all, but guaranteed all Afghans freedom of belief, along with other fundamental rights, in a National Democratic State. Even in the section subtitled 'moral education', the Action Programme did not mention Islam or religion; it pledged the future National Democratic State to promulgate a series of 'mental and moral principles' such as 'loyalty to the aspirations of peace, national democracy, national independence, social welfare and progress, love and respect for the working people, and irreconcilability with reaction, despotism, injustice, exploitation, colonialism, imperialism, bellicose enemies of the people and foes of national and international progressive ideas among the people ....' The PDPA, then, proclaimed itself a completely secular party; the National Democratic State it aspired to was to be a totally secular state, in which all people were to enjoy the same equal right to belief, but the state would promulgate only secular values.

With the proclamation of the Democratic Afghan Republic, the PDPA took care to assure the Afghan people that the State would protect their religious faith and that they would be free to observe their religious rites and customs. The regime appeared to be sensitive to the key role played by Islam in Afghan society and politics, and far from itching for a confrontation with Islam, the regime's propaganda machinery seemed to be anxious to placate the religious leaders and to reassure them that their traditional role was secure in the new dispensation. Nevertheless, as the radical reforms began to be implemented in October 1978, the clergy rose in protest, and by January 1979, the traditional ruling elements—the property-holders and the clergy—joined together to mobilize large segments of the urban–rural people in all Afghanistan to offer armed resistance to the Marxist regime. It was not before the second phase of the Saur revolution—discussed later in this volume—that began after the Soviet intervention and the installation of Babrak Karmal as President of the DRA that the

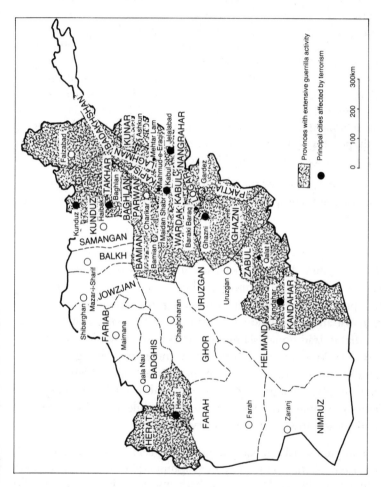

4. Guerrilla and terrorist activity

regime candidly recognized the special role that Islam enjoyed in Afghanistan. Early in 1982, a Soviet reporter recorded after a journey through the Balkh province of Afghanistan,

Mullahs and ulems have always played an important part in the country's life, and this is not to be disregarded. Mazar-i-Sharif [the main city of the province] has 200 mosques, but the St. Ali cathedral mosque stands out among them and is highly revered by all of Afghanistan's Sunnites. Each spring dozens of thousands of pilgrims flock to its cupolaed building to celebrate the red tulip festival. There are nearly one thousand mullahs in the province, and about 320,000 in the whole of Afghanistan, of which 280,000–290,000 constitute the poorest section of the clergy. The ulema organisation of Mazar-i-Sharif includes 120 persons. The mullahs maintain stable contacts with the people's regime. In particular, each Friday—the Moslem day of rest—they pay a visit to the Governor of Mazar-i-Sharif.[1]

This kind of concern for the Islamic clergy and for the role of Islam in Afghanistan was conspicuously missing in the first phase of the revolution.

Soviet scholars recognize the importance of religion, especially Islam, in the political ferment in the traditional societies of the seventies and eighties. A Soviet social scientist writes that in the concrete situation of individual countries, religion can be used 'for retarding social progress and also for stimulating the growth of the anti-imperialist and anti-exploiter sentiments of the popular masses.' She notes that in traditional Islamic countries in the seventies and eighties 'all modern Moslem mass political movements are coming out for the restoration of the fundamental principles of Islam.' Islamic fundamentalism plays an anti–imperialist, nationalist role in certain specific situations in some of the Muslim countries, while in others it is used to defend conservative, even reactionary regimes.

Fundamentalist social and political theories are being used today for various political aims—both as a form of protest against exploitation and as a banner of counter-revolution. However, in both instances, they are oriented in supporting petty proprietors and the non-proletarian sections of the population.[2]

The Taraki–Amin regime did not realize, or else refused to recognize, the constant and dynamic role that Islam and the ideals of *jihad* (religious war) had played in the history of Afghanistan since the eigh-teenth century. Indeed, political and religious concepts merged in Islam, which became the most powerful legitimizing element in the eyes and minds of the people. The Afghans waged *jihad* against the British colonial power based in India. It was by using the concept of *jihad* that Abdur Rahman was able to consolidate the power of the central government over the tribes and local chiefs. In 1919, soon after becoming king, Amir Amanullah declared *jihad* against the British in order to gain complete independence for Afghanistan. When he won his political battle, Amanullah, now a national hero, sought to project his image within and outside Afghanistan as a defender of Islam, both in the temporal and the religious sense. However, his efforts to establish a modern, secular state brought him into conflict, first with the vested interests in rural–urban Afghanistan, particularly the khans, and later, in 1928, with powerful *ruhani*, or Sufi spiritual leaders of Kabul. The *ruhani* were able to mobilize the Muslim masses against Amanullah with the help of 'foreign mullahs'—clergy on the payroll of the British, and the movement against Amanullah became a *jihad* to save Islam. The struggle was fought not over political or ideological issues, because these issues did not exist, but on elemental passions and prejudices stirred up by the traditional vested interests, aided and abetted by the powerful British entrenched on Afghanistan's southern borders.[3]

Nadir Khan came to power after the overthrow of Amanullah as founder of the Musahiban dynasty riding the crest of a conservative, even reactionary counter-revolution spearheaded by Islamic leaders, and this fundamental reality governed the politics of Afghanistan for the next forty years. Nadir Shah could not be expected to challenge the forces of reaction; he had to adopt a policy of accommodation and co-operation, and he invoked Islam to legitimize his rule.

The Musahiban strategy of coopting traditional leadership proved effective—at least in the short run . . . the new structure of power relations had impor-tant long-term local and national effects. On the local level, many of the traditional leaders who relied on community consensus, their own power of persuasion, and exemplary authority, were now effectively transformed into an official ruling elite with an independent source of coercive power and authority. Their association with government and often spatial isolation from their communities resulted in the gradual weakening of their ties and credibility as community leaders, creating a parallel structure to deal with community concerns. Nationally the new official elite began to perpetuate itself through rampant nepotism and a patronage system, thus effectively reducing social and political mobility for those who were not already part of the ruling structure.[4]

However fragmented the rural power structure of Afghanistan— fragmented by tribal, linguistic, social, economic and even religious divisions—the tenuous links between government and community increased the importance of traditional leaders. At the same time, for most Afghans, Islam provided the order and cohesion without which no social organism can survive. In the perception of the ordinary Afghan, the state and Islam were indivisible; government service was service to Islam; government was the protector of Islam and thereby the protector of the Afghan identity. This was known to all rulers of Afghanistan from Nadir Shah to Daoud, and it should have been known to Taraki and Amin, although they were Marxists. In their revolutionary zeal, they abolished the Islamic judicial system, the one living link between individuals and the state, and a powerful symbol of an Afghan's identity as a Muslim. Going a fatal step further, they ordered the ideologically converted schoolteachers not to support the basic Islamic tenets, but to propagate the fundamental principles of the Saur revolution.[5]

In 1979, the PDPA regime confronted two Islamic rebellions. One was politically conservative in nature, the other fundamentalist. The conservative Islamic elements consisted mostly, if not entirely, of propertied people dispossessed by the reforms; they raised the banner of Islam with the willing co-operation of conservative mullahs who saw the new rulers in Kabul as communists and therefore enemies of Islam. The conservatives feared radical politics, even if couched in Islamic terms. They had long enjoyed the patronage of Kabul which had given them control of local affairs and to whom they had rendered valuable service in the form of the loyalty of the mass of the Afghan people. The conservative Islamic elements had no appetite for government intervention in the life of Afghans; they had lived for a long time in peace with Kabul's doctrine of minimum government, which ensured their own control of local affairs. They saw the role of government primarily as defender of Afghanistan's independence and sovereignty, as well as the traditional power and influence of local leaderships; they needed government to legitimate the system of Islamic justice, manned and administered by officials who loyally obeyed the Sharia't. As we shall see in the next chapter, the conservative Islamic elements rose in rebellion primarily as a result of DRA's frontal attack on the local power structure, and were able to mobilize the masses by exploiting the Marxist regime's attack on certain hoary symbols of Islam in Afghanistan.

The other Islamic rebellion was fundamentalist in political perspective and ideology. A fundamentalist Islamic movement had existed in Afghanistan since the sixties; its manifestation in Kabul was in the Jawanan-i-Musulman—Muslim Youth—which had sprung up in 1965 as a prompt response to the emergence of the PDPA. As the rebellions spread in 1979, three conservative or traditionalist Islamic groups emerged parallel to four fundamentalist groups. The conservatives organized around a pattern of personal loyalties. Amongst them were leading figures of the former regime, tribal chiefs and traditionalist religious leaders trained in private *madrasas*. They were found mostly in Pushtun-dominated southern Afghanistan, close to the Pakistani border.[6] The traditionalists' objective was given out as the safeguarding of the independence of Afghanistan and the defence of Islam. They lacked a programme of reforms, they favoured the restoration of the monarchy. An alliance of three traditionalist groups responded positively to an appeal made by the former King, Zahir Shah, in July 1983, to join him in the formation of a National United Front against the Soviet-Karmal forces. The traditionalists have strong family and business connections in the West, especially in the United States, Canada and Britain, and access to Western social scientists and journalists. They want direct and increasing military and political support from the United States as well as Saudi Arabia and Egypt. In the Western mass media, they are often described as 'moderates'.[7]

The Islamic fundamentalists are revolutionaries of a different hue from the Marxists of the PDPA. They want a radical restructuring of Afghan society based on an unequivocal and explicit Islamic mandate. They want to eliminate ethnic distinctions between Pushtuns and the non-Pushtun tribes or national groups because they believe these distinctions are un-Islamic and only weaken the Afghan state by keeping its population divided and at war with itself. They want a new order based on authentic brotherhood and the equality of all nationalities. They regard the pre-1978 political system in Afghanistan as seriously flawed; they reject the restoration of the monarchy. The fundamentalists want an assertive central government—government's role must be activist, intrusive, doctrinaire.[8] One of the fundamentalist resistance groups, the Afghan National Liberation Front, projected its political programme in the following language:

The Afghan National Liberation Front strongly believes that the sincere and true application of Islamic principles is the only way to ensure the survival and well-being of our nation. Therefore, we shall struggle for the establishment of a government founded on Islamic teachings and our own traditions of democracy.

. . . The ANLF . . . opposes emphatically the re-establishment of one man or one party dictatorship depriving our people of their right to self-determination.

ANLF will fight against ethnic discrimination, class distinction, economic exploitation in Afghanistan, and will strive for establishment of an economic and social order consistent with the Islamic concept of social justice.

ANLF will fight for the protection of individual rights, the right to live, the right to be free, the right to equality before justice, the right to equal opportunity, and the right to personal property.

ANLF will fight all elements of imperialism and feudalism which hinder the establishment of a politically independent, economically prosperous, and socially progressive Afghanistan.

ANLF . . . will re-establish, according to Afghanistan's traditional policy, a true and constructive neutrality.[9]

For the Islamic fundamentalists, then, it is not enough to liberate Afghanistan from Soviet occupation and to defend Islam; it is equally important to establish an Islamic political and social order. They hold the Musahiban dynasty directly responsible for the plight of Afghanistan. They are basically anti-Western, or, more precisely, anti-American. As one of their leaders put it, 'The Afghan mujahidin are now well aware that imperialism and communism are like the two blades of a pair of scissors for the purpose of cutting the roots of our beloved religion: Islam.'[10] They do not believe that the United States is interested in a quick solution to the conflict in Afghanistan.[11] The

Islamic fundamentalists in Afghanistan evidently see themselves as part of the anti-imperialist and radically nationalist stream of Islamic fundamentalism which triumphed in Iran in 1979 under the leadership of Ayatollah Khomeini, and which has its following in several Muslim countries in the Middle East, the Persian Gulf and South Asia, including Pakistan.

Several attempts have been made to bring together the seven Islamic resistance groups into a single coalition or alliance, but none has met with success. The three traditionalist organizations—the National Liberation Front, led by Sibghatullah Mujahidi, the Islamic National Front of Sayyid Ahmad Gailani, and the Islamic Revolutionary Movement, led by Mawlawi Muhammad Nabi Muhammadi, have at times worked together in loose alliances. Gailani and Mujahidi belonged to a reputed *ruhani* family with strong ties with the Musahiban dynasty and officialdom. Muhammadi, on the other hand, was a traditional Islamic scholar trained in the *madrasa*, but he too had strong ties with the royal household.

The four fundamentalist or revolutionary Islamic rebel organizations are the Islamic Society of Afghanistan (JIA) led by Burhanuddin Rabbani; the Islamic Party of Gulbudin Hikmatyar; a second Islamic Party, formed after a split, of which the leader is Mawlawi M. Yunus Khalis; and the Islamic Alliance for the Liberation of Afghanistan, led by Abdur Rabbur Rasul Sayyaf. Rabbani and Sayyaf had been students at the Islamic Studies Department of Kabul University and at Al-Azhar University in Cairo; at the time of the Saur revolution, both were teaching at Kabul University. Khalis had been educated in a *madrasa*, but was nevertheless a rather radical Islamic preacher and intellectual. He broke with Hikmatyar as a result of personality and tactical conflicts. Hikmatyar's group is still the largest of the Islamic rebel groups. He was a former engineering student at Kabul University. Selig Harrison wrote in 1981 that Hikmatyar's 'piety is manifested in a facial expression that foreigners have never seen crease with a smile. His fighters have recently taken to carrying Super-8 movie cameras to battle to supply the world with visual evidence of their exploits.'[12]

Islam *per se* has not been an insuperable barrier to communism. The Indonesian Communist Party (PKI), the largest party outside the communist world in the early sixties, consisted of millions of Muslim peasants; its support base was also among the Muslim peasantry. The Marxist struggle in Yemen in the sixties was not unduly impeded by the Islamic factor. It was supported by a powerful Muslim neighbour—the Egypt of Nasser—and opposed by another powerful Islamic power, Saudi Arabia. The Soviets had succeeded in overpowering Islamic resistance in the Central Asian republics of the USSR in a long civil war of attrition, and the Chinese communists had not met with irreducible resistance from the Muslims of Sinjiang.

Afghanistan's Islamic factor proved to be particularly difficult for the leaders of DRA because Islam had for centuries been a popular political-religious ideology of the people of that country; it had been woven into the emotional and symbolic myths of Afghan nationalism. The DRA leaders singularly failed to mobilize Islam on behalf of the revolution; they antagonized it and succeeded in being seen by the Afghan masses as the enemy of Islam. For this, their own revolutionary zeal and impatience was to a large extent responsible, as we shall see in the following chapter. At the same time, the triumph of the Iranian revolution over the Shah of Iran and his great patron, the United States, was undoubtedly a very important factor, which Amin totally failed to take into account. The fundamentalism of the Iranian revolution had a strong impact on the Islamic fundamentalists of Afghanistan. As Fred Halliday put it,

As far as Afghanistan is concerned, the Shah's regime would have been less menacing than that of Khomeini; although the organizational ability of the previous regime to assist the counter-revolution might well have been greater, the power of ideological mobilization would have been much less, especially if it is remembered how much the Shah's previous interference in Afghan affairs had been resented.[13]

The fundamentalist Islamic upsurge against the Saur revolution in 1978-9 in Afghanistan was not without its own weakness, however. Its greatest weakness, as noted, lay in the failure of the several fundamentalist groups to unite and offer a credible political alternative to DRA. Apart from the four main fundamentalist groups, there were dozens of smaller ones, including the Afghan National Liberation Front, a part of whose political programme was quoted earlier (pp. 62). The emergence of Islamic fundamentalism in Afghanistan alarmed the Soviet Union no less than the United States and Pakistan. The Soviets were able to get some sympathy from the United States and other countries when in 1980-1 they were able to project Afghanistan's Islamic fundamentalism as an existing and potential threat to the Central Asian republics of the Soviet Union. Americans had little sympathy for the Iranian brand of Islamic fundamentalism as it appeared to prevail in Afghanistan. The same was the case with Pakistan. Its military dictator, General Zia-ul Haq, was trying cautiously to introduce his own variety of Islamization modelled by and largely on Saudi fundamentalism. Indeed, the Pakistan military regime and the Jamaat-i-Islami, which was given responsibility for attending to the huge mass of Afghan refugees who had assembled in the North-West Frontier Province, have been determined to keep Afghanistan's anti-imperialist Islamic fundamentalism at bay. The Afghan fundamentalists were also affected by the unending, gradually escalating Iraq-Iran war. The Islamic revolutionary regime of Iran could not extend to the Afghan fundamentalists as much help as it might have done if it had not been locked in a wasting war with Iraq.

In the second phase of the Saur revolution, DRA, under the leadership of Babrak Karmal, wasted no time in launching a strong campaign to placate the Islamic clergy and to make amends for the errors committed by Amin. However, the Soviet military intervention and the presence of over 100,000 Russian troops in Afghanistan armed the rebels with an emotive *nationalist* cause; they were now fighting to rid Afghanistan of foreign invaders, they told the masses. Their claim was confirmed on the ground as the rebel groups faced offensives mounted by the Soviet troops directly or in co-operation with the seriously depleted troops of the DRA. However, as will be seen in later pages of this study, overcoming the Islamic resistance became perhaps the single most important preoccupation of the Karmal regime through the mid-eighties, and, since 1983, it has seemed to be slowly gaining ground among sections of the Muslim clergy, especially in the non-Pushtun areas.

6   Revolution on the Verge of Collapse

Within twenty months, the Saur revolution was brought to the brink of collapse. The reasons were two-fold. By April 1979, the one-year-old PDPA regime was under seige from within. However, the mounting resistance was not the only factor that drove the regime to the precipice. An equally contributory factor was the war within the revolutionary leadership. Afghan factionalism proved fatal for the Khalq phase of the revolution. It also denied the resistance its chance of offering a credible alternative to the Afghan people.

The first six months of the revolution passed off reasonably quietly. The United States embassy in Kabul was not sure that the DRA was a Marxist-controlled, pro-Soviet state. Harking back to America's China experience, Washington's attitude was one of waiting and watching rather than rushing to an apocalyptic conclusion. The Shah of Iran had begun to hear the first ominous rumblings of the Islamic funda- mentalist revolution, as mentioned before. Pakistan's Zia-ul Haq was still trying to cement the foundations of his less than one-year-old military regime. The Soviets had hastened to confer diplomatic recog- nition on the DRA, and Soviet political, security and economic support was quickly coming in, but the world did not see the new regime as having been propped up by Moscow or as coming rapidly under Moscow's control.[1]

The Afghan peasant was busy in his fields. From early spring to early fall, rural Afghans 'place the stone of the mountain'—in other words, bury the hatchet—in order to give themselves to the agricultural and herding cycle. The Saur revolution had only occurred in Kabul; the rest of Afghanistan took a little time to react to it. Both Khalq and Parcham parties were city-based without any organizational reach to the rocky depths of rural Afghanistan. But the revolutionary regime was impatient to bring about radical structural change in Afghanistan's tradition-bound, backward society. The initial Afghan reaction to the revolution was far from being either uniformly positive or negative. The leftist intellectuals in Kabul and the major provincial cities were jubilant. Islamic activists were dismayed. But 'there was little reaction from the majority' of Afghan people. The Khalq-Parcham coalition was carried to the provinces and thence to the sub-provinces. For a short while, they worked together. In Badakhshan province alone, Khalq party membership increased by two hundred. 'The new members were mostly urbanites from district centers, a few with rural backgrounds from the central districts, and substantial numbers from the peripheries, especially Shughnan, where peasants reportedly joined as well.'[2] What happened in Badakhshan, the province of Afghanistan that borders the USSR, and where the Saur revolution did better than elsewhere, was certainly not repeated all over the country. But the general mood of the Afghan masses was to wait and see what the new regime would do, how it would behave, whether and in what manner it would be different from the previous regimes that had prevailed in distant Kabul. One single group of Islamic fundamentalists, led by Gulbudin Kikmatyar, broke the general mood of tense waiting. Members of this group fled to Pakistan immediately after the proclamation of DRA, and began to conduct sporadic attacks from Pakistan territory as early as May/June 1978.

The DRA had two options while inaugurating its regime of reforms. It could proceed slowly, cautiously, adopting a tactical line of gradualism, rapidly building up its rural network, and pursuing a policy of adoption and exploitation of the ethnic and cutural divisions and animosities in Afghan society. Or it could plunge headlong into action, relying more on coercion than on persuasion, arguing that caution and gradualism would only allow the resistance to growth in strength. The dominant Khalq faction in the PDPA adopted the second option after defeating the Parcham faction in a bitter and tense internal debate; almost all representatives of the Parcham faction in the Cabinet and the Revolutionary Council were banished to ambassadorial jobs, as we have already seen.

Fred Halliday, in a Marxist critique of the Saur revolution, has identified four aspects of the rural structure of Afghanistan that gravely complicated the programme of social transformation.[3] The first was that the peasants of Afghanistan did not perceive social relations in the rural areas in class terms. Tribal, ethnic and religious factors intersected economic divisions in rural Afghanistan. 'Any attempt to reform such a system by appealing to the class interests of the poor and landless peasants was bound to run into considerable difficulties.' The ethnic, religious and tribal factors were the strongest in the Pushtun areas, but they were not much less strong in the northern plains where land-owning relationships are most differentiated. This difficulty was further compounded by the fact that about 15 per cent of the Afghan population still lived mainly by their nomadic flocks, and knew very little of class relationships or ownership patterns.

The second vital aspect of rural Afghanistan that, in Halliday's analysis, created considerable problems for the Saur revolution, was the 'traditional independence of the mountain tribes'. These tribes had in the past been paid subsidies by the Government in Kabul; among them 'the bearing of arms was a natural feature of adult life'.[4] A number of the reforms, particularly those relating to land, and the regime's attempts to eradicate smuggling, angered many of these tribes. The government in Kabul was their traditional adversary. The PDPA could have overcome these difficulties posed by the armed tribes if it had had an organization among them: it had none. The third obstacle was the 'weight of Afghan political traditions', which affected the PDPA as it had done all Afghan political groups. 'Afghanistan is a country where political and social issues have tended to be settled by the gun and where the room for peacefully handling conflicts within the state, or between the state and its subjects, is extremely limited.' The fourth adverse condition for the revolution in Afghan society was the people's attitude to Islam.

Halliday also mentions three other problems which contributed to the checking of the initial dynamic of the revolution. The first was 'the disunity and the extremely undemocratic internal structure of the PDPA itself.' Not only did the Khalq and Parcham factions fall out with one another within weeks of the revolution, within Khalq also, factional in-fighting broke out in no time, and these disputes were settled by bullets rather than by votes. The second problem was the deteroriation of the regional climate, in particular, the impact of the Iranian revolution. Khomeini lost little time in making the cause of Islamic Afghanistan his own, and his victory in Iran, over the combined power of the Shah and the United States, provided the fundamentalists in Afghanistan with a passionate ideology to fight the 'anti-Islamic'

Marxist regime. The third problem, in Halliday's view, was the impact of the Sino–Soviet conflict on Afghanistan. The PDPA regime was aligned with Moscow; but in the initial months, it tried to placate the Chinese leaders too. In order to keep Beijing in good humour, it broke with South Korea and established diplomatic relations with the North. Taher Badakhshi, leader of a Maoist faction, was given a berth in the Cabinet. But the Chinese were not pleased. They never extended support to the Saur revolution, did not in fact recognize it as a Marxist revolution. Halliday believes the reason for the Chinese antipathy was the PDPA's failure to mention even a nominal independence of Moscow, within the narrow margin that was available to it. The PDPA did not support the Iranian revolution until November 1978, waiting for the CPSU to give the lead. It extended diplomatic recognition to the Heng Semrin regime in Kampuchea. The alliance with Badakhshi soon collapsed and he quit the Cabinet and took up armed opposition. Early in February 1979, around the time of the Chinese invasion of Vietnam, it became known for the first time that China was sending arms to the Afghan rebels via Pakistan. During the Sino–Vietnam war, there were apprehensions in Moscow that the Chinese might attack Afghanistan across the Hindu Kush to compensate for the setbacks in Indo-China. In June 1979, Chinese hostility to the Afghan revolution became explicit. *Beijing Review*, in its issue of 15 June, stressed Soviet strategic and economic interest in Afghanistan and quoted 'public opinion abroad' suggesting that Afghanistan was becoming the 'sixteenth republic' of the Soviet Union.

Since the summer of 1978, the man who was actually in control of the PDPA Government in Kabul was Hafizullah Amin: he was Deputy Prime Minister, Foreign Minister and Politbureau Secretary, and he held complete sway over the armed forces, and over Aqsa, the new secret police force established with Soviet assistance immediately after the revolution.[5] The outbreak of armed resistance in the fall weakened Taraki's position. On 28 March 1979, in a dramatic (and ominous) reshuffle of the Cabinet and the Government, Amin became Prime Minister while retaining the foreign affairs portfolio. Taraki remained President, Secretary-General of the PDPA, and Commander-in-Chief of the armed forces. All the ministers in the new eighteen-man Cabinet were Khalqis, including some who had been members of the Parcham faction earlier but had defected to Khalq. Only two of the eighteen were new faces: Sadiq Alam Yar, an engineer, who became Minister for Planning, and Khayal Mohammad Katawazi, who was put in charge of radio and television.[6] Together with the new Cabinet, a nine-member Homeland High Defence Council was set up to run the security forces. At the same time, the Soviets took a more active and visible part in the whole government machinery. This was evidently the result of the treaty of peace and friendship that the Soviets had signed with the DRA in November 1978. The treaty gave the Soviets legitimacy in assisting the revolutionary regime to secure internal stability as well as to defend itself from external intervention or attack. On 6 April 1979, a high-level Soviet delegation led by General Alexei Yepishev, First Deputy Defence Minister and President of Political Affairs of the Soviet Army and Navy, arrived in Kabul. Yepishev is known to be one of the most hardline Soviet generals.[7]

Soon after Yepishev's visit, Vassily Safronchuk, a councillor in the Soviet embassy in Kabul, was made co-ordinator of Soviet and Afghan efforts to deal with the swiftly escalating armed resistance. He took up an office next to Taraki's in the People's House in Kabul. By the end of the summer of 1979, up to five thousand Soviet civilian advisers were helping the PDPA streamline its administrative machinery:

large sums of money, running into millions of dollars a day, were being used to subsidize the state, and Russian responsibility for the military campaign became more direct. Russian forces took over the Bagram air base north of Kabul, officers were posted down to the company level, and from the spring onwards, most Afghan military planes flew with at least one Russian pilot, to counter political dissatisfaction in the air force. This was an especially important development, since, as the situation on the ground deteriorated, the government came to rely more and more on air power to fight the rebellion.[8]

The way in which the situation on the ground deteriorated has been described by a number of American anthropologists who have done field-work in Afghanistan and who claim to have first-hand information or knowledge of how the people of a number of provinces reacted to the radical reforms put through by the Marxist regime. These scholars have agreed on four errors committed by the regime and on two of its fundamental weaknesses as major contributing factors to the rapid spread and strengthening of the resistance between the fall of 1978 and the winter of 1979. The errors were, first, the wholesale sacking of experienced administrators and technocrats who were not regarded as committed supporters of the revolution. Afghanistan was so short of competent hands in government that this action soon left the PDPA regime without the personnel essential to maintain a minimum level of administrative efficiency. Second, too much was attempted in too short a period in a country long-accustomed to traditional torpor and inertia; a more gradualist, incremental approach might have given better results. Third, the biased language of Marxist–Leninism in which the projection of the reforms was couched was foreign to the Afghan villager who had long been accustomed to a purely Islamic political language and society. And fourth, too much force was used to suppress even the initial acts of resistance that were necessarily of a low level of violence. The two fundamental weaknesses of the revolutionary regime, which contributed in a big way to its failure to mobilize rural support were, first, the PDPA's lack of an organizational base beyond the main towns and cities, and, second, the alienation of its city-based youth cadres from the rural population, their customs, passions, prejudices, culture and behaviour.[9]

The rebellion began in Nuristan, which is a 5,000-square mile region strategically located in north-western Afghanistan. Since early times, caravans, pilgrims, traders, explorers, travellers and soldiers have traversed routes through and around Nuristan that link the fertile valleys of central Afghanistan and the Amu Darya (Oxus) basin to the plains of the South Asian subcontinent. On 4 October 1978, a combined resistance force from the Kom, Mumo and Kato tribes of the Landay Sin Valley of Nuristan attacked the Kamdesh district government post near a village named Yurmur. After a three-day battle, the outpost fell to the attackers. In a few weeks, the whole of eastern Nuristan came under the control of the rebels. 'Thus began the first sustained insurgency against the Communist government in Afghanistan', writes Richard F. Strand, of the Wesleyan University of Connecticut. 'In the ensuing six months the Nuristanis fought successfully against Communist counterattacks. By April 1979 Communist forces had been totally repulsed from eastern Nuristan; six months later most of the rest of Kunar province was free of Communist control.'[10]

According to Strand, the Nuristanis were angry with the Marxist regime because it had sacked 'their people' from the Government, thereby breaking their links with the centre. Nuristanti elites thus lost their 'personal ties' with government, which they had established during the reign of Daoud. They had already labelled the Marxist regime anti-Islamic; now, they saw it also as hostile to the Nuristani ruling elite. The Marxists arrested a number of eminent Nuristani tribal leaders; some of them were local heroes. The aggrieved tribal leaders were able to mobilize youth and the clergy. The Marxists tried to exploit inter-tribal rivalries. They declared that the Nuristanis had abandoned Islam and become apostates. They mobilized a number of other tribes and appointed a Gujar leader, Gul Muhammad, as commander of the 'tribal irregulars'. The Nuristani rebels defeated the tribal irregulars and the rebel leader, Muhammad Anwar, a charismatic Kom tribal chief, established a form of rebel government in a cluster of Kom villages with traditional tribal leaders charged with specific duties. In 1979 Nuristani rebels received arms from one of the conservative rebel groups camping in Peshawar, but the leader of a fundamentalist group, Gulbudin Kikmatyar, tried to divide the Nuristanis in an effort to recruit followers from among them. In 1980, Nuristani rebel leaders set up their own office in Peshawar and sought support from 'foreign governments'. However, 'the lack of response embittered them toward what they perceived as an international conspiracy to force them under the domination of the Peshawar guerrilla organizations.'[11]

The situation was different in the Vaygal Valley in Nuristan, homeland of 8,500 people divided into nine corporate communities called *des*. All these communities are known as Kalashas. During Daoud's time, the Kalasha elite had forged links with central government. However, the Kalashas preferred minimum intervention by Kabul in their local affairs. Kalashas are profoundly Islamic: they see state and Islam as indivisible. The massive purges conducted by the PDPA regime 'virtually eliminated Kalasha links to the top government level. . . . Many urban Nuristanis who were not arrested fled to the relative security of their mountain villages.'

David J. Katz, of Washington University, Seattle, says that Kalashas found the Marxist bid to establish a strong, all-powerful government in Kabul repugnant to their culture and political traditions. The announced reforms threatened to penetrate the fabric of their social, economic and political life. The Kalashas were alarmed when they found that, unlike previous regimes, the Marxist regime took the reforms seriously and meant to implement them. They found the new government's pronouncements 'antagonistic and confrontational.'[12]

The Marxist Government had not mobilized popular political support before launching its reform programme. It had won some support by promising to accommodate ethnic minorities neglected by the previous regimes. The majority of the Kalasha, however, saw the Marxist regime as dominated by the Pushtuns. 'Kalasha had no reason to expect that these (Pushtun) leaders would either tolerate or accommodate the legitimate interests of non-Pakhtun ethnic populations.'[13] Insurgency in the Vaygal Valley was ignited in 1978 by the arrest by the government of a number of Safi religioius activists. The government had tried to defuse a Safi uprising by negotiation, but had failed. Other uprisings followed. In 1979, however, the situation in the Vaygal Valley was very mixed. The resistance was divided between Islamic conservatives and fundamentalists. There was little co-operation or co-ordination between the two. Katz did not see Islam as the single determining factor in the Kalasha's break with the Marxist regime. In his view, 'the critical abiding interests of Vaygal Valley Kalasha are with preserving security, peace and control over their resources and lives. Through their rebellion, whatever the particular ideological rationale, Vaygal Valley Kalasha show that they do not believe the current government can satisfy these interests.'[14]

R. Lincoln Keiser has given an account of the resistance in Darra-i-Nur, a side valley within the Kunar River Valley system, located about 65 miles from the city of Jalalabad, and inhabited by about 10,000 people, speaking a variety of dialects, the principal one being Pashai. Fighting between the people of Darra-i-Nur and troops of the PDPA Government broke out in the winter of 1979. The rebel forces were led by Mir Beg, who was able to bring under one banner of rebellion a number of tribes over a wide region that had seldom come together before to fight for a common cause. For this uncommon achievement of the rebels, Keiser found four main reasons. First, the traditional animosity between the people of Darra-i-Nur and the Pushtun-dominated Government in Kabul, which had not changed as a result of the Saur revolution. Second, the Marxist Government was seen to be striking at the root of corruption and nepotism which had fed the local administration for a very long time. Third, there was the 'introduction of Communist ideology and the debunking of Muslim beliefs in the primary schools.' The fourth factor which helped the rebels to mobilize on pan-tribal lines was the Government policy on increasing military conscription. Keiser writes:

The symbolic linking of Islam with unified political opposition would not have occurred if either the Communist government had retained the Muslim judicial system which symbolically identified previous regimes with Islam, or government teachers and officials in Darra-i-Nur had at least publicly supported basic Islamic tenets. However, because the government both secularized the system of justice and publicly attacked Islamic beliefs, it became identified with kafirism.[15]

The responses to the Saur revolution of the people of Badakhshan were very different. These ranged from 'active support of the Communist government in Kabul, to passive acceptance of its rule, to an exodus from the area, to armed uprisings challenging the legitimacy of the regime', reports M. Nazif Shahrani, of Pitzer College, Claremont, California.[16] Badakhshan, as already noted, borders the USSR; its Soviet neighbour is the Tajik SSR. It also shares borders with China and Pakistan. Its land area of 40,886 sq. km. is economically and infrastructurally one of the most backward in Afghanistan. It has hardly any industry, and it has been a victim of chronic neglect at the hands of the Pushtun-dominated governments in Kabul. Over the whole province there are practically no roads that can be used throughout the year. Little effort has been made over the decades to improve Badakhshan's agriculture and animal husbandry. The population is ethnically highly heterogenous. The major linguistic groups are the Uzbeks and the Tajiks.

In Badakhshan the traditional rural leaders had pursued a policy of avoidance rather than confrontation regarding the state. However, attitudes began to change with the advent of education. Beginning in 1930, the Government opened a network of modern schools in the province; in the 1950s, when foreign aid started flowing into Afghanistan, the schools were upgraded. Graduates of these schools were sent to Kabul to train as teachers, agricultural experts, technicians and theologists. In 1958, students from Badakhshan were admitted to the military high school in Kabul. Many of these students were drawn to the leftist movement in the 1960s, and became members of either the Khalq or the Parcham parties. Three of these people, Mansur Hashimi, Tahir Badakhshi and Burhanuddin Rabbani, rose to leading roles in provincial as well as national politics. Hashimi joined the Khalq faction following his higher education at the Teachers' College of Columbia University in New York and became one of the four or five known Khalq party members from Badakhshan. Badakhshi, too, joined the Khalq party in 1965 and became a member of the central committee of the PDPA. When the PDPA split, he joined Babrak Karmal's Parcham faction. His second wife happens to be a sister of Sultan Ali Kishtmand, prime minister in the government set up in the last days of 1979 with Karmal as president. Rabbani, on the other hand, took a leading part in founding the Muslim Youth Group, of conservative Islamic orientation, and went into resistance when the Democratic Republic of Afghanistan was established. He went into self-exile first to Saudi Arabia and then to Pakistan, from where he has been leading his resistance faction within Afghanistan.

The first major armed insurgency in Badakhshan occurred a year after the Saur revolution. In April 1979 a group of educated youth, of Maoist persuasion, attacked an army post at Baharak, and captured the sub-district centre. The army retaliated with brute force, killing forty members of the group, and capturing and executing others. The regime unleashed a reign of repression, with mass imprisonments, torture and murder of suspected enemies. 'Hundreds of respected local 'ulama, ruhani teachers and pious individuals were drowned in the Kukcha river, a major tributary of the Amu Darya.'[17] By August 1980, as many as three thousand people had reportedly been executed. The repression helped a group of Islamic conservatives to organize resistance and establish links with similar groups of resisters. They also sent representatives to Peshawar to meet with Rabbani. The group known as Jamaat-i-Islami (JIA) set up its headquarters in Peshawar.

'Since the beginning of the rebellion, the battle lines have not changed', wrote Shahrani in 1983.

The Isma'ili population near the Soviet borders has either sided with the government or accepted the new order without resistance . . .. In the central areas of Badakhshan, the mujahidin were in virtual control (with the exception of the garrison and the airstrip in Faizabad) from September 1979 to June 1980, when the Soviets began an air offensive and began sending armoured divisions . . . to the embattled areas. In July 1980 the mujahidin estimated a combined Soviet and Afghan force of 12,000 in the province. They also estimated human losses to be between 15,000 to 20,000. Up to 90 per cent of the Sitami Milli (Maoist) in the province are believed to have been killed—not only by the mujahidin, but by the Khalqis and Parchamis as well.[18]

Thomas J. Barfield, of Harvard University, has given a perceptive list of the failures of the PDPA regime in the first phase of the Saur revolution.[19] The revolution's fundamental weakness was that it only happened at the national level, in Kabul, with practically no base in the villages. At the same time, its reform programme was sweeping in scope. 'This program was bound to raise issues that had been buried since the fall of Amanullah, yet the DPDA did not see provincial opposition or difficulties in implementation as insurmountable obstacles.' The PDPA's confidence was based on its control of the army. It overlooked the fact that Afghanistan had been ruled and its internal peace maintained not by the army but by the linkages that the previous regimes had forged with the local chieftains in the countryside.

The PDPA regime's second great mistake was to depend on the civil and military bureaucracies to implement radical reforms. The provincial administration was soon found to be woefully inadequate in discharging the responsibilities assigned to it. The reforms could not be implemented because the arguments advanced by the regime were alien to the common Afghan. Also, because the regime lost the ideological battle, at the local level, tribal and religious leaderships were better organized than the revolutionary government.

'The PDPA failed not only to analyse the objective state of Afghanistan's economic and social development, but also to put the party's propaganda in a form that would attract a broader base of support outside the party itself.' In spite of the fact that Afghanistan's economy was almost exclusively agricultural, and Afghan society was both bound and split by bonds of kinship and religion, the PDPA declared that the Saur revolution was proletarian in nature. 'As a result, it appealed consistently to class interests in a country where the political idiom was still tribal or religious.' The PDPA also failed to consider the ramifications of its actions. 'Many of the issues it considered purely economic had social components, and many of its social reforms affected such basic values as family honor.'

Perhaps the most basic difficulty faced by the national government was its own weakness at the provincial and subprovincial levels. Under the Musahiban dynasty, traditional tribal and religious leadership had grown weaker in the face of growing government authority. Nevertheless, villagers still sought out non-governmental leaders when they wanted solutions to many problems. The existence of such an alternative power structure, while of minor importance in normal times, provided a ready-made political structure to organize against the new government. At the local level, traditional leaders had the ability to bring their neighbours together using kinship and personal contacts. Unlike the PDPA, opposition leaders used the old political language of Afghanistan, calling on their followers to defend the faith of Islam, the honor of their families and country, and their property. The parochial nature of this type of opposition made it pervasive but non-centralized, resulting in the seeming paradox of the PDPA government becoming weakened to the point of collapse without an easily identifiable enemy at the national or international levels.[20]

Hugh Beattie, of the School of Oriental Studies, University of London, has given a first-hand account of how the people of Nahrin, a town located about one hundred miles north of Kabul in the northern foothills of the Hindu Kush, reacted to the reforms promulgated by the Marxist regime.[21] The town contains the administrative headquarters of the sub-province of Nahrin, which had in 1974 a population of 70,000, of whom Pushtuns were in a majority, and Uzbeks and Tajiks strong minorities. Beattie says that after the new Decree reforming marriage and bride price laws had been promulgated, 'it looked as though the people in Nahrin would try to observe its provisions'. Weddings were less elaborate. There were rumours that two people had been prosecuted for breaking the new laws. However, the new laws were not popular. 'People with unmarried daughters resented the decree most because they could no longer expect to receive brideprice payments for them when they were married.' The Decree was particularly unpopular because 'it represented a threat to male honor. By banning brideprice—and especially by declaring that women could marry whom they pleased—it threatened to undermine the strict control over women on which the maintenance of male honor depended.'

Under the PDPA regime, Beattie adds, the local administration was more accessible to the poor than in the past. However, although the new sub-governor came from a poor family and an unsophisticated background, and was young and energetic, he soon proved to be as much of an autocrat as his predecessors. Little effort was made by the sub-governor to build a party organization although he allowed his house to be used as the headquarters of the PDPA.

Taken together, the Khalq government's reforms and the manner in which they were implemented in Nahrin amounted to a vigorous if not always well-conceived attempt to change existing economic and political relationships and to alter many patterns of customary behaviour. . . . [Therefore] in spite of the popularity of one or two of the new policies, it is hardly surprising that the overall reaction was one of irritation and anger at the extent to which the new government was interfering in people's lives. The irritation and anger were compounded by the fact that most people in Nahrin felt a deeper loyalty to Islam than to the Afghan state. Islam, it was believed, sanctioned most, if not all of their cherished customs, particularly those concerning the status of women and marriage. Hence it was felt that in trying to change these, the Khalq government was attacking Islam.[22]

In a neo-Marxist critique of the first phase of the Saur revolution, Fred Halliday found that the strategy to enforce a regime of radical reforms in a traditional, change-resistant society that Amin and his principal Soviet adviser, Safronchuk, designed in 1979, rested on three main points.[23] First, there would be a relentless military response to all signs of resistance or counter-revolution. In 1979 the Air Force was given a crucial role in the growing military response. Second, it was decided to deny the insurgents food in order to cow them still further. In the Kunar Valley, crops were burnt by Soviet-Afghan aircraft, creating a severe shortage of grain in Afghanistan in 1980, which the Soviets had to meet through exports. The third part of the policy was to reach an understanding with Pakistan. Halliday believes that Amin expected elections to take place in Pakistan in 1979 in which he was convinced that political forces sympathetic towards Afghanistan would come to power, and in 1979 he was in touch with the leaders of some of these forces, notably Khan Wali Khan, of the National Awami League, a constituent of the Movement for Restoration of Democracy (MRD), a nine-party coalition of banned political groups, of which the leading faction was the Pakistan People's Party founded by the late Zulfikar Ali Bhutto.

General Zia-ul Haq had no intention of holding party-based or even party-less election in Pakistan; the Pakistan aspect of Amin's strategy therefore misfired. As the vicious circle of resistance and military action spread from province to province, engulfing the countryside and threatening several provincial towns, the Government increasingly fell back on repression, using the secret police, Aqsa, and the Sarandoy, a military police force.

Government forces carried out a number of large offensives and some of these met with a measure of success. However, large numbers of troops, sometimes whole brigades, defected; the vast majority of PDPA cadres in the towns and villages were killed. Soviet military personnel became increasingly involved in directing the Government's military operations, and a number of them were killed, wounded or taken 'prisoner'. The secret police resorted to large-scale torture, using such modern methods as electrodes for the first time in Afghanistan. 'The very brutal traditions of Afghan politics have therefore not only been used by the opposition, but have corroded and shaped the response of the PDPA itself.'[24]

The lack of success of the Government's military operations and the rapid spread of the insurgency inevitably intensified factional in-fighting in the PDPA. In July 1979 Amin took over the defence portfolio, displacing Colonel Watanjar, who was believed to be close to Taraki. A huge personality cult grew around Taraki, but, ironically, he was being rapidly neutralized and reduced to a mere symbol of the revolution. Straining under the pressure of the insurgency, the regime's policies began to betray a lack of cohesion and consistency. On the one hand, both Taraki and Amin tried to demonstrate their own, and the revolution's Islamic credentials; Taraki joined in mass prayers in the glare of television cameras, and the Government's propaganda machinery spouted out a lot of Islamic rhetoric. On the other hand, the PDPA regime was promoted as a 'worker's state'. On this Marxist theoretical point, differences surfaced between Taraki and Amin. Taraki sought to downplay the proletarian aspect of the Saur revolution, while Amin justified it by describing peasants as 'potential workers', claiming that the 'originality of the Afghan revolution lay in its making the transition from feudalism to socialism'.[25]

In 1979 the Islamic revolution in Iran had an immediate impact on the civil war in Afghanistan. The Hazara tribe, the most oppressed of the Afghan nationalities, being Shia, was particularly susceptible to Khomeini's Islamic voice. In the summer of 1979, the regime lost nearly all its non-Pushtun cadres and looked very much like an all-Pushtun set-up. The regime itself appeared to have lost sight of the great diversities of Afghan society.

Indeed official PDPA statements gave very little sense of any attempt by the leadership to comprehend the specificity of Afghan society, to face up to the complexities of the country beyond their offices in Kabul. The appeals to Islam and their meetings with tribal chiefs were a façade, a substitute for any serious political strategy based upon the social forces at play.[26]

In September 1979 the Soviet Union pressed Taraki to change the PDPA political line which was alienating vast portions of the Afghan population from the Marxist regime. On 10 September, on his way back to Kabul from Havana, Taraki halted in Moscow and was received by Brezhnev with an unusually warm display of Soviet commitment to the Kabul regime. We have no knowledge of the exact nature of the conversations that took place between Taraki and the Soviet leader. However, reports say that Brezhnev persuaded Taraki that a new political line of moderation and conciliation was essential in order to win the civil war. Taraki reportedly met with several Parcham leaders who were self-exiled in Moscow.[27]

The hands of the CPSU leaders had been strengthened by the emergence of a strong dissident group within the People's Democratic party. Since the summer of 1979, the Soviets had been pressing Amin and Taraki to broaden the base of the Government and rectify the left-deviationist mistakes committed by the Afghan party. Partly under

Soviet pressure and partly because the rebellion was spreading at an alarming rate, the regime announced its intention to set up a 'united national front' of all 'progressive public and political forces', and the move was immediately welcomed in Moscow.[28] *Pravda* reported another welcome Kabul plan: the creation of a 'national organization for the defence of the revolution'.[29] Towards the end of August, an underground document issued by 'Khalqis who favour unity' was circulating in Kabul. It denounced Amin for the costly excesses committed in the name of the revolution. He was accused of 'selfishness and personality cult', of setting up 'a centralized leadership instead of a democratic leadership', of using the party and the revolution for personal and family benefits, 'displacing and dismissing loyal revolutionary leaders', 'attacking religion and tradition', indulging in 'violent acts and the use of military force', 'collusion with foreign enemies and giving domestic enemies important positions', and of 'ignoring the promises made to the people', failure to provide 'democratic freedom and personal security' and 'putting thousands of Khalqis in jail who did not come to terms with the "Loyal Student",' the identity that Amin had given himself more than a year before.[30]

Amin knew that the Soviets were displeased with the way the revolution was going under his pilotage. Under the twin pressures—from Moscow and from within Afghanistan—Amin began to behave in a confused manner. Immediately after dismissing Colonel Watanjar from his post as Defence Minister, Amin got rid of three other cabinet ministers whom he thought to be close to Taraki—Major Sherjan Mazdooryar, Minister for Frontier Affairs, Colonel Sayed Mohammad Gulabzoy, Minister of Communication, and Asadullah Sarwari, head of the secret police. In August 1979 Amin's Cabinet was virtually an all-Pushtun body; all or most of the non-Pushtun members were either dismissed for suspected activities against him or neutralized as political agents.[31]

Amin looked upon Taraki's talks with Brezhnev with grave suspicion. He had two very important 'spies' working with Taraki. One was Taraki's aide-de-camp, Major Sayed Daoud Taroon, and the other, Foreign Minister Shah Wali. Both must have kept him informed of what was going on in Moscow. Taraki was given a grand welcome when he returned to Kabul on 11 September. 'The great leader of the people . . . today returned to the beloved country and was warmly and unprecedently received by tens of thousands of our noble and patriotic people carrying flowers and revolutionary slogans', glowed a Kabul Radio commentator. The same day Taraki telephoned Amin to ask him to come to the presidential palace for discussions. After demurring for a while, Amin agreed to come. The Soviet ambassador, Alexander M. Puzanov, reportedly guaranteed his personal safety. But when Amin came to the palace there was a shoot-out. A number of people were killed, but Amin was not one of them. He was saved by Major Taroon who took bullets aimed at Amin. Amin then returned to the palace a little later with his own men and took Taraki prisoner. The next day the Revolutionary Council announced that Taraki had 'asked to be relieved from party and state posts on health grounds'; a second announcement, on 9 October, said that Taraki had died from 'the serious illness from which he had been suffering for some time'.[32] It later transpired that Taraki had been killed by Amin's men in the dark night of 8 October.[33]

Outwardly, everything was friendly between Amin and Moscow. When Amin appointed himself president of the DRA, a congratulatory message came from Moscow. Beneath the surface, however, the two were at loggerheads. The Soviet ambassador in Kabul showed his displeasure with the regime in various ways.[34] Moscow put heavy pressure on Amin to change his entire political approach. Amin, for his part, tried to show his own displeasure with the way Moscow was treating him. At a meeting with the ambassadors of the communist countries, Foreign Minister Wali accused Ambassador Puzanov of hiding the four ministers who had been sacked by Amin in July/August. He asked the Kremlin to recall Puzanov. Amin had several meetings with the American chargé d'affaires, and expressed his desire to improve relations with the United States. It could not have been more than a gesture to warn Moscow that he had an alternative. In reality, Amin could not ease Afghanistan out of Soviet influence even if he seriously tried to do so. In the last three months of Amin's rule, the Soviets appeared to support him, but in reality they were looking for ways to ease him from the leadership of the PDPA. They sent him $6.7 m. worth of military equipment and a number of KGB experts to revamp the Afghan secret police and, in October, the Soviet–Afghan economic commission held its meeting in Moscow. Amin tried to tighten his grip of the army and the police; fearing assassination, he changed his residence several times. At the same time, he moved fast to implement some of the reforms he had already promised. He set up an Organization for the Defence of the Revolution, with people belonging to 'all strata' of Afghan society. He tried to mobilize the support of tribal chiefs. He launched a vigorous campaign to enlarge the membership of the PDPA, and expanded the politburo by adding several more military officers as members. Amin also tried to pacify the Islamic elements in Afghanistan. Mosques were repaired or whitewashed. Thousands of copies of the Koran were distributed. Amin presided over Islamic functions, peppered his speeches with invocations to Allah, and even went to the length of declaring that the 'great Khalq revolution is totally based on the principles of Islam'. He organized a Jamaat-i-Ulama or council of religion, with a number of traditional Islamic leaders attending, who proclaimed him Olelamar—a secular leader who rules with the authority of Allah. Amin promised his people a new constitution, created the new slogan of 'Security, Legality and Peace'. He released some political prisoners and promised to let off many more. He promised the Afghans a regime in which no one would be arrested without charge, none would be pressurized to act against his religious custom and traditions, and everyone would enjoy 'full liberties and inviolable democratic rights'.[35]

But all this proved to be too little, too late. In the fall of 1979, the American embassy described the situation in Kabul in the gloomiest of terms: 'an atmosphere of mortal fear and dread pervading the country as virtually every Afghan (even some "loyal Khalqis") wonders if tonight is his night to fall into the clutches of the security authorities, perhaps to disappear into one of the country's overcrowded prisons, never to be heard from again.'[36] A mutiny broke out in the 7th Army Division at the Rishkor base, south of Kabul. In October, Amin launched a major offensive against the rebels in Paktia province. The rebel bases were overrun, and some 40,000 Afghans fled to Pakistan. But when government troops withdrew, the area passed under rebel control again. In December, the insurgents were active on the very outskirts of Kabul.[37]

In early December, Amin sent an urgent message to Pakistan's

General Zia-ul Haq, asking for an early meeting. Zia-ul Haq sent his Foreign Minister, Agha Shahi, to Kabul. Shahi had a two-hour meeting with Amin, in which the Afghan leader said he was under tremendous pressure from the Soviet Union to surrender Afghanistan's sovereignty and independence, and he would like to explore what the United States would like to do to come to his help. Amin asked Shahi if Pakistan could help to get the United States involved in Afghanistan. However, Amin was far from clear in his mind on what he would give as the price of an American rescue operation if that were at all possible. He was not willing to reverse the process of the Saur revolution, which, in many ways, had been his own revolution. Amin wanted the United States to help him resist Soviet pressure. Shahi promised to relay the message to Washington, but was personally doubtful whether the Americans would intervene in Afghan affairs in a big way. The Soviet embassy in Kabul came to know the substance of Amin's dialogue with Shahi and immediately brought it to the notice of the Kremlin.[38]

Since November, the Soviets had been preparing the alternative of last resort—a military intervention in Afghanistan in order to save the Saur revolution. Washington knew of Soviet troop movements in areas close to the Afghan border, but the skeletal personnel in the American embassy in Kabul had no knowledge of it whatsoever. On 27 December, the Soviets intervened with a 'limited contingent' of 85,000 troops, overpowered troops loyal to Amin without a major battle, and Amin died fighting. Babrak Karmal was proclaimed President of Afghanistan in a regime now openly protected by Soviet arms. The second phase of the Saur revolution had begun.

7 Soviet Intervention and American Response

Afghanistan had long been in the Soviet sphere of influence, as has been shown in previous chapters. The Soviets had played a crucial role in the development and modernization of Afghanistan since the late fifties, and no government in Kabul, monarchical or republican, tried to pursue policies detrimental to Soviet interests. The Soviets had acquired extensive and intensive knowledge and understanding of the social, political, cultural and economic realities of Afghanistan; according to one source, in the two hundred years preceding the Saur revolution, as many as six thousand monographs on Afghanistan had been published in Tsarist Russia and the Soviet Union.[1] The Soviets had nothing to do with the actual revolutionary seizure of power in Kabul in April 1978, but they instantly adopted the Saur revolution and extended to it considerable economic, military and other assistance. In less than eight months after the Saur revolution, the Soviets concluded a treaty of peace and friendship with the Marxist regime in Kabul, Article 4 of which contained an explicit commitment on Moscow's part to the security of the new Afghan regime. It stated,

Acting in the spirit of the traditions of friendship and goodneighbourliness, as well as the United Nations Charter, the parties to the treaty will consult each other and, with mutual consent, will take appropriate measures to ensure the security, independence and territorial integrity of both countries. In the interests of reinforcing the defence potentials of the parties to the treaty, they will continue to develop cooperation in the military sphere.

The Soviet leaders justified the despatch of 85,000 to 110,000 troops into Afghanistan in December/January 1979–80 by their obligations under the 1978 treaty as well as by Article 51 of the UN Charter. Amin had been asking for Soviet military help since the winter of 1979 when the insurgency began to spread in the countryside. The Soviets sent him several thousand military advisers, and kept anxious watch on the range and scale of fighting in the Afghan civil war. In the spring of

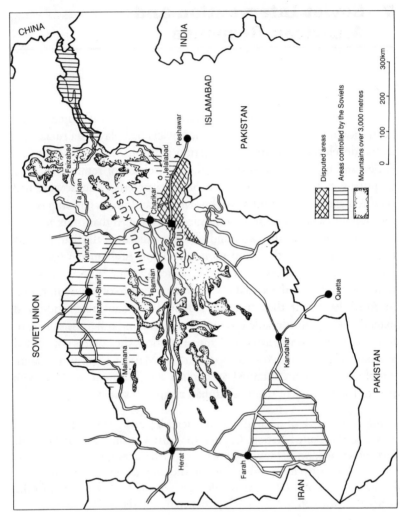

5. Soviet presence

1979, General Alexei A. Epishev, chief of the Main Political Admini-stration of the Soviet armed forces, made an inspection tour of Afghanistan. The tour resulted in larger supplies of Soviet weapons and advisers to the Kabul regime. In the summer of 1979, the situation in Afghanistan became highly complicated. On the one hand, the repressive policies of Amin were not working in the provinces; they were only reinforcing popular resistance to the regime. On the other hand, Amin's leadership of the PDPA was being challenged by a fairly large number of his Cabinet colleagues. Amin asked the Soviets for an unspecified number of Soviet troops in the summer, and some negoti-ations did take place between Kabul and Moscow. In August, Brezhnev sent General Ivan G. Pavlovskii, Commander-in-Chief of the Soviet ground forces, to Afghanistan to make a thorough survey of the entire terrain. Pavlovskii spent three months in Afghanistan conducting the survey. The Soviets, then, had, or should have had, an accurate idea of the condition of the civil war in Afghanistan, of the strengths and weaknesses of the two sides, when they finally determined to intervene. The political-strategic implications of the intervention were debated and decided at the Politburo of the CPSU, and this difficult exercise took into account, as Brezhnev disclosed after the intervention, all aspects of the traumatic projected Soviet action, especially its impact on Soviet-American relations, and on political alignments in the strategic regions of the Persian Gulf, southern Africa and South Asia.

The civil war in Afghanistan has continued for five years; it has involved not only the PDPA and its opponents in Afghanistan, but a number of external nations, notably the Soviet Union, the United States, China, Pakistan, Saudi Arabia, Iran, Egypt and India. In a way, Afghanistan has ignited an international civil war, polarizing the Soviet Union and its allies against their enemies and adversaries on a global scale. It is not Afghanistan as a piece of real estate that has triggered this international confrontation: Afghanistan became the dramatic symbol of Soviet 'expansionism' and American 'retreat' on a global scale in the 1970s, the hinge of global power alignments in the 1980s.

This volume does not attempt to study the Soviet intervention in Afghanistan except in its relevance to the Afghan revolution and the Marxist regime in Afghanistan. The Soviet intervention or invasion has been studied at length by American and other Western scholars and journalists in the context of the century's prolonged confrontation between the Soviet Union and the United States as leaders of two contending international political systems. Relatively less attention has been given to the Marxist regime in Afghanistan as it has tried to assert itself in that landlocked, mountainous country for five years under the protection of Soviet arms. However, since the protection of Soviet arms has proved to be inseparable from the survival of the Marxist regime and its gradual, slow process of gaining political ground in Afghanistan, this volume must pay some attention to the Soviet armed intervention of December 1979 and the American reaction to that landmark event.

It is now known that the CPSU Politburo arrived at the decision to intervene after an intense debate lasting for several days, in which every member was not equally enthusiastic. The most forceful advocate of intervention was the late Suslov; he was supported by Brezhnev, Ustinov and Gromyko. Yuri Andropov expressed considerable doubts and was perhaps supported by more than one other Politburo member.[2] During the debate, every aspect of the intervention was thoroughly examined, especially the ways in which it would impact on Moscow's relations with the United States, and its fortunes in Western Europe, the Persian Gulf, the Middle East, the Indian Ocean and the South Asian subcontinent. Much attention was given to what a Soviet analyst later described as 'the atmosphere under which the decision of rendering Soviet assistance to Afghanistan was taken.'[3] In Soviet perceptions, the United States had decided since 1977 to downgrade *détente* and adopt a strategy of confrontation with the Soviet Union. The confrontational strategy began with the election of Jimmy Carter as American President; its principal architect was his national security adviser, Zbigniew K. Brzezinski. It started with the presidential directive of August 1977 calling for the creation of a Rapid Deployment Force, and was carried forward, brick by brick, through the NATO promise of May 1978 to increase the military spending of the member countries, the NATO decision to employ new medium-range missiles in Western Europe 'directed against the Soviet Union and its allies', the virtual freezing of the SALT II agreement by President Carter, and by the semi-strategic alliance forged between the United States and China. There were other antipathetic American actions that the Soviet leaders reportedly took into account—the sharp downgrading by the Carter administration of the importance of improving relations with the Soviet Union; the decision to deny the Soviet Union a role in settling problems and disputes in regions close to the Soviet Union, such as the Middle East; 'the intensified build-up of US naval presence near the USSR's southern borders'; 'an active drive to modernize American strategic weapons' and 'the refusal of the Carter administration to carry on a constructive American–Soviet dialogue.'[4] The Politburo came to the grim conclusion that *détente*, as it had come to flourish during the Nixon administration, was dead, and that a new era of American–Soviet confrontation had begun.

Developments in the area around Afghanistan particularly were taken into account by the Soviet leaders as they arrived at the decision to intervene. The principal event was the fall of the Shah of Iran and his American-backed regime. The great American debacle in Iran pleased the Soviet leaders, but they watched the grotesque unfolding of the Islamic revolution under the Ayatollah Khomeini with considerable misgiving, if not alarm. As the Saur revolution debouched in 1979 under Amin's revolutionism, the Soviets were deeply concerned to protect Afghanistan and the Central Asian republics of the Soviet Union from an invasion of revolutionary Islamic fundamentalism.

For the United States, the Soviet invasion of Afghanistan was an absolutely unacceptable assertion of Soviet military might, beyond the 'legitimate' frontiers of the Soviet bloc. As an American scholar put it:

As the 1970s progressed, the problem of Soviet military intervention in Third World conflicts came to assume an increasingly prominent place on the US foreign policy agenda. The USSR attempted—by means of diplomacy, military advisers, arms shipments, and occasionally troops—to influence the course of at least eight localized conflicts during the decade. The list of those conflicts reads like a roll call of the decade's most dangerous international crises and hot spots: the Indo–Pakistan war, the Yom Kippur war, the war in Vietnam, the Angolan civil war, the Ogaden war, the intra-Communist clash in Indo-China (Vietnam's invasion of Cambodia and China's incursion into Vietnam), South Yemen's brief clash with Yemen and the civil war in Afghanistan. The USSR had been involved militarily in local conflicts before, of course, but the magnitude, scope and apparent success of its efforts in the 70s were perhaps without precedent.[5]

Afghanistan has turned out to be a watershed in Soviet–American relations. It provided President Carter with the occasion to formally launch the second cold war. Later, with Ronald Reagan in the White House, the United States embarked upon the greatest peacetime military build-up in history, with the declared objective of regaining strategic superiority over the Soviet Union. The contest between the two giants joined strategic issues with Third World rivalries, in which medium-range missiles and Star Wars became as much symbols as did Afghanistan.

The authoritative pronouncements made by Soviet leaders justifying the intervention (or invasion) in Afghanistan sketched the Soviet self-image as well as Soviet images of the United States at the turn of the decade of the 1980s.

The Soviet leaders now clearly saw the Soviet Union as an equal of the United States. In their vision, the socialist system had gained in economic, political and military strength during a period of continuing decline of world capitalism. The Soviet Union was no longer a junior superpower. The United States had been forced to concede strategic parity with the Soviet Union; it must now also concede parity of influence in the vital geo-strategic regions of the world, especially in those areas in which the Soviet Union also had vital interests. The United States could no longer claim regions like the Persian Gulf and the Middle East as exclusively its own, or the West's, areas of vital interest. Soviet might and power demanded world-wide parity, not just equality in the strategic field.

By defending with military force the Marxist revolution in Afghanistan, the Soviet Union signalled two important messages to the rest of the world. First, the countries comprising the world socialist system—its members, associate members and 'observer' status members—could depend upon the Soviet Union for military help, if not protection; therefore, no external power would easily invade them or try successfully to destabilize them. Second, the time had come for a realignment of forces in the Third World, to identify the vanguard of radical change and militant anti-imperialism as well as its firm and reliable friends and allies, and to differentiate these nations from those who had chosen, or had been forced to choose, to toe the capitalist-imperialist line.[6]

In the Soviet perception, the Afghan operation was entirely defensive; their objective was to secure a friendly neighbouring state as a Marxist regime, as well as to protect the southern flank of the Soviet Union from intervention by alien forces, i.e., Islamic fundamentalism, and American imperialism operating through a number of anti-Soviet countries such as Pakistan, Saudi Arabia, Egypt and China. At the same time, Moscow was well aware of the linkages between Afghanistan and the changed strategic situation in the Persian Gulf. Soviet pronouncements implied that just as the United States was trying to operate a comprehensive strategy for Iran, the Persian Gulf, Pakistan and Afghanistan, so were the Soviets pushing a comprehensive counter-strategy for the entire area with a view to reducing American influence, enhancing Moscow's own, and turning the regional balance of power, if not against the United States, then, at least in favour of a Soviet presence on a par with America's in regional stability and conflict-management.

The Soviet armed intervention in Afghanistan brought out into the open some of the changes that had already occurred in global and regional power equations. The year 1979 brought a severe political jolt to the American-orientated political order spanning most of the developing world as well as to the American-orientated world economic order. Much of the world that had somehow recovered from the shock of the skyward leap in world oil prices in the early seventies was deeply shaken by the second large increase in oil prices in the late seventies. With the advent of the eighties the planet was caught in a severe recession; the economic policies adopted by Ronald Reagan undermined the political unity of the industrialized capitalist nations. As the United States resolutely embarked on a programme of massive arms build-up, aimed quite candidly at restoring American military superiority over the Soviet Union, the importance of strategic nations sharply increased for both superpowers. The United States needed a string of friendly nations that would co-operate in the building of a strategic consensus for the containment of Soviet power and influence. The Soviet Union needed strong and viable allies in strategic regions of the world in order to fend off the American offensive. The Soviet intervention in Afghanistan helped the United States to mobilize a large number of Third World nations to condemn, deplore or regret the

Kremlin's action at the World Islamic Conference and at the United Nations.

However, when it came to the forging of a strategic consensus, which would imply the granting of bases or facilities to the United States for operating its global anti-Soviet strategies, most of the friends and allies backed out, and the search was given up by the Carter administration and was not renewed by the Reagan White House. The West European allies stuck to the agreement to deploy middle-range missiles from the United States, but without much conviction and in the face of a considerable popular protest movement. When it came to applying economic and trade sanctions against the Soviet Union, most of them demurred, and the Soviets were able to build the trans-Siberian gas pipeline with large-scale financial assistance from Western Europe. Americans noticed a rising tide of 'neutralism' in Western Europe, while the Soviets were perturbed by the escalating nationalism of the East European elites, especially those belonging to the younger, post-war generation. Unlike cold war I, cold war II was by and large an American enterprise, mounted on America's unilateral global military build-up and finally ending up with Ronald Reagan's $500 bn. minimum Strategic Defence Initiative (SDI) or Star War weapons project.

If Afghanistan was the staging ground of a Soviet military-ideological offensive, paradoxically, it threw the Kremlin into a defensive posture on a wide political-strategic front. While the Soviet troops got bogged down in Afghanistan in a prolonged civil war, brutal and gory in its daily, weekly and seasonal operations, and highly expensive in political terms, when it came to Soviet prestige and image in the community of developing countries, the Soviets fought defensive battles on several major fronts against American diplomatic-strategic offensives, lost some of the battles, won a few, and drove its adversary into a stalemate in the others. The intervention in Afghanistan had a strong impact on the struggle between the regime and the people in Poland; Moscow was under the compulsion to go extremely cautiously in the use of force in Poland in view of adverse world reaction to its Afghan action. At the same time, the very extremity of the Soviet action in Afghanistan cautioned the United States against overt action in Poland which might provoke strong retaliatory Soviet military action.

On the medium-range American missiles issue, the Soviets lost to the United States an important strategic-diplomatic battle in Western Europe, but were able to collect some compensation when a broad-based Marxist-dominated regime took over in Nicaragua, throwing the volatile politics of Central America into a new, class-orientated ferment. In the Middle East, the American military–diplomatic initiatives in Lebanon ground to a halt; in the Persian Gulf, the two superpowers were constrained to act along parallel lines to see that the seemingly unending war between Iraq and Iran did not create a situation compelling either, and therefore, both, of them to intervene.

Coming back to the specific point of Soviet intervention in Afghanistan, it is significant that in the last week of December 1979, the Soviets were as apprehensive of an imminent American move into Iran as were the Americans of a probable Soviet push into Pakistan or Iran from the vantage point of Afghanistan. Cyrus Vance wrote in his memoirs: 'There were background news stories coming out of Washington to the effect that there was a possibility of some form of US military action against Iran.' Vance realized that 'US military presence in the area would make a collapse of the Kabul regime more dangerous for the Soviets and thus enhance the possibility of Soviet intervention.'[7] Marshall Shulman, who was Secretary Vance's chief adviser on Soviet affairs, told an American journal that it was his belief that the Soviets invaded Afghanistan because of a 'broad fear' of 'the creation of a crescent of militant Islamic anti-Soviet states on its southern borders, with the added possibility of Chinese or US influence, and not because it seeks to gain access to the Indian Ocean and control over the Middle East.' Shulman added that the Soviet action in Afghanistan 'opens up the possibility' that the Soviets might attack Iran or Pakistan, although he did not believe that was the intention of the invasion.'[8] Brezhnev himself justified the intervention as a defensive action to ensure the security of the southern borders of the Soviet state. The Soviets, he said, saw

a real threat that Afghanistan would lose its independence and be turned into an imperialist military bridgehead on our southern border . . . The time came when we could no longer fail to respond to the request of the government of friendly Afghanistan. To have acted otherwise would have meant leaving

Afghanistan a prey to imperialism, allowing the aggressive forces to repeat in that country what they had succeeded in doing, for instance, in Chile . . .. To have acted otherwise would have meant to watch passively the establishment on our southern border a seat of serious danger to the security of the Soviet state.[9]

A high-ranking Soviet scholar, speaking in Rome four months after the intervention, confirmed earlier reports that the decision to inter-vene had not been an easy one. 'This was in fact a very difficult decision', said Academician Evgenii Primakov, Director of the Institute of Oriental Studies of the Soviet Academy of Sciences. 'When all the positive and negative aspects were weighed from the point of view of revolutionary operation in Afghanistan and the general situation of forces in the world, it became clear that it was necessary.'[10]

The decision to intervene, then, was taken in the context of three principal factors: the fate of the Afghan revolution, the security of the southern flank of the Soviet Union, and the world pattern of forces at the end of 1980. In the Soviet judgement, the three factors were part of a whole: one could not be separated from the other two. By putting forward the three-factor explanation, the Soviets claimed that they had the legitimate right to intervene with significant military force to protect a Marxist revolution in a friendly country with whom they had concluded a security-orientated treaty of friendship only a year before. The claim to legitimacy of the intervention derived its justification from the geographical location of Afghanistan—it bordered a sensitive flank of the Soviet state. Its borders have been a matter of grave concern for Moscow since the time of the Tsars; the Russian and the Soviet states had had to face six invasions across their borders since 1812, as against none into the United States. However, it was the 'general situa-tion of forces in the world' which made the crucial decision necessary and possible.

The collapse of trust and understanding between the United States and the Soviet Union, together with heightened tension and crises in regions of vital interest to both constituted one aspect of the general world situation in December 1979. The Carter administration systematically dismantled the confidence-building mechanisms that had been built between Washington and Moscow by Nixon, Kissinger and Ford. The collapse of the Shah of Iran, the Khomeini revolution, and the hostage crisis seemed to put American vital interests in the strategic Persian Gulf in serious jeopardy. All of a sudden, the future of the entire 'arc of crises'—extending from Turkey through Pakistan to the Horn—seemed to be gravely uncertain. This was a time when a certain mutual trust and confidence between the world's two most powerful nations was of the utmost importance in order to enable either of them to know what the other would and would not do in specific crisis situations. Not only was mutual trust and confidence completely lacking between Washington and Moscow in December 1979, but both laboured under the fear that the other was about to embark on military action in Iran that would gravely injure its vital security interests.

Under these circumstances, there was inevitably a lot of hyperbole in the Soviet action and the American reaction. In order simply to save the Afghan revolution, the Soviets did not have to despatch to Afghanistan, in a matter of ten to fifteen days, a contingent of more than 100,000 troops. A much smaller force, of perhaps 25,000, would have been adequate to pull Amin down, instal Karmal as head of the DRA, give an entirely new direction to the regime's policy and programme, and wait to see how the new regime fared against the widespread resistance. The Soviet intervention did not have to be blamed entirely on the 'imperialists', that is, the United States. With some candour, Brezhnev could have articulated Soviet apprehensions of Iran-type Islamic fundamentalism sweeping Afghanistan in the case of a collapse of the DRA regime, and he might have received some sympathetic hearing in the United States. In December 1979, almost a million Afghans had assembled in the Peshawar area of Pakistan, and many of them were armed. But the United States was not extending to the Afghan insurgents more than token military and financial aid. Brezhnev, however, had his own reasons for not blaming the Khomeini revolution as a gravely destabilizing factor: the Soviets were anxious to have Iran on their side, if this were at all possible, or at least, not to be hostile to the Soviet Union in the extremely volatile build-up of forces in the Persian Gulf region. The Soviet show of military strength in the Afghan intervention was unnecessarily provocative; the rhetoric accompanying it was even more so.

The size of the Soviet 'limited contingent' of armed forces and the rhetoric of assertive military power provoked an American response that went far beyond Moscow in a counter-assertion of American military might. The Carter administration's obsession with the Iranian situation inevitably made it perceive the Soviet intervention as a threat to Iran, Pakistan and indeed the entire mosaic of American and Western interests in the Persian Gulf region. Carter described the Soviet intervention in Afghanistan as the 'greatest threat' to peace since World War II, saw it as a threat to both Iran and Pakistan, and as a 'stepping stone to their possible control over much of the world's oil supplies', and 'a quantum jump in the nature of Soviet behaviour'.[11] The President's perception was echoed and refined by Drew Middleton, military correspondent of *The New York Times*. There were no military forces in the immediate area that were collectively, much less individually, capable of deterring any Soviet military action in Iran or Pakistan, Middleton wrote. Soviet forces could make further moves into Iran or Pakistan and command the entrance and exit to the Persian Gulf. China was willing to help, but its military capability in that area was extremely limited. To some analysts in Washington, Middleton added, a turbulent Iran appeared to be most vulnerable to further Soviet intervention.

Pakistan and Afghanistan share a rugged frontier that should make transferring the munitions of war difficult. A more reasonable objective of the United States military policy would be to supply Pakistan with modern fighter aircraft, tanks, anti-tank and anti-aircraft missiles and armoured personnel carriers. The chief political drawback seen by some officials in Washington is that such a step would frighten India and possibly move that country closer to the Soviet Union, thus shifting the power balance in Asia even more toward Russia.[12]

That is exactly what happened. The United States made Pakistan a 'front-line' state in its own strategy for resisting the Soviets in Afghanistan, and offered it, in 1980–1, a package of military and economic aid valued at $3.1 bn. in six years, plus forty F-16 aircraft, paid for with a hefty loan from Saudi Arabia. The Indian Government refused to condemn the Soviet intervention and accepted its rationale and its justification at least in public pronouncements.[13] For New

Delhi, the transfer of modern, sophisticated American arms to Pakistan constituted a greater security threat than the Soviet military presence in Afghanistan. The American arms transfers to Pakistan led to a substantial Indian military build-up with willing Soviet collaboration. The traditional cleavage in the subcontinent between Pakistan and India was deepened by the Soviet intervention in Afghanistan and the American response to it. So were the political cleavages within Pakistan. The military regime of Zia-ul Haq was strengthened by the powerful support it received from the United States, China, Saudi Arabia and other states. But the political elements that remained deeply alienated from the regime refused to recognize General Zia's Afghanistan policy as suitable for the national interests of Pakistan. Gradually, over a period of five years, a strong stream of public opinion developed in Pakistan which regarded the Afghan policy pursued since January 1980 as having been imposed on Pakistan by the United States, and this opinion advocated a political settlement of the Afghan crisis through direct negotiation between Pakistan and Afghanistan. As Pakistan moved in 1985 towards a transition from military to civilian rule, demand for direct negotiation with Kabul began to crystallize into a national demand, which Zia-ul Haq found increasingly difficult to resist.

The geopolitical weight of the Soviet military intervention in Afghanistan forced out of public awareness the other, perhaps more important, aspect of the intervention: how the Soviets tried, with a mixture of military force and a moderate political programme executed through the Babrak Karmal regime, to salvage the Saur revolution, with what failure and what success, and what kind of a Marxist regime was being built in Afghanistan's rugged terrain soaked with the blood and sweat and the long agonies of its people. To these crucial questions we turn in the following chapter.

8   Soviet Wings for the Saur Revolution

The Soviets did not send a 'limited contingent' of armed forces into Afghanistan in order to conquer that country, but to protect the Saur revolution. The mission was more than a rescue operation. The revolution had not only to be saved but also to be made viable, capable of standing on its own feet; the Soviets aimed to bring the ravaged economy and political system of Afghanistan back to a process of orderly revolutionary reconstruction. In the discharge of this mission, unprecedented in Soviet experience, the USSR was pitted against a formidable array of obstacles: widespread Afghan resistance—call it counter-revolution or struggle for national liberation; significant military assistance to the rebels by a group of enemy countries led by the United States; an incompetent, faction-ridden PDPA which had neither the organizational base nor the cadre strength to take on the challenge of revolutionary reconstruction; an outraged and hostile world public opinion, and, last but by no means least, the Kremlin's own lack of resources and lack of experience in handling a complicated, prolonged guerrilla war situation in a backward, rocky, mountainous Third World country.

Afghanistan was not the only instance of a Marxist revolution provoking hostile reaction in capitalist countries and armed intervention by hostile external forces. Indeed, from the Bolshevik revolution in Russia to the Vietnam revolution, internal resistance and external intervention have worked together to create problems for Marxist revolutions, including the problem of survival. What makes the Afghan Marxist revolution different from other Marxist revolutions or take-overs of the post-World War II period is that, first, it was brought about by an exceedingly weak communist party that lacked the wherewithal to ensure its effectiveness, and, second, it had to depend on Soviet arms for survival. The United States had had the experience of defending pro-American regimes or overthrowing regimes perceived to be detrimental to American interests in more than one Third World region. The Soviet experience in this regard was confined to Eastern Europe until the Saur revolution dragged Moscow into the Third World as armed defender of a Marxist revolution.

The Soviets knew the Afghan terrain well. High Soviet officials had been closely associated with the PDPA regime from the moment of its inauguration. For almost a year before the military intervention, ranking officers of the Soviet army closely inspected the rising tide of civil war. Yet, when the Soviet army entered Afghanistan and immediately got involved in direct clashes with the rebels, it became doubtful whether the military planners in Moscow understood the true nature of the war that lay ahead of their troops in the rugged mountainous terrain of Afghanistan. Clausewitz has always been a favourite military authority with Soviet military planners, yet the latter seemed to have had an insufficient grasp, in getting locked into the resistance in Afghanistan, of his famous warning:

The first, the grandest, and most decisive act of judgement which the Statesman and General exercises is rightly to understand . . . the War in which he engages, not to take it for something, or wish to make of it something, which, by the nature of its relations, it is impossible for it to be. This is . . . the first, the most comprehensive of all strategical questions.[1]

The military intervention was unavoidable if Kabul were to be saved from the rebels. In the words of *Pravda*, 'the fiery ring of counter-revolution backed actively from abroad became tighter and tighter round the capital.'[2] In its first flush, however, the military intervention was intended to provide diplomacy with a punch and to frighten the rebels and their foreign backers into caution, circumspection, and, finally, submission. The astonishing size of the Soviet force was intended to have a stunning impact on surprised enemies and adversaries. Brezhnev later affirmed that the Politburo had pondered 'all' short- and long-term implications of the intervention before taking the final decision. For the first week or so, the emphasis was on perfect execution of the military operation. The terse announcement of 27 December stressed the intervention's legitimacy as well as objectives. Legitimacy rested on the Soviet–Afghan treaty of 1978. The request for military help came from the 'political leadership' of the Saur revolution rather than from the government headed by Amin. The objective was to 'defend the gains of the April revolution', and to prevent the imperialist powers from converting a 'neighbourly country with a border of great length into a bridgehead for penetration of imperialist aggression against the Soviet state.'[3]

The diplomatic initiative that accompanied the military intervention focused not on the United States but on Pakistan, Syria, India and Iran in the region, and on France, West Germany and other NATO members that were more perturbed than enthused by President Carter's unilateral declaration of cold war II. The first capital visited by Gromyko after the intervention was Damascus, the second, New Delhi. The diplomatic offensive against Pakistan was conducted simultaneously on three levels: direct pressure on the border, raising the grim prospect of Soviet troops penetrating Pakistan territory in hot pursuit of rebels; pressure on Islamabad from Moscow not to toe the American line; and diplomatic–*realpolitikal* pressure from the PDPA Government now headed by Babrak Karmal. Syria's help was sought to counter American–Pakistani–Saudi efforts to arouse Islamic nationalism against the Kabul regime and the Soviet Union. India was accorded top priority because Moscow needed India's benign neutrality, if it could not get India's political support. The Soviet leaders could not be certain that Mrs Indira Gandhi would return to power in the elections for the Indian Parliament scheduled for the first week of January 1980; they had to take account of having to deal with a government in New Delhi of those opposition parties not as kindly disposed towards Moscow as the Congress I party of Indira Gandhi. France and the German Federal Republic immediately became major targets of Soviet diplomacy because of their refusal to walk with the United States the full length of the second cold war.

When Moscow's diplomatic rhetoric took on the United States, the Soviet posture was a combination of adamant strength and a willingness to recognize the legitimate interests and concerns of America and its Western allies if the United States were to do the same with regard to the concerns and interests of the Soviet Union. Brezhnev conceded the partial legitimacy of American and West European concern over the uninterrupted and free flow of petroleum from the Persian Gulf, and *Pravda* asserted that Moscow had no designs on West Asian oil and no intention of pushing through to the warm-water ports on the

Indian Ocean. Brezhnev also declared that the Soviet troops would not be in Afghanistan longer than necessary. 'We want to state very definitely that we will be ready to commence the withdrawal of our troops as soon as all forms of outside interference directed against the government and the people of Afghanistan are fully terminated,' announced Brezhnev in his interview with *Pravda* on 22 February 1980.

More relevant to the situation immediately created by the Soviet military push into Afghanistan were the firmness and precision with which the Soviets reiterated their determination to defend the legitimate interests of national security and a fraternal revolution. The burden of Moscow's carefully orchestrated articulations was that the United States was turning Nelson's blind eye on the changes that had occurred to the global balance, that it was determined to take the world back to the wasted epoch of cold war, and that this exercise in muscle-flexing would fail because the Soviet Union had emerged as an equal of America and could not be cowed by threats of military superiority. In its first reaction to Carter's State of the Union message of January 1980, which incorporated the now nearly forgotten Carter Doctrine, and which asserted 'vital US interests' in the Persian Gulf region, Moscow objected that the President should have 'arbitrarily proclaimed the area of the Persian Gulf which lies thousands of miles away from the American shores, a sphere of US vital interests'. The purpose was 'to keep the dominant position of American monopolies in the region'. Brezhnev affirmed Soviet power in unmistakable phrases and accents. 'Nobody will intimidate the Soviet Union', he declared. 'Our strength and possibilities are tremendous. We and our allies will be able to stand up for ourselves and rebuff any hostile sallies and nobody will succeed in provoking us.' *Pravda* added with greater lucidity,

The Soviet Union will not remain passive in the face of actions against our security. Everything will be taken into account and nothing will be left without a response, be it establishment of military bases, deployment of new American missiles near the Soviet frontiers or attempts to instigate the states lying near the Soviet Union to take unfriendly acts towards the USSR.[4]

The force that was sent to Afghanistan in the last days of December 1979 and the first days of January 1980 was, except for the airborne units, Category-C units, manned primarily by Central Asian reservists. The initial idea was not to deploy Soviet troops on a significant scale in direct combat with the insurgents, but to use them to occupy the main cities, defend Kabul and major military installations close to the capital city. *The Guardian*, of London, printed a report in January 1980 which suggested that the Soviet troops were required to keep a low profile.

The Red Army has orders to return fire but not to initiate shooting. . . . The officers believe with what seemed to be a very real sincerity that they are not an occupation army and certainly do not reckon with being the biggest threat since World War II. 'We are here to help a friendly country', said one. 'This was not an invasion, we cannot understand why the BBC and the Voice of America are saying these things.' They see their roles as saving Afghanistan from Chinese and Pakistani interference.[5]

But the role of the Soviet troops changed quickly. They were soon involved in direct clashes with the rebels. The Afghan army became useless because of desertions and lack of morale, and had to be rebuilt with young conscripts, which took time. In the summer of 1980, the Central Asian reservists had to be replaced with regular combat troops but, in nearly six years of fighting, the overall troop level was maintained at between 100,000 and 110,000. Soviet military tactics have generally tended towards reliance on motorized rifle and tank troops employed in sweep or 'hammer and anvil' operations. The Soviet units were inhibited by the mountainous territory and poor off-road terrain. They resorted to increasing air assault and airborne operations, usually of company or battalion strength, in conjunction with motorized rifle units. Some of the larger operations involved the open build-up of forces close to targets and long air and artillery preparations, so that battle plans became known not only to the guerrillas but even to the Western press.

It is extremely difficult to attempt an objective assessment of the military operations of the Soviet forces in Afghanistan. The data base is practically non-existent. Most of the information on which American and West European assessments have been made has come either from Afghan rebels or from European reporters who were able to witness some of the operations for short periods of time as guests of the rebel forces. The Soviets themselves only began to report casualties in 1981, though as early as May 1980 *Pravda* conceded that 'struggle against the bandits is no easy matter'.[6] Sifting through a large quantity of American and West European reports on the nature of the fighting within Afghanistan, it appears that, throughout 1980, the Soviet troops tried to avoid large-scale direct combat. The principal Soviet focus was on diplomacy. The Carter administration was not willing to pay a heavy price for Pakistan's logistical support for a programme to feed arms to the Afghan rebels. Rejecting Washington's 'peanut' offer of $400m. in military and economic aid in the first year of an imprecise aid package, the military regime in Pakistan was musing loudly about making up with 'our great neighbour to the North'.[7] Prime Minister Indira Gandhi of India appeared to be willing to play the role of an honest broker between Moscow and Washington.[8] The situation changed, however, with the inauguration of the Reagan administration. The United States now determined to strengthen Afghan resistance as far as possible, and was ready to pay an adequate price for Pakistan's co-operation as a 'front-line' state. All diplomatic contacts with Moscow were cut off. The Reagan administration's anti-Sovietism paralleled that of John Foster Dulles in the early 1950s. Afghanistan became a symbol of Soviet expansionism and hegemony. As with Poland, it was also a symbol of the second cold war.

In August 1980, a high-level Soviet military delegation arrived in Kabul to reorganize both the Soviet forces and what remained of the Afghan army. Earlier, on 29 July, the *Washington Post* reported that the Soviet troops had launched their largest land and air offensive to put down a mutiny in an Afghan army division. By the end of October, it seemed that the Soviet troops would have to bear the brunt of the growing Afghan resistance alone. The years 1980 and early 1981 saw two meetings in Moscow between Brezhnev and Babrak Karmal, one in mid-October, the other in February 1981 at the time of the 26th congress of the CPSU. At the first meeting, according to *Tass*, the two leaders gave high priority to achieving an agreement with Pakistan that would end Pakistan's support to the Afghan rebels.[9] In March 1981, the overall military-political situation was summed up in the following words by Richard P. Cronin for the Congressional Research Service of the United States Library of Congress:

Published reports on the situation in Afghanistan suggest that the war has been essentially a standoff since early 1981, with the Soviets entrenched firmly in Kabul and other population centers but with the rebels controlling perhaps 75–80% of the countryside. In actuality, however, this stalemate favours the Soviets and the situation for the rebels has been described as increasingly desperate due to shortages of weapons, ammunition, and, critically, food. The Soviets seem content with their existing force level of 85–90,000 troops and have emphasized improving the efficiency and tactics of their forces.

The health of the guerrilla movement remains a matter of dispute. Some feel that with a modest flow of small arms and some limited quantities of anti-aircraft and anti-tank weapons, the guerrillas can hold out indefinitely and make the Soviets pay a heavy price for their occupation. Others see the imminent collapse of the movement as the refugee exodus and Soviet operations aimed at denying the rebels access to food and supplies take their toll. . . .

Many observers see a long-term strategy to remake the country by training new military and civilian cadres and educating a new generation of Afghans to accept a state moulded on Soviet lines and quasi or outright satellite status. At the same time, the rebels also see a prolonged struggle leading up to the formation of an exile government and an escalating guerrilla campaign to convince the Soviets that their position is not worth the cost.[10]

The fighting escalated in 1982–83. With Pakistan's co-operation (officially denied), the CIA put through a programme of funnelling Soviet-made arms, purchased from Egypt, Somalia and other sources, to the rebels; a certain number of Chinese arms were also supplied across the Sino–Afghan border and through Pakistan. While the Afghan army was still being made battle-fit, the Soviet forces launched a number of major offensives to clear several heavy rebel concentrations. One of the largest of these operations was directed against a three thousand-strong rebel force led by a charismatic Islamic fundamentalist leader, Ahmed Shah Massoud, in the Panjsher Valley. The Soviets had reportedly made four earlier attempts to flush out the Panjsher Valley guerrillas. None had been successful. Massoud's rebel force continued to harass Soviet lines of communication, to ambush Soviet–Afghan convoys, capture Soviet arms and subvert Afghan soldiers. At least once were they able to penetrate the Bagram air base near Kabul. In May 1982, after a week-long air bombardment, Soviet and Afghan forces were introduced by helicopter into the narrow Panjsher Valley. The rebels, however, had received warning of the Soviet battle plan and had escaped down the side valleys or along the top of the ridges. A *Pravda* correspondent, covering the operations, reported that the first waves of Soviet–Afghan attackers faced a 'multi-level system of fire prepared in advance'.[11] Three days later, a tank/motorized rifle force entered the valley, bringing the total Soviet and Afghan force to between 12,000 and 15,000. A series of tough engagements followed. In the month-long fighting, 200 rebels were killed, 80 per cent of the houses in the valley were destroyed, and about 1,200 civilians—more than 1 per cent of Panjsher's population—perished. Rebel sources claimed to have destroyed thirty-five Soviet helicopters and fifty vehicles.[12]

Soviet forces withdrew in mid-June but mounted another offensive in September. In January 1983 the Soviet–Afghan forces and Massoud's guerrillas concluded an unwritten truce which, for a while, was held up by the Kabul media as a new pattern of relationship emerging between the Marxist regime and local resistance groups. The truce, however, broke down in April 1984, by which time Massoud had reportedly repaired his logistical base in the valley and recruited and trained two thousand new guerrillas. In April 1984 the Soviets launched another major offensive against Massoud's rebel force. 'Preceded by more than 40 Tu-16 strategic bombers and dozens of Su-24 fighter-bombers—both types being flown from bases inside the USSR—more than 20,000 Soviet troops entered the valley.' The Soviets, as well as Kabul, claimed a big victory and a 'final solution' to the rebellion in Panjsher Valley. Soviet and Afghan units set up a garrison in the lower part of the valley. But Massoud was reportedly still at large, and rebel sources claimed that his resistance force had not been crushed.

The military operations against Massoud's guerrilla force in Panjsher Valley have a particular political significance. Panjsher has been the centre of the strongest fundamentalist group in Afghanistan since the early 1970s. Massoud's mentor is the Peshawar-based fundamentalist leader, Burhanuddin Rabbani, who has wide contacts with Pakistan's Jamaat-i-Islami, the fundamentalist party that has been in charge of relief and care of the over three million Afghan refugees living on Pakistani territory. The Panjsher fundamentalists are pre-dominantly Tajik nationals. The Soviet forces in Afghanistan have been deployed in strength since 1982–83 to flush out large concentrations of guerilla forces in areas where the possibility of forming a rebel government exists. Except for Panjsher Valley, the cities of Kandahar and Herat and parts of Ghazni district, the guerrilla forces have failed to establish a collective identity in spite of intense pressure from the United States and Arab capitals. Even in these regions, the collective effort so far has been limited to co-ordinating resistance to the Soviet–Afghan forces rather than political issues affecting an Afghanistan liberated from Soviet-backed Marxist rule. In 1983–4 Soviet forces succeeded in bringing Kandahar and Herat under Kabul's control, but rural areas around these urban centres continued to remain outside the firm control of the Marxist regime.

Selig Harrison, after a visit to Afghanistan in 1984, wrote that the number of Afghans on the Soviet-subsidized payroll of Kabul was some 375,000, including about 60,000 in the army, another 75,000 in various paramilitary forces and at least 25,000 in the secret police. The army was still plagued by desertions, but 'the desertion rate appears to have levelled off. As for the resistance, the number of organized *mujahidin* with regular links to base camps in Pakistan and to external inputs of weaponry and financial aid appears to be 35,000.' The guerrilla fighters continued to be deeply committed to their religious and patriotic causes. Harrison did not find a matching motivation in the Afghan army, but found that 'their communist officers and junior officers are highly motivated'. Factional divisions in the Afghan officer corps 'are less severe than in the past and [the Afghan army] is becoming a useful adjunct to the Soviet military machine.'[13]

In early 1985, the Soviet forces in Afghanistan, the 40th Army, were composed of seven divisions and five air assault brigades, backed up by a few *spetsnaz* (special purpose commando) units, 500 helicopters, several squadrons of MiG-21s and 23s, and at least one squadron of Su-25 (Frog Foot) attack aircraft, which represents the first deployment of this ground-attack aircraft anywhere in the world.[14] Divisional deployments are geographically balanced, with about a third of the total ground forces in the Kabul area, and other major deployments at Mazar-i-Sharif and Quandoz in the north, Herat and Farah in the west, Kandahar in the south, and Jalalabad in the east. The seven major air bases are located in Herat, Shindand and Farah in the west, Kandahar in the south, Jalalabad in the east, and in Kabul and Bagram.[15]

The most brutal war is a civil war, and Afghanistan has been no exception. Soviet 'terror tactics' have ranged from the use of booby-trapped toys to wholesale carpet bombing of guerrilla positions. Human rights observers have reported systematic violation of human rights and dignities and war tactics designed to deny food to the rebels and their supporters. Certain areas have been bombed for seven days running; village after village has been 'rubble-ized'. The guerrillas in turn have been equally brutal. Neither side believes in taking prisoners except for exhibition purposes. The United States State Department has accused the Soviets of using chemical weapons in at least thirty-six cases between 1980 and 1982. The allegations have been strongly denied by Moscow as well as Kabul. Kabul has also denied large-scale violation of human rights of Afghans resisting the Marxist regime, and has pointed out that, since January 1980, it has adopted a series of administrative, legal and constitutional measures to protect the basic human rights of the people of Afghanistan.

The Soviets have tested or experimented with many new items of equipment in the Afghan civil war, including the Su-25 attack aircraft, the Hind gunship, and the AGS-17 automatic grenade launcher. 'The use of helicopters is perhaps the most significant of these tests. Helicopters are used for resupply, reconnaisance, troops transport, fire support, and command and control. The Soviets view pilot training in Afghanistan as superb.' The Soviet military command has drawn several lessons from the fighting experience of their troops in Afghanistan. There have been numerous articles in the Soviet military press on mountain training and some emphasizing the need to develop the 'initiatives' of field commanders and the physical fitness of fighting men. Mountain training has been given considerable importance in Soviet military training in the last five years.[16]

Estimates of Soviet losses in Afghanistan vary enormously, and so do estimates of what Afghanistan has been costing the Kremlin. United States State Department estimates, based on reports received from resistance sources, puts the number of Soviet casualties between 1979 and 1984 at 13,000 dead and 40,000 wounded. The Soviets are said to have lost 5,000 vehicles and 600 helicopters. The war has cost the

Kremlin $17bn. The total number of Afghans dead, including army, resistance and civilians, is approximately 150,000 since 1980.[17] British estimates of Soviet casualties are considerably lower—5,000 dead up to 1984.[18]

Selig Harrison's overall picture of the political–military situation in Afghanistan in 1984 was one of a 'deepening stalemate'.

On one side, the Soviet subsidized Communist regime is slowly but steadily building a stable Afghan city-state in Kabul and its environs, buttressed not only by Soviet forces but also by an elaborate Afghan military, paramilitary and secret police apparatus. On the other, scattered groups of dedicated resistance fighters, while better coordinated militarily than in the past, continue to lack the political infrastructure that would be necessary to follow up their military successes by establishing secure liberated areas in the countryside.

The prevailing Western image of the Afghan struggle is grossly distorted because it denies the reality of a political stalemate. In this simplistic imagery, there is a sharp dichotomy between an illegitimate Kabul regime, unable to establish its writ beyond the capital, and an alternative focus of legitimacy collectively provided by the resistance fighters, who are seen as controlling most of the country's land area. It is true that the Kabul regime does not have a grip on much of the countryside, but neither does the resistance. In reality, most of Afghanistan, now as in past decades and centuries, is governed by free-wheeling local tribes and ethnic warlords.[19]

Writing for the Congressional Research Service in January 1985, Richard Cronin drew up a more or less similar political–military land-scape in Afghanistan. 'The Soviets are in firm control of Kabul . . . and the neighbouring military complex at Bagram, and now reportedly control Herat, and Kandahar. . . . The mujahidin retain free movement over most of Afghanistan's mountainous countryside, and the ability to mount limited rocket, mortar and small arms attacks on Soviet garrisons in urban areas.' In Panjsher Valley, Richard Cronin reported that the Soviets were in occupation of the mouth of the valley, but the guerrillas had returned 'in force' to its upper reaches and had reportedly resumed fighting.

Notwithstanding its difficulties, the Soviet Union has made some clear gains that it would not willingly relinquish. It has kept a communist regime in power in a sensitive border region and has gained some strategic advantages, including an expanded airbase at Shindand, in southwestern Afghanistan, which puts Soviet tactical aircraft within range of the Straits of Hormuz, in the Persian Gulf.

Soviet strategy seems to be to maintain control of Afghanistan with a minimum military commitment while seeking to train a new generation of Afghan communist leaders loyal to Moscow. It is reportedly training as many as 10,000 Afghans annually in the Soviet Union both to rebuild the Afghan army and to staff the administrative bureaucracy.

The Soviets, Cronin added, had resorted increasingly to heavy and indiscriminate air and artillery attacks on resistance villages. Their objective clearly was to deny the *mujahidin* vital access to the local population for their support.

These tactics may in time seriously handicap the ability of the resistance to carry on effective military operations. While the depopulation of the countryside removes the need of the *mujahidin* to defend their families and farms, it also eliminates the prime asset of the guerrilla—the ability to blend into the population and live off the land. At a minimum, Soviet tactics will tend to increase guerrilla dependence on external supplies and on more extensive supply lines.[20]

Cronin's overview of the impact of Soviet military operations in Afghanistan has been confirmed by other American sources. The *New York Times* reported in mid-July 1984 that Western intelligence sources had concluded that 'savage Soviet military campaigns' against Afghan villages had gone a long way to drying up popular support for the insurgents. Rural populations had fled combat areas, and the rebels were thus denied supplies, without which they could barely survive. The Afghan population of 15.5 million had been reduced to 11.5 million, with 3 million taking refuge in Pakistan, half a million in Iran, and another half million killed, wounded or driven from their homes.[21]

According to an Afghan scholar working at Columbia University, New York City, who has kept close track of the fighting within Afghanistan, the Soviets have had significant successes in several areas. Perhaps their two most important successes have been, first, the failure of the resistance groups to unite politically and to set up an alternative government on 'liberated Afghan territory', and, second, the fighting between and among insurgent groups. Both successes have their roots in the fragmentation of Afghan society into mutually hostile tribal groups. The Soviets are believed to have put together an effective state security service of 20,000 Afghans, and to have trained another 30,000 Afghans belonging to the PDPA armed forces. According to the Afghan scholar, Zalmay Khalizad, less than 20 per cent of the Soviet troops now participate in actual combat, the main onus of which has been passed on to the Afghan army. The Soviets have inflicted much heavier costs on the Afghans than vice versa, are relying increasingly on air strikes to destroy resistance hold-outs, and have made considerable progress in 'sovietizing' the Afghan economy and education system, training a new generation of Afghans in the Soviet Union to rebuild Afghanistan on the Soviet model. Meanwhile, most people in the West have lost interest in Afghanistan, and the West Europeans have been nudging the Reagan administration to mute its protests against Soviet activities in that country. A continuation of these trends, Khalizad suggests, could in time lead to a consolidation of Soviet power in Afghanistan.[22]

Since 1983, the Soviets have increased pressure on Pakistan, both militarily and diplomatically, while making tantalizing offers of large-scale across-the-board development assistance at the same time.

According to Pakistani sources, there have been hundreds of violations of Pakistani airspace and border areas by Soviet planes and artillery since 1983. In 1984 Soviet aircraft began to bomb Afghan outposts located on the Pakistani side of the border; Pakistani sources claim that several hundred people have been killed or wounded in these hot pursuit attacks. There have also been several cases of large ammunition explosions in the Afghan refugee camps on Pakistani territory, suggesting that among the refugees there are pro-Soviet elements intent on sabotaging resistance activity. In retaliation, Afghans murdered a couple of Soviet prisoners taken to the refugee camps in Pakistan, and the incident was given a lot of publicity, creating embarrassment for the Pakistan Government which pretends that Pakistan territory is not being used to train resistance personnel, or to supply arms to insurgents within Afghanistan.[23]

These systematic Afghan-Soviet forays into Pakistan—which were equally systematically denied by Kabul and dismissed as politically-motivated Pakistani propaganda—were evidently aimed at mounting pressure on Pakistan to cut off supplies to Afghan insurgents and to agree to negotiate with the Karmal regime a political settlement of the Afghan crisis. In the summer of 1985 these two Soviet objectives appeared to be somewhat closer to realization than at any time in the past five years. The Pakistan Government's stoical refusal to retaliate—despite the substantial military assistance given it by the United States since 1981—aroused considerable public protest. In the National Assembly members demanded retaliation, mainly in order to further embarrass the military regime which did not wish to get involved in a military conflict with Soviet-backed Afghanistan. Members also demanded direct negotiation with Afghanistan, for which the military regime was not prepared. On 12 June, the National Assembly held a thirty-minute debate on Afghanistan. The Foreign Minister, Yakub Khan, in a spirited speech, declared that the Government would 'spare no sacrifice for the defence of the motherland against provocations and inhuman violations of its territory', but gave no assurance that it would retaliate against the violations. Yakub Khan, on the other hand asked the members

to appreciate that we must always keep the objective of a negotiated political settlement uppermost in our minds. This requires us, on the one hand, to remain firm in our resolve not to accept unprincipled compromises under pressure of military threats and violations, and, on the other hand, not to allow ourselves to be provoked into retaliatory measures which could harm the prospects of a peaceful solution.[24]

In mid-1985, as will be seen later in this volume, the Soviets seemed to be more confident than at any time since December 1979 of bringing the Afghan drama to a denouement which was to their liking. Soviet spokesmen were hopeful that, given time, the Karmal regime would be able to gradually take over the direction of the civil war as well as rebuilding the ravaged Afghanistan. They had given complete support to the regime since they had themselves helped to instal it in Kabul in the immediate wake of their military intervention. Not only had they committed their great military might to the defence of the regime and the revolution, they had expended a large slice of their not unlimited resources to keep the Afghan economy going. Under the protective wings of Moscow, Babrak Karmal has been trying, since January 1980, to put the Saur revolution together again. Whether the Soviets will withdraw their troops from Afghanistan, and when, will depend entirely on the Marxist regime acquiring the internal strength necessary for its survival when the Russian soldiers have gone.

9 Saur Revolution:
the Parcham Phase

With the death of Amin and the take-over by Soviet troops, the Khalq phase of the Saur revolution came to an unlamented end. The Parcham phase of the revolution began under the Kremlin's protection and overall supervision and guidance. Babrak Karmal, leader of the Parcham faction of the PDPA, was proclaimed President of Afghanistan and General Secretary of the Party, three or four days after the Soviet takeover. Although Babrak Karmal later claimed that he was very much in Kabul at the time of the Soviet arrival, he was probably flown to the Afghan capital in a Soviet plane after the death of Amin. Karmal's mandate was two-fold: to rectify the errors and mistakes committed by Amin and Taraki by mellowing the reforms that had battered the socio-cultural fabric of Afghan society, and to build the broadest possible support base for the regime; and second, to re-organize the Afghan army and secret police with Soviet help in the shortest possible time so that Afghans loyal to the regime could themselves take on the resistance. Karmal decided to attempt both tasks within a rigorous framework of total loyalty to the USSR. 'The pursuance of eternal friendship and solidarity with the Leninist Communist Party of the Soviet Union and friendship between our countries and our peoples are the basic measures and yardsticks for the appraisal of the work of every member of the party from top to bottom, and of the party and government from top to bottom', declared Karmal in a broadcast to his people on 13 November 1980.[1]

Karmal made his first broadcast to the Afghan people on 27 December 1979, although doubts exist as to whether the broadcast was made by him personally from Kabul or whether Kabul Radio played a recorded broadcast brought by the Soviets along with their armed forces. In less than a week, however, Karmal announced his Government's new programme on Afghan television. It carried the banner 'Forward towards Peace, Freedom, National Independence, Democracy, Progress and Social Justice'. It pledged the regime to six immediate acts: the release of all political prisoners and the abolition of executions; the abolition of all anti-democratic and anti-human rights regulations and a ban on all arrests, incarcerations, arbitrary persecutions, house searches and inquisitions; respect for sacred principles of Islam, freedom of conscience, belief and religious practice, protection of family unity, and of legal, lawful, just and private ownership; the revival of individual and collective security and immunity, the restoration of revolutionary tranquillity, peace and order in Afghanistan; ensuring healthy conditions conducive to democratic freedoms such as the freedom to form progressive and patriotic parties and mass or social organizations, freedom of the press, of demonstrations, and immunity of correspondence and communications, travel and domicile; and, finally, the extending of serious attention to the younger generation, school, college and university students and the intelligentsia.[2]

In a series of speeches and official announcements, Karmal told the Afghans that there would be no attempt to change Afghan society rapidly. He introduced himself as a good Muslim, and began each and every speech with an invocation to the Almighty. He said progressive and democratic political parties and mass organizations would be allowed, and constructive dissent tolerated. The regime ordered the release of several thousand political prisoners and declared an amnesty to all resisters if they laid down arms, and promised rehabilitation to all refugees if they returned to their villages and towns. The regime promised to hold elections when suitable conditions were restored. It promised equality to all nationalities as well as the preservation of their distinctive cultures, traditions and values.[3]

Babrak Karmal also sought to widen the base of his Government by including in the Cabinet and administration people with differing shades of political view—some even described as rightists. In all, more than forty politicians, diplomats, civil servants and technocrats were rehabilitated, some of them for the first time since April 1978. Among the over one hundred senior appointments made there were some people whom Karmal had known from the days of the Daoud regime, who were not Marxists but in whose patriotic integrity he had complete confidence. The Khalq members of the Government and the bureaucracy, as well as of the higher organs of the party, were retained in their respective positions (see Table 3). Asadullah Sarwari, a Parcham leader who had been jailed and tortured when Taraki was in power, became Deputy Prime Minister. Khalqis outnumbered Parchamis in the Government, and even more so in the army. Factional in-fighting did not disappear, however. In June 1980 Sarwari was sent away to distant Mongolia as ambassador. Following the arrest of a Khalqi commander of the 14th Armoured Division, the soldiers mutinied. There were reports of plots against the Government in June, July and October of 1980 and again in February 1981.[4] Since then, however, Karmal has succeeded in keeping the party together, no split has occurred, no plots have been reported, and Karmal has acquired certain aspects of a father figure, a national unifier under the umbrella of Soviet arms.[5]

The Government set out to reorganize the Afghan armed forces which had been mutilated in the civil war and weakened by large-scale defections. Much greater emphasis was put on the political reliability of the soldiers than on their numbers. Officers began to be sent to the Soviet Union for training. The PDPA took over the task of the political education of the soldiers. In the summer of 1980 compulsory military training and three-year service was introduced for all able-bodied men between 20 and 50, but the measure was never rigorously enforced because it was very unpopular. In 1983, conscription was reduced to two years.

In April the Revolutionary Council proclaimed a new Afghan constitution. Its official name was the Fundamental Principles of the Democratic Republic of Afghanistan. It defined the rights and duties of citizens as well as the functions of the national and provincial executive and judicial agencies. The constitution guaranteed the 'democratic rights' of the Afghans, including the right to peacefully assemble and demonstrate. No one could be arrested except by warrant; no one could be tortured in prison; trials of political prisoners had to be open to the public and each of the accused had the right to self-defence. Freedom to profess and practise Islam was also guaranteed. Article 5 of the Fundamental Principles stated, 'Respect and defence of the holy religion of Islam are ensured in the Democratic Republic of Afghanistan. All Moslems are guaranteed and ensured complete freedom in the performance of Islamic religious rites'. The same freedom was guaranteed to people of other faiths too. At the same time, the government

Table 3. Membership of the leading party and state organs of the People's Democratic Republic of Afghanistan, 10 January 1980

Revolutionary Council	Presidium of the RC	Political Bureau	Secretariat	Central Committee CC	Alternate CC	Government Post
Total number 56	7	7	3	36	8	17
Babrak Karmal	×	×	×			Prime Minister
Assadullah Sarwari	×	×		×		
Sultan Ali Kishtmand	×	×		×		
Nour Ahmad Nour	×	×	×	×		
Major General Abdul Qader	×			×		
Lieutenant-Colonel Mohammad Aslam Watanjar	×			×		Minister of Communications
Lieutenant-Colonel Gul Aqa	×			×		
Dr Anahita Ratebzad		×		×		
Dr Saleh Mohammad Zeary		×	×	×		
Ghulam Dastagir Panchsheri		×		×		
Dr Raz Mohammad Paktin				×		Minister of Water and Power
Sayed Mohammad Gulabzoi				×		Minister of the Interior
Shah Mohammad Dost				×		Minister for Foreign Affairs
Lieutenant-Colonel Sherjan Mazdooryan				×		Minister of Transport
Abdurrashid Aryan				×		Minister of Justice
Abdul Majid Sarbuland				×		Minister of Information and Culture
Abdul Wakil				×		Minister of Finance
Fazul Rahim Mohmand						Minister of Agriculture and Land Reforms
Lieutenant-Colonel Faiz Mohammad					×	Minister of Frontiers and Tribal Affairs
Mohammad					×	Minister of Higher Education

Minister of Mines and Industries
Minister of Commerce

Minister of Defence
Minister of Public Works

Mohammad Khan Jalalar
Lieutenant-Colonel Mohammad Rafic
Eng. Nazar Mohammad
Imtiaz Hassan
Suraya
Jamila Palwasha
Dr Habib Mangal
Major Khalilullah
Khalilullah Kohistani
Major Dost Mohammad
Sayed Ikram Paygir
Dr Sayed Amir Shah Zarra
Sayed Taher Shah Paikargar
Suleyman Laiq
Eng. Abdul Zohoor Razmjo
Abdus Samad Azhar
Abdul Qayoum Noorzai
Azizur Rahman Saeedi
Ghulam Sarwar Yuresh
Dr Ghulam Farouq
Feda Mohammad Dehnishin
Mohammad Hassan Bareq
Mohammad Hassan Paiman
Mohammad Ayan Ayan
Lieutenant-Colonel Mohammad Nabi Azimi

Source: Bogdan Szajkowski (ed.), *Documents in Communist Affairs–1980*, London, Macmillan, 1981, pp. xxiv–xxv.

was determined not to allow religion to be 'turned into a weapon of anti-popular propaganda'.

The new constitution ensured equal rights of women as well as 'genuine equality' of all large and small national groups and tribes in Afghanistan, providing them with equal opportunities to develop their traditions, languages, literature and arts. It forbade discrimination on national, linguistic, racial or tribal grounds. Special status was conferred on the 'numerous Pathan tribes inhabiting southern and south-western Afghanistan.' The government would go on building its relations with them on the basis of trust, peace and co-operation.

The constitution provided for a mixed economy, committing the government to encourage, protect and preserve 'different forms of ownership'. The economy and productive forces were to be developed through 'planned, dynamic and mutually complementary cooperation between the public, mixed and private sectors.' The public sector would extend chiefly to the production of capital goods, power development and transport. The main concern of the private sector was to manufacture traditional handicraft goods, operate the service industry, and run small and medium-size shops. The state would provide retailers with goods. Private businessmen wishing to take part in building industries or public catering and service establishments or in the setting up of transport companies would remain untouched, except in the case of large landlords. Agriculture would not be collectivized. The economic thrust of the constitution was clearly aimed at assuring Afghanistan's one million small traders and businessmen and the great bulk of its peasants that their interests were safe and secure in Marxist Afghanistan.[6]

The constitution came into force on 15 April, seven weeks after a week-long demonstration of popular resentment at the presence of Soviet troops in Afghanistan. The demonstrators paralyzed life in Kabul and several provincial capitals, reportedly stunning the Parcham leadership no less than the Soviets. It began as a general strike in Kabul on 21 February, backed by almost 95 per cent of the traders, and developed into mass civil disobedience. There were reports of sporadic fighting between Afghan government troops and rebels. Soviet soldiers kept to their barracks, leaving the Afghan troops and PDPA cadres to persuade the shopkeepers not to close their shutters. The demonstrations

warned the Soviets as well as Babrak Karmal of the extent of Afghan
alienation from the regime, and of Afghan resentment of the Soviet
military intervention.[7]

However, the February demonstration was the last public protest on
a mass scale in Kabul or any other large city in Afghanistan against the
Soviet military presence and/or the Karmal regime. It hastened well-
orchestrated counter-measures by the regime and its Soviet patrons.
Karmal announced the Fundamental Principles as a major political
drive to win popular confidence. Both Kabul and Moscow launched
parallel 'peace offensives'; at the same time, military operations against
the resistance were intensified. The rebels were not getting more than
token military assistance from American, Pakistani, Chinese and other
sources. The Carter administration was not willing to pay a high price
for Pakistani co-operation in a bloody opposition to the Sovietization
of Afghanistan. The number of refugees in Pakistan did not touch the
million mark. There was time for the Karmal regime to launch its
political offensive and for the Soviets to launch their military action.

In 1981 Karmal succeeded in broadening the political base of his
regime. In April he presided over the inaugural session of the National
Fatherland Front, which was designed to be a coalition of nationalist,
patriotic, democratic and progressive forces from different classes,
strata and groups of the Afghan people. The first session of the NFF
was attended by delegates from the PDPA, the trade unions, unions of
agricultural co-operatives, democratic youth organizations, unions of
journalists, writers, artists, schoolteachers, university lecturers and
professors, chambers of commerce and industry, the supreme council
of ulemas and the assembly of tribal representatives. A lot of time and
effort had been spent in building these constituents of the NFF before
its first session was held. The charter of the NFF, adopted at the first
session, visualized it as the principal instrument of mass mobilization
on behalf of the Marxist regime. It was to serve as 'the basis of working
people's rule'; it was to popularize the PDPA's policies amongst the
masses and draw them into the administration and into public affairs; it
was to ensure that Islam and Islamic practices and customs were given
the respect due to them under the Fundamental Principles.[8] The NFF
that met in April 1981 was far less than representative of the Afghan
people. However, the conference was attended by religious and tribal

leaders as well as representatives of business and industry. In 1982 the NFF was given a crucial role in the implementation of land and water reforms. These reforms, announced in June 1981, were much mellower than those decreed within weeks of the Saur revolution.[9] Peasants were allowed to keep up to 25 acres of high-grade land. The laws relating to debts and bride price were suspended, and no more was said of them.

In 1981 the PDPA began its campaign of holding local *jirgahs* and set up a network of local government on traditional Afghan lines, but with the full legitimacy of the more liberal laws of the regime. Tribal chiefs were asked to take over much of the local administration and the Islamic judicial system was restored. Throughout 1981 the PDPA and the Government campaigned jointly for the first 'countrywide conference' of the party, which was scheduled for March 1982. The conference was held in Kabul on 14 and 15 March. No data were released on the composition of the 'countrywide' conference, nor on the number of delegates present. Karmal, in his inaugural address, described the session as the 'beginning of a new stage' in the 'work and struggles' of the party. The CPSU central committee claimed, in a message, that 'the social base of the progressive regime is expanding . . .. The representatives of various strata of the population are joining in the ranks of the active builders of the republic.'[10] The report of the PDPA central committee to the 'countrywide' conference did not mention the total strength of party membership, but said that 60 per cent of the new recruits came from working-class or peasant families.[11]

The report was an important political document since it defined with some clarity the class character of the Democratic Afghan Republic as well as the objectives and the methodologies of the Afghan national democratic revolution. The revolution, it said, was developing 'in peaceful as well as non-peaceful forms'; it was taking place in a country with a 'complex national and tribal composition', the majority of people being followers of the 'holy religion of Islam'. The Saur revolution must move forward stage by stage, one leading on to the next. In the present stage of the revolution, 'broad and progressive programmes of action' had to be implemented to improve the material condition of the toilers, to continue with the land and water reforms, improve the provision of essential goods, and the development of commerce, culture and education. The report claimed that the 'bases of a new political system' had been created, lending the revolution its 'democratic substance'. The new bases consisted of two state organs: the National Fatherland Front, which the report described as the 'bastion and stronghold of the power of the working people', and the Front's 'inherent' social and popular organizations. 'A new political system has been created and is functioning', it affirmed. The system's economic base would be 'multi-form', the state sector enjoying preference. The main economic aim was the abolition of feudalism, and in this task the 'national capitalists' would be encouraged to play their own role.[12] The 'countrywide' conference adopted an 'action programme', which was projected as the PDPA's first action programme since the one adopted in 1965.[13] It made the Marxist–Leninist theoretical point that the basis of political power in the DRA was an 'alliance of workers and peasants', backed by all democratic, patriotic and progressive forces. The workers formed the vanguard of the revolution.

In 1982 Karmal and other Government and party leaders began to travel to provincial capitals. *The Kabul New Times* carried reports of rebel activities in different areas, the rebels being described as 'bandits'. Karmal visited Moscow twice, the second time for a meeting with Yuri Andropov. Afghanistan started building up a network of political and economic relations with the Soviet bloc socialist countries, and concluded a treaty of friendship and co-operation with Hungary. In an interview given to the BBC, Karmal disclosed that the PDPA membership in 1982 stood at 70,000. He claimed that his Government controlled all the cities of Afghanistan. 'For the first time in the history of Afghanistan, a strong and powerful central government is formed, the local organ of whose power exists in all the far-flung areas of the country', he asserted.[14] In August 1982, the PDPA central committee held its 9th plenary session. Karmal's report conceded that the party organization was still weak in most of the provinces; party unity had improved but was still insufficient, the party was still to gain the trust and 'optimism' of the masses. However, the NFF had set up committees in 23 provinces, 15 districts and 3 cities outside Kabul, where it now had 78 councils. Of the 70,000 members of the party, 28 per cent were workers and peasants, but 48 per cent had been recruited since the holding of the 'countrywide' conference.[15]

On 20 December, Karmal addressed a press conference in Moscow.

He reported a 0.5 per cent increase in the area under cultivation in the first six months of the year, and a 5.1 per cent increase in wheat production over the output of 1981. He said that, compared to 1981, agriculture and livestock production in 1982 had grown by 3 per cent, and industry, power and mining by 3.7 per cent. 'The prices of foodstuff remained three times lower than in Iran and at least two times lower than in Pakistan.'[16]

With the summit conference of the non-aligned nations in New Delhi in mind, the PDPA offered, in February 1983, to hold a grand *jirgah* with tribal chiefs who had fled to Peshawar, and reiterated its readiness to settle the Afghan crisis in direct negotiations with Pakistan and Iran. It set hopes high for the mediation effort of the UN envoy, Diego Cordovez.[17] In an interview with *Patriot* of New Delhi, Karmal claimed that about 21,000 'erstwhile counterrevolutionaries' had surrendered to the government.[18] The Afghan delegation to the non-aligned summit was led by Prime Minister Sultan Ali Kishtmand, who met with several NAM leaders separately before addressing the plenary session. Among these were Prime Minister Indira Gandhi, Fidel Castro, of Cuba, Yasser Arafat, of the PLO, President Assad of Syria, and the Prime Ministers of Vietnam, Libya and Algeria. No contact, however, took place between the Afghans and the Pakistanis and Iranians attending the NAM session.

Kishtmand only came to the situation in Afghanistan at the end of a long speech delivered at the Non-Aligned summit. He said that 300,000 landless peasants had been given land, free of cost, since 1978, and the cancellation of land revenue had benefited 200,000 poor rural families. He reported a large literacy campaign which had already made 300,000 adults literate and was giving literacy lessons to more than 600,000. The Kabul regime, he claimed, was enjoying 'ever greater support' from 'all strata', of the Afghan population; the political base of the regime was being expanded and state organs made stronger. Kishtmand bluntly told the conference that the Soviet troops would not withdraw from Afghanistan as long as foreign interference in the country's internal affairs was not completely halted.[19]

The year 1983 was projected by the Kabul regime as a year of steady gains for the revolution. Government leaders visited more provincial capitals in 1983 than in the previous year. The party gave high priority to mobilizing the support of the Islamic clergy and traditional village elders who were not feudal lords (most of the latter had fled the country or joined resistance groups). A great deal of emphasis was given to the mobilization of women and children. It was disclosed that 60,000 children had been enlisted as pioneers since 1978.[20] Several resistance groups were reported to have announced their support for the revolution. One of these was led by Ghulam Rasul, of Herat province, who was described as the leader of the 100,000 people of his tribe, and who joined 'the side of the revolution' in March.[21] In May, another resistance group, Afghan Millat, reportedly dissolved itself and decided to co-operate with the regime.[22] The holding of local *jirgahs* was given high priority in the party and Government programme. The crushing of the resistance continued to receive the highest priority, but the regime and the PDPA seemed to be focusing more and more on economic issues and on repairing the crushed civic life of the nation.

Addressing the 11th plenum of the PDPA central committee in March, Karmal said that the civil war had taken a toll of 24bn. afghanis, 'perhaps more'. The Soviets, he said, were doing everything in their power to help Afghanistan rebuild itself, but, said Karmal, Moscow could not solve Afghanistan's economic problems: 'we must take decisions ourselves'.[23] An emphasis on self-reliance amidst immense dependency on the Soviet Union was noticeable in the Outline of the Development Plan for 1983–84, released towards the end of May. It envisaged an investment of afs.12.8 bn., of which 55.5 per cent was to come in foreign aid which was flowing in, mostly from the Soviet Union, with several East European governments chipping in with relatively small contributions. Institutional aid from the World Bank and the International Monetary Fund was cut off in 1982-3. The main emphasis in the annual plan was on land reforms, increasing agricultural outputs and expanding the socio-economic services such as education and public health, jacking up foreign trade and the 'rehabilitation of damaged institutions'. The plan aimed at a 6.6 per cent increase in the GNP by making the public sector strong.[24] The plan put the 'strengthening of national defence' rather low on the list of identified priorities, which probably meant that reorganization of the Afghan army was being completely financed by the Soviet Government. In November Karmal addressed the first national conference of secretaries of primary party organizations of the Army and stressed the need to streamline the political education of soldiers, especially the youth who were being recruited from the provincial towns and villages.[25]

In a progress report in December 1983, the overall situation in Afghanistan was regarded as being modestly positive. The economy had begun to pick up, the report claimed. Large quantities of inputs had been supplied to cultivators; seven mechanized farms had been set up in as many provinces; 296,000 hectares of first-grade land had been distributed to poor peasants. For the benefit of farmers, the purchase price of cotton had been raised by 60 per cent, that of sugar beet by 40 per cent. Income from the sale of natural gas has increased considerably. Two power lines from the Soviet Union have been constructed and work on a 700 kW power-station in Kunar was to have been completed in 1984. Altogether, 243 development projects, 'of which 50 are new and the remaining transitional' were nearing completion.[26]

The year 1984 began with more news of economic development, with Soviet help, of course. Sheberghan, capital of Tauzjan province, 'one of the cradles' of Afghan communism, was said to be fast developing into a 'big industrial sector'. It earned the distinction of being the first city in Afghanistan with piped natural gas both to industrial plants and workers' housing. The city is now connected to the main supply line at the Jarqudok mine, with a twelve-kilometre pipeline.[27] On 28 January, electricity from Soviet Central Asia began to flow into the Hairatan river port in Afghanistan and adjacent populated areas through a high-voltage cable built across the Amu Darya. The cable is being extended to Mazar-i-Sharif. More powerlines are being built from Soviet Central Asia, with a capacity of 200,000 kW of electricity for Afghanistan.[28]

Since 1983 the rebels in Afghanistan have been getting larger and better supplies of arms from the base camps in Pakistan, and reports printed in the Afghan press often speak of 'intensified fighting with bandit gangs'. However, the rhetoric of the regime suggests an increasing confidence in the eventual victory of the revolution. The central committee of the PDPA held two plenums in 1984; Karmal's reports to the plenums were a mixture of increasing self-confidence and admission of major failures on the part of the Government and the party in accomplishing vital talks. The regime earnestly engaged in the task of setting up a network of 'local organs of power'. The law defining the powers and functions of local organs was announced in February after 'profound analysis and debate' in a commission consisting of representatives of the various national groups and tribes. The local organs were to be elected all over the country, from the village to the provincial level, keeping the existing geographical and administrative boundaries intact, on the basis of universal franchise (but open ballot 'in the prevailing circumstances'), and the councils thus elected would administer the laws and mobilize popular support for and participation in the struggle against the counter-revolutionaries. The controversial matter of conscription, which had met with considerable resistance and criticism in the country, was also left to decision by the local councils. The minimum age for a 'people's deputy' was fixed at 18, despite some opposition, and it was laid down that candidates could only be nominated by the National Fatherland Front or one or the other of its constituent bodies. The local *jirgahs* were to be the 'highest state organs' in their respective areas, looking after political, administrative, economic and cultural matters'.[29]

The DRA budget and annual development plan for 1984–85, announced in March, claimed that GDP had increased by 6 per cent and GNP by 4.5 per cent in the preceding twelve-month period. The plan gave an idea of the volume of development assistance Afghanistan was getting from the USSR. 'In the past two years', stated the annual plan document, sixteen big projects 'which have a major role in the growth of the national economy of the DRA', were built with Soviet assistance and were now in operation. The public sector, built almost entirely with Soviet help, was producing 70 per cent of the country's industrial products. Sixty per cent of Afghanistan's external trade was with the Soviets. 'Every year, the Soviet Union renders us a huge quantity of consumer goods needed by the public and the industry gratis or on a long-term credit basis.'[30]

In a long report published in the CPSU journal *Party Life* (June 1984), Noor Ahmad Noor, PDPA Secretary, claimed that in 1983 Afghanistan's GNP and national income had 'for the first time' since April 1978 exceeded the level of before the revolution. Industrial production for that year was valued at afs. 82.5 m. The PDPA organization network now consisted of 30 provincial party committees, 61 precinct and city committees, 207 district and sub-district committees, and 3,000 primary committees. Party membership had increased from 18,000 at the time of the Saur revolution to 151,000. This was 80,000 more than the figure of 70,000 given by Karmal to a BBC reporter in 1982. Noor said that over 7,000 party members had received theoretical training in the USSR and other socialist countries and in the Institute of Social Sciences of the PDPA central committee.[31]

Babrak Karmal delivered three important speeches in 1984: his reports to the 13th and 14th plenums of the PDPA central committee held in March and September respectively, and his speech at a party seminar in Kabul in June. Each address combined sharp criticism of the party's many failures with claims of significant gains by the regime since January 1980. A common theme in the three speeches was the party's failure to win the trust and confidence of the village poor, even to reach out to them at their hearths, in their homes in the rugged depths of the Afghan countryside: 'we have not been able to convey the voice of the revolution and its cause and demands to the ears of all', said Karmal in June. 'We should have conveyed to all peasants the reality that the revolution is in the service of the peasants and in their interests. Peasants still do not know that the distributed land belongs to them so that they have to defend their land.' He set three main tasks before the party: consolidation of state power, strengthening the armed forces, and extending the party organization to the far corners of the country. Karmal stressed in all three of his speeches that the party members had to realize that they belonged to the ruling party and that the demands of the people on their time, ability, integrity and dedication were much greater now than in the past.[32]

Babrak's report to the 13th plenum of the party central committee was remarkable for its candid admission of indiscipline and factional in-fighting still prevalent in the PDPA. He severely warned party leaders against 'meddling in affairs not related to them' and against causing indiscipline in the armed forces. He regretted that neither the state organs nor the party committees were working seriously to recruit soldiers for the armed forces, with the result that the army itself had to spend a lot of time and effort enlisting new recruits, instead of fighting the rebels. Relations between the party and the army were still not entirely harmonious, Karmal added.[33]

In his report to the 14th plenum, Karmal claimed that the political-military situation in Afghanistan had 'improved to a certain extent'. Government forces had inflicted 'considerable defeats' on the insurgents; the 'big bandit groups' in Panjsher and Andarab had been 'suppressed'. The overall situation, however, was still 'complicated'. The class struggle had gained 'an extraordinary intensity'. The resistance compensated for every defeat by devastating the economy and the social fabric of the areas they were expelled from. The latest session of rebel leaders in Peshawar had been attended by representatives from twenty-six countries, including the United States, France, Western Germany, Egypt, Pakistan, Iran, Japan and China. The decisions taken at that meeting 'envisage further expansion of the undeclared war against our revolution'. The revolution faced not only its internal class enemies, but also 'the vast intrigues of imperialism headed by the United States'. In spite of the significant gains made by the revolution, it could not be said that there had been a 'decisive turn' in its favour. For a decisive turn, Karmal said, it was essential to consolidate the party's relations with the masses, to expand the 'social pillars' of the revolution, to realize that the counter-revolution would not end soon but would be there for a long time, which meant that the revolutionary state organs, the PDPA and the armed forces must forge an iron discipline and invincible unity amongst them and also with the masses. The bulk of the speech was devoted to an elaborate enunciation of what the party must do at its various levels in order to achieve greater discipline and unity so that it could meet the battles still lying ahead.[34]

The year 1985 started with a big celebration of the 20th anniversary of the founding of the PDPA. On 10 January, Karmal inaugurated the 'grand meeting' in Kabul in the presence of fraternal delegations from twenty-seven foreign communist parties, and one from the ruling Congress I party of India.[35] His speech covered a wide area of ground, but was chiefly interesting for what it said about the Afghan Marxist party, the resistance, and the economic ground the regime claimed to have gained since the revolution. The PDPA, said Karmal, was a 'new type of party'; in its short history it had gone through experiences hardly encountered by similar parties in the developing world. The party's membership stood at 120,000, of whom 32,000 had been recruited in the Afghan year of March 1983 to March 1984. Thirty per cent of the members came from the working class and the peasantry, but the percentage was over 50 for members recruited since January 1980. It was a truly national party, with representatives from twenty national groups and tribes. The party organization had spread to 'every nook and corner' of Afghanistan. Karmal disclosed that 60 per cent of party members were actively engaged in the armed struggle against the resistance as members of the Afghan armed forces.

About the economic and social ground covered by the PDPA regime, Karmal gave the following additional information: one million Afghans had been made literate, while literacy courses were being given to 400,000 others. The circulation of daily newspapers had expanded by two-and-a-half times; radio and television broadcasting hours had doubled. Hospital beds had increased by 84 per cent and the number of medical doctors by 45 per cent. Hundreds of Soviet professors were teaching at the Institute of Social Sciences of the PDPA central committee.

Karmal was satisfied with the 'consolidation of Afghanistan's position in the world'. The DRA had been recognized by eighty countries, while the PDPA had active relations with 103 communist parties. Among the parties with which the PDPA signed protocols of co-operation during the 'grand meeting' were the two Indian communist parties—the CPI and the CPI-M, and the communist parties of Pakistan, Saudi Arabia, Iran and Syria.

Karmal spoke passionately about the international help the resistance had been getting through Pakistan. More than one hundred rebel bases were operating on Pakistan territory, he alleged, and from these bases thousands of 'mercenaries' were sent into Pakistan every month. A commentary in the *Kabul New Times* a little later described Pakistan as a 'haven' of counter-revolution, and alleged that the Pakistan military itself was training Afghan rebels at thirty-four paramilitary camps, each training course being attended by one thousand to two thousand insurgents.[36] *Pravda*, in a report in February, said that the civil war had caused property and other losses in Afghanistan valued at $800 m.[37]

Karmal spoke warmly of the contributions of the Soviet Union towards Afghanistan's economic development. Ninety-nine projects built with Soviet assistance were in operation, he said, while ninety more were either under construction or undergoing feasibility study. Afghanistan received 94.7 per cent of all its foreign aid from the socialist countries, 70.1 per cent from the USSR alone, an official announcement said in March.[38]

The 15th plenum of the PDPA central committee met in March to hear a major policy announcement from Karmal. The party's Politburo had decided, as a matter of policy, that the border with Pakistan would be 'sealed, protected and defended', Babrak Karmal told the plenum. It was the first decision of its kind in Afghanistan's entire history. Evidently the decision could not be implemented immediately; it required the active co-operation of the Pushtun tribes inhabiting the border areas, which was totally lacking. Karmal himself conceded that. The army and the border forces alone could not effectively seal the border with Pakistan, he pointed out; for this, the army commanders and party units had to cultivate local support. But he visualized a time when the PDPA would be able to mobilize the Pushtun tribes for the defence of the border. The immediate implications of this policy decision were three-fold. It implied that the Afghan forces backed by the Soviets would be operating close to the border and would engage in hot pursuit of rebel groups retreating into Pakistani territory. It was, in this respect, not only a warning to the Afghans living in refugee camps close to the border, but also to the Pakistan Government that the border would be getting 'hot' in the near future.

Karmal also admitted that the resistance still commanded the active or tacit support of a majority of Afghans, but this, he asserted, was a 'temporary' phase. The combination of the class enemies of the revolution and the imperialists had created a formidable problem, and although the PDPA regime had gained a lot of ground, and had inflicted many defeats on the resistance groups, 'the necessary turn has still not taken place' in the struggle for the mobilization of mass support. Karmal implied that most of the people who had not joined the resistance or had seemingly accepted the regime were sullen in their minds and alienated in their attitudes. The broad masses had not been attracted to the revolution; they were not working for its success. The weakest link in the party organization, Karmal noted, was the 'village circles'. Hundreds of village *jirgahs* had been held and village administrators elected, but 'we are still not leading the people in a struggle for total victory'.[39]

The claims that Karmal and his colleagues made for the gains of the revolution were certainly exaggerated, as were the claims made on the other side by leaders of the resistance and their international patrons. The hard facts of the situation in Afghanistan, independently verified, were impossible to obtain at any time after January 1980; these became even more scarce after the civil war escalated. However, the failure of the resistance groups to forge a common political platform, set up an alternative government on Afghan soil and thus offer a credible political alternative to the Afghan people, appears to have doomed the future of the insurgents. In the spring of 1985 Pakistani newspapers began to report the return of resistance groups to Afghanistan, and the launching of big Soviet offensives in a number of provinces close to the Pakistan border. Ten thousand Soviet troops were reported to have started an offensive against resistance bases in Kunar province in May. They broke the ten-month-old guerrilla capture of the Barokot garrison just a mile from the Pakistani border and were determined to cut supply lines from Pakistan to other resistance bases. The garrison fell when two hundred Soviet commandos made a surprise attack on an unprepared guerrilla force.[40] On 1 June the United States Government protested to Moscow against the establishment of a 'large militarised fort' across the Pakistan border. 'It appears that Soviet troops, helicopters and vehicles have been moved to staging areas near Jalalabad', the American note added.[41] A Quetta report printed in *The Muslim*, of Islamabad, said that an important Afghan spiritual leader, Abdullah Agha, 'who has millions of followers both in Pakistan and Afghanistan', had 'returned to his country and joined hands with Karmal.' He was the second Islamic spiritual leader to join the side of the revolution in two months, the first being Asmatullah Muslim.[42]

10 Prospects for a Political Settlement

'Time's glory is to calm contending kings', wrote Shakespeare in *The Rape of Lucrece*. Has time begun to calm the contending forces within and outside Afghanistan that have been locked in a grim struggle for nearly six years? Is there a credible prospect of the Afghanistan crisis being finally resolved, not in the rugged depths of the Hindu Kush but at negotiating tables in Moscow, Islamabad, Kabul and Geneva?

In the gory revolutionary drama of Afghanistan, the 'contending kings' are five. Three are directly involved: Afghanistan, the Soviet Union and Pakistan. Two others—the United States and the three million Afghan refugees gathered in Pakistan—are also directly involved, though more in the process of the civil war than in that of negotiation. The two parties most directly involved are Afghanistan and Pakistan. The resistance could not have assumed the proportions it has if Pakistan had refused to harbour the refugees or allow them to wage *jihad* against the Marxist regime. The Soviet Union and the United States were involved at a low level from the beginning of the revolution, the latter at a much lower level than the former. The Soviets became the armed defender of the revolution with their intervention in the last week of December 1979. The American cold war riposte made Washington the principal opponent of the Soviet intervention. The Afghan resistance carried out large-scale guerrilla operations, with generous assistance from Pakistan, the United States and several other countries. Pakistan cast itself in a key role. It reserved for itself effective control of the movement of arms and weapons mobilized by the CIA for the Afghan resistance. Pakistan has been the recipient of a $3.2 bn. package of military and economic assistance from the United States spread over the period 1980–86.

Of the five parties involved in the Afghan problem, the positions of three—the United States, Pakistan and the Afghan resistance—are weakened by inherent contradictions and gaps between their avowed objectives and the resources they are willing to deploy, and are capable of deploying, for the achievement of their goals. The positions of the two other parties, the Soviet Union and the Marxist regime in Kabul, are also weak, but the weakness is derived more from the hard, intransigent realities in Afghanistan than from the external forces that are committed to make their political objectives difficult and expensive to attain.

In the last five years or more no serious attempt has been made to find a solution to the Afghan problem which is both desirable and practicable. Indeed, a fundamental contradiction exists between the two since what is desirable for the United States, Pakistan and the Afghan resistance, namely, the liberation of Afghanistan from Soviet occupation and control, and the restoration of its status as a non-aligned sovereign state with a government that represents the political preferences of the majority of its people, is not practicable. The United States has neither the political will nor the military power to fight the Soviets out of Afghanistan. Pakistan is not even prepared to allow guerrilla warfare in Afghanistan to escalate beyond a moderate threshold lest it has to face large-scale Soviet retaliation. The Afghan refugees operating from Peshawar, in Pakistan, are divided into a dozen or more feuding factions and unable to offer the people of Afghanistan a credible political alternative to the Marxist regime in Kabul. The resistance groups within Afghanistan lack both the level of forces and the level of weapons to inflict crippling damage on the Soviet–Afghan forces. Besides, there is no political cohesion and unity amongst them, even if there exists a limited measure of co-ordination of guerrilla efforts.

Clearly then, the three parties cannot, even with their combined resources, reasonably expect to throw the Soviets out of Afghanistan. The Soviet Union, for its part, cannot eliminate the resistance except over a long period of time.[1] Moscow has dug in for a long haul, and time is its ally in Afghanistan. The parties have recognized that the Afghan problem is amenable to a political rather than a military settlement. However, there is a fundamental difference over which *part* of the problem is negotiable. The Soviets have made it clear that the situation *around Afghanistan* is politically negotiable, the situation within Afghanistan is not. The United States, on the other hand, perceives itself committed to no political change in Pakistan as an essential input of a settlement. Negotiations for a political settlement have run into deadlock since 1983. Not only are the Soviet and American positions mutually irreconcilable, but the United States and Pakistan have different priorities which determine their respective approaches to a political solution. For Pakistan, the return of the Afghan refugees to their homeland is of the utmost importance; Islamabad is willing to live with a Marxist regime in Kabul if it can persuade the bulk of the refugees to go back. The United States, on the other hand, has a visceral problem with the Marxist Government in Afghanistan which it perceives to be a forced transplant by the Kremlin onto the tradition-ally non-aligned and ruggedly nationalist soil of Afghanistan; the American priority therefore is on political change in Kabul, with the consent and approval of the resistance.

Over the past three years, a narrow tunnel of negotiations has been bored by the UN mediator, Diego Cordovez, through the granite walls that separate the three main parties—the Soviet Union, the United States and Pakistan. The negotiations, however, have been stalled by fundamental disagreements between Moscow, Islamabad and Washington. The fifth anniversary of the Soviet intervention was marked by a reiteration of the old rhetorics in Western capitals and in Islamabad, and by the re-adoption of old resolutions at the United Nations and other international forums. However, with each passing year, these rhetorics seem to carry less conviction with those who routinely pronounce them. The blunt reality of the Afghan situation is that the Soviets will not withdraw their troops except, by and large, on their own minimum terms, that their adversaries are unable to wrest from Moscow concessions that go against the grain of Soviet objec-tives and that the Reagan administration is unwilling to accept an arrangement that would mean the 'loss' of Afghanistan to the 'evil empire'.

The Soviet position on Afghanistan has remained stubbornly consistent. Brezhnev declared in his first major statement after the military intervention that 'the USSR will withdraw its military contingents from Afghanistan as soon as the reasons that caused their presence there disappear and the Afghan government decides that their presence is no longer necessary.' He added in the same breath,

I want to state very definitely that we will be ready to commence the withdrawal of our troops as soon as all forms of outside interference directed against the government and people of Afghanistan are fully terminated. Let the US, together with the neighbours of Afghanistan, guarantee this and then the need of Soviet military assistance will cease to exist.[2]

The minimum Soviet conditions stem from the premises on which the military intervention was mounted in December 1979. Six basic premises can be distinguished from a mountain of Soviet pronouncements on Afghanistan, beginning with an article in *Pravda* of 31 December 1979 by political analyst A. Petrov, right up to the comments in the Soviet press in the first six months of 1985, including, in this broad sweep of time, numerous authoritative statements by Brezhnev, Andropov, Chernenko and Gorbachov. These are:

(1) The Soviet Union intervened in Afghanistan with military force in order to defend the country from what Brezhnev called in his statement of 13 January 1980, 'external aggression (and) crude interference from outside'. Brezhnev was more specific when he said that 'imperialism together with its accomplices launched an undeclared war against revolutionary Afghanistan'.

(2) The Soviet Union intervened in Afghanistan in order to maintain the security and stability of its southern, central Asian, flank. As Andropov told a Western interviewer on 1 April 1984, 'We have a long common border, and it does make a difference to us what kind of Afghanistan it will be. By helping Afghanistan we defend our national interests.'

(3) The Soviet action in Afghanistan is aimed at preventing a spill-over of Islamic revivalism to the Tajik, Uzbek and Turkmen Republics of the Soviet Union.

(4) The Soviet Union has gone into Afghanistan with military force to defend a fraternal Marxist regime from imperialist-aided local counterrevolution.

(5) The Soviet action in Afghanistan is aimed at preventing the United States from advancing its spheres of influence in a region very close to the Soviet Union's southern frontiers. Making this point, a *Pravda* editorial on 29 January 1980 said, 'Washington, it seems, proceeds from the assumption that it is enough to declare Iran, Afghanistan and other countries or areas thousands of kilometres away from the American shores as zones of America's vital interest—to be more precise, of the biggest monopolist and the military industrial complex of the USA—for everybody to accept this.'

And (6) The Soviet military action in Afghanistan was aimed at countering possible American military action or the threat of military action in the Persian Gulf. This assumption is confirmed in numerous Soviet pronouncements beginning with a TASS despatch from Washington on 5 January 1980 which saw in Jimmy Carter's State of the Union message an attempt 'to keep the dominant position of American monopolies' in the Persian Gulf region unchallenged and accused the United States of having concentrated the biggest ever armada of naval forces in the Gulf region.

These six Soviet premises have remained unaltered in the five and a half years of Soviet military presence in Afghanistan. They have remained constant in spite of the casualties which Moscow has suffered and the losses it has had to face in the Third World in terms of prestige and respect.

Indeed, Soviet losses in Afghanistan have been more in terms of prestige and image in the Third World than in the financial and human costs of the military operations. At each successive session of the UN General Assembly, the Soviets have had to stoically bear with over two-thirds of the member nations collectively asking it to pull out its troops from Afghanistan. However, UN resolutions in recent years have been somewhat less stinging than in the first two years of the Soviet invasion of Afghanistan.[3] Moreover, with the UN Secretary-General engaged in the delicate process of mediation among the rival parties, the Afghan mood of the General Assembly has undergone a visible change. The Afghan Foreign Minister and Kabul's permanent representative at the UN are no longer ignored by the majority of Third World delegations as they used to be in 1980-81. The American 'sanctions' against the Soviet Union did not bite the Kremlin: they stopped neither the flow of American grain nor of West European technology and credits to the USSR. The stubbornness with which Moscow has stood by its fraternal ally in Kabul has enhanced the value of Soviet friendship in the eyes of several Third World regimes. In any case, international rejection of a Soviet action sparked off by the United States only enhances the release of adrenalin into the arteries of the Soviet State. It makes Soviet resistance stubborner, not weaker.

The cost of warfare, as we have seen in Chapter 8, has been bearable. The cost seems to be largely compensated for by economic and logistical gains: the wholesale import of Afghanistan's increasing supplies of natural gas, the exploitation of the country's rich mineral resources, and the installation of a Soviet military presence in the Persian Gulf region that would counsel caution and restraint for the builders of a formidable American military strength in that area under the Reagan administration.

Those in the United States and elsewhere who had hoped that Afghanistan would develop as Moscow's Vietnam have been proved wrong. The fighting in Afghanistan is not unpopular in the Soviet Union; if anything, it has stirred the patriotism of the Russian people. This was conceded in a Moscow-dateline report published in the *New York Times* of 3 December 1984.

As the Soviet occupation of Afghanistan draws towards its fifth anniversary this month, it is clear that the war is not resulting in the domestic backlash that the Vietnam war stirred in the United States. In talks with people around Moscow, both young and old, no sign emerges of a discontent that could force Kremlin leaders to bring the boys back home soon.

The reporter, Seth Mydans, stated that ever since the Soviets had sent troops into Afghanistan, the action had been portrayed in the Soviet media 'as a rescue mission on behalf of a pro-Soviet Government under siege' from counter-revolutionaries aided and abetted by the United States. The Soviet media have drawn parallels between the Afghan war and the Russian defence of its own homeland against the Nazi invaders in World War II. 'This is how Russia wins its wars', an unidentified Soviet scholar told the *New York Times* reporter. 'People defend the Russian land. And in this they are ready to undergo any hardship, any loss.'[4] Indeed, a Soviet journalist told this writer that the second cold war had led to a general tightening of the belt by the Soviet people and to a delay in much-needed economic and administrative reforms. It has certainly delayed the process of evolution along liberal lines.

The Kremlin leaders are preparing their countrymen for a long-drawn-out war in Afghanistan, the outcome of which, they are convinced, can only go in Kabul's and Moscow's favour. The Soviet press have been saying that there is no light yet at the end of the Afghan tunnel. As *Izvestia* put it in early December 1984, 'Judging by the current attitudes of Washington and Islamabad toward the political regulation of the situation around Afghanistan, war against Afghanistan is more dear to them than that peace in Southwest Asia.'[5] It took the Bolsheviks more than ten years to tame the Central Asian republics and to yoke them fully to the Soviet State. The Soviets have drawn up long-term plans for Afghanistan. Moscow's visions of the future can be gauged from the nature of the television coverage of happenings in Afghanistan. In a television programme in November 1984 a Colonel told of showing a film about Lenin to a group of Afghan villagers. 'A fire burned in their eyes. They listened with attention and joy. They were full of questions: Who was Lenin? How did we set up our revolution? How did we overcome our opponents?'[6] The Soviets have accepted some 20,000 Afghan youths, nearly half of them school-children, for long-term training in the Soviet Union.

From the beginning, the American response to the Soviet invasion of Afghanistan has been a matter of dispute between the administration and dissenting sections of the foreign policy elite. Jimmy Carter, as noted, described the Soviet action as a 'stepping stone to . . . possible control over much of the world's oil supplies'. Almost immediately, a dissenting note came from James Reston, indicating differences within the administration with regard to the actual meaning of Mr Carter's rhetoric. Reston wrote in the *New York Times* that 'It is important not to exaggerate the Afghan tragedy . . . it is not the considered view of this government that Moscow is actually engaged in a reckless rampage to control the fuel and sea lanes around the Persian Gulf.'[7] Split between the heightened cold-warlike vision of the Soviet action and the intransigent realities on the ground, the American dilemma has remained unchanged: how to mount a credible challenge to the Kremlin in Afghanistan. The arms supplies to Pakistan, the speeding up of the construction of the Rapid Deployment Force, the concentration of a huge naval armada in the Persian Gulf and the Indian Ocean, the unsuccessful search for a strategic consensus with friends and allies in the Gulf area, and the verbal invectives of the new cold war do not add up to an actual commitment to throw the Soviet forces out of Afghanistan. The amount of covert American aid to the Afghan resistance has risen steadily. With $280 m. earmarked for the Afghan resistance for FY 1985 (which will not be available until 1986), total American aid to the guerrillas comes to $625 m. in six years—or roughly $100 m. a year.[8] This is not the kind of investment that can enable the Afghan resistance to push the Soviet troops out of Afghanistan. But it is enough to keep the resistance alive and kicking for as long as the aid is there.

There are two contradictory versions of American aid to the Afghan resistance. As a correspondent pointed out in the columns of the *New York Times* of 26 November 1984, the first version is generated by high-ranking CIA bureaucrats and other officials of the administration, giving a 'glowing picture of superb cost-effective CIA operations, top-notch and daring'. The second version consists of independent field reports by Americans and Europeans, including one commissioned by the Pentagon. These reports indicate that the Afghans have received three types of weapon through covert American operations. The first type includes weapons that are unsuitable for guerrilla warfare in Afghanistan, such as SAM-7 and 82 mm medium-range Soviet-made mortars, instead of the more accurate French Redeye, Stinger or British Blowpipe surface-to-air missiles, or the long-range British or Finnish 81-mm medium-range mortars. The second category is one of weapons that have been tampered with and have therefore become useless, such as anti-tank and anti-personnel mines that are missing their demolition components. To the third category belong weapons which are good but have so little ammunition that they are out of operation 95 per cent of the time. The best examples of this category are the 12.7 mm and 14.5 mm heavy machine-guns, the Afghans' only defence against incoming aircraft and gunships.

On the vital question of how the Russians and the Kabul regimes are doing in Afghanistan and the success of the guerrillas operations, too, there are sharp differences among Americans as well as between American and British intelligence agencies. Officials of the State Department and the CIA say that the fighting is not going well for the Soviet–Afghan government troops and that the rebels are well supplied. Other intelligence sources and experts outside the American government assert that the Russians are making gradual progress. It is generally conceded that 15 to 40 per cent of the arms earmarked for the resistance are skimmed off by the Pakistanis and by the Afghan exiles. The system for supplying arms to the Afghan rebels is that American dollars are used to buy mainly Soviet-made arms from countries like China, Egypt and Israel at exorbitant rates. The arms are then delivered to Pakistani ports. At that point, by agreement between the CIA and Pakistan, the supplies pass under Pakistani control for delivery to the political leaders of the Afghan insurgency in Peshawar and elsewhere. They, in turn, are supposed to pass on the arms to the guerrillas. There is hardly any accounting procedure. Pakistan is given full control, on the grounds that it is running the risk of incurring Soviet displeasure and possible military retaliation.[9]

The unsatisfactory nature of the supplies to the Afghan rebels has been stressed in several expert reports. A staff report of the Senate Foreign Relations Committee written in April 1984 reported icily that 'the signs of Western aid are indeed scarce.'[10] A more detailed report was given at the end of September 1984 to the Senate Intelligence Committee by Alexander Alexiev of the Rand Corporation working under a Pentagon contract. To him the problem was the quality rather than the quantity of arms being delivered. 'The most glaring deficiency continues to be the lack of any effective means to compete with Soviet jets and helicopters', Alexiev reported. 'The Soviets are able to operate with virtual impunity in the air, which, given the fact that perhaps 80 per cent of all Soviet combat and logistics operation depend on the air, virtually precludes any significant and lasting Mujahideen military gains.'[11]

Nearly two years ago, on 4 December 1983, Drew Middleton reported in the *New York Times* that resistance to the Soviets had diminished in Afghanistan as a result of 'a shortage of anti-aircraft and anti-tank weapons and rivalry between pro-western and pro-Iranian rebel groups'. At least three of the six groups of guerrillas were said to be pro-Iranian, a discovery that lent a measure of substance to Soviet fears of the contagion of Islamic fundamentalism spreading to their Central Asian Republics. Middleton quoted both American and British intelligence reports as saying that the

Russians, with the Afghan army's help, can police the country with one division, about 1,000 men. The rest of the occupying force, estimated at 110,000 to 120,000 men, is being trained in an environment unfamiliar to Soviet army trained for operations in Western Europe and northern China.

Middleton added that 'western analysts, surveying the present situation, say they wonder whether the trend toward Soviet domination is irreversible.' This was perhaps an American way of expressing doubt that Afghanistan could ever be extricated from Soviet influence.

In 1984, the level of weapons supplied to the guerrillas was raised, but it is quite clear to objective observers that it is not the United States but Pakistan which determines how 'effective' the resistance can be. While Pakistan is very willing to keep resistance on-going, it is mortally afraid of offending the Soviets beyond a maximum level of tolerance, and it is no less afraid of the Iranian variety of Islamic fundamentalism getting the upper hand in Afghanistan and among the three million Afghan refugees assembled on Pakistani territory.

There is a mock heroic touch in the resolutions that get extraordinarily rapid passage through the United States Congress calling for 'effective support' by the administration to the Afghan guerrillas. The latest of these resolutions was adopted in October 1984 by a vote of 97 to 0 in the Senate and without a single dissenting vote in the House of Representatives, practically without debate. It was the culmination of a two-year battle, however, between the State Department and Capitol Hill, the former claiming that the resolution was not necessary because the resistance was progressing very well. It is not without interest that the same Congressmen and Senators who oppose American financial and military aid to the counter-revolutionaries in Nicaragua enthusiastically pump money to the resistance in Afghanistan, thereby dramatically demonstrating their anti-Soviet spleen. They cannot be ignorant of the fact that only a fraction of the funds would be actually used by the resistance movement.

If Pakistan does not allow the United States to escalate Afghan resistance, the United States does not allow Pakistan to tread the road to a negotiated political settlement that would answer its own, rather than Washington's, priorities and preferences.

Despite repeated denials by numerous American officials, it is widely believed that the Reagan administration has not helped, has, in fact, halted, the process of the 'indirect negotiations' between Islamabad and Kabul sponsored by the UN mediator, Diego Cordovez. This is for the simple reason that American and Pakistani priorities do not jell. The American conditions for a political settlement were spelled out quite precisely in a statement handed exclusively to the author in the autumn of 1983 by the then Assistant Secretary of State for South Asia, Harold Schaffer.[12] 'We have maintained', the statement said,

> that any negotiated political settlement for Afghanistan, besides including the withdrawal of Soviet troops, the return of the non-aligned and independent status of Afghanistan, and the return of the refugees, must include self-determination for the Afghan people. We have not said how this (the accord) must come about, but that the issue of how the Afghan people will be allowed to form the type of government they wish must be addressed.

From the American position, the consent of the Afghan people to the type of government that exists in Kabul is of the first priority, and the consent must presumably come primarily from the resistance groups in Afghanistan and the refugees who have taken shelter in Pakistan. Pakistan, on the other hand, has been willing since 1982 to live with the Marxist regime in Kabul if effective ways can be found for the return of the refugees. The Reagan administration knows that the Soviets would neither change the regime in Kabul in accordance with the political wishes of the rebels nor restore a regime in Afghanistan which Mr Reagan could recognize as non-aligned and independent. It has no means of forcing the Kremlin to do so. Hence the American stand that it does not wish to say how its conditions are to be fulfilled, except that there shall be no political settlement without them.

This rider has proved to be an adequate brake on Pakistan's initial earnest intention to seek a solution to the Afghan problem through the UN negotiation process. Pakistan's dilemmas are many and it has to ride the wave of several contradictions. The American connection is all-important for the military regime in Pakistan, but it is not enough to get Pakistan out of the binds created by the Soviet push into Afghanistan. General Zia has got a great deal of political and strategic-economic mileage out of the Soviet invasion, but he cannot get the Soviet forces out by means of his American ally, or by means of the Afghan resistance. While the steadily souring problems created by the prolonged presence of three million refugees on Pakistani territory persist, General Zia must find a way to send the bulk of them back to Afghanistan and he just does not know how he can do it. Indeed, Afghanistan presents a problem of *two* invasions—the Soviet military invasion of the country and the Afghan refugee 'invasion' of Pakistan.

Pakistan is to bear the brunt of *both* invasions alone. General Zia cannot afford to buy a political settlement of the Afghan issue from the Soviet Union that might provoke large numbers of the refugees to train their guns on his regime. At the same time, he cannot afford either to allow the number of refugees to multiply, which is inevitable if the military operations within Afghanistan escalate, or to allow the refugees to continue to live in Pakistan for an indefinite period of time. He cannot afford to succumb to Soviet blandishments or threats and he cannot afford to antagonize the Soviets beyond a point of the Kremlin's tolerance.

In the last two years two significant developments have surfaced in Pakistan. The first is what one would like to call the emergence of a Soviet constituency amongst the Pakistani elites; the second is a steadily growing demand that the Afghan problem be solved in direct negotiations with Moscow and Kabul. The Soviet constituency is evidently the offspring of a co-operative bilateral relationship that has grown between Pakistan and the Soviet Union during the last four years, despite Pakistan making itself a 'frontline' state. In an interview with the author in June 1983, Foreign Minister Shahebzada Yakub Khan described the essence of Pakistan's strategic perception as 'a quest for security in the South Asian region, taking into account all the realities existing here and also of the changes that are likely to occur in the foreseeable future.'[13] Pakistan foreign policy strategic thinking has been trying to take into account the grim reality that Pakistan must learn to live with two powerful neighbours, the Soviet Union and India—mutual friends—with both of whom Pakistan's relations conflict. How to improve relations with the Soviet Union and India without downgrading its all-important American connection is the most demanding dilemma of Pakistan's foreign relations policy-makers. Pakistanis are painfully conscious of the fluctuations in American commitments to their country and the basically limited and derivative nature of these commitments. They are worried and afraid that the United States would, over time, lose interest in the Afghan resistance; that improvement in Washington's relations with Moscow would inevitably lead to a withering of American involvement in the Afghan issue; that, lured by expectations of expanding relations with India, Washington would sooner or later change its policy towards

India, which Pakistan would find less than reassuring to the stability of the military regime, if not the security of Pakistan. These Pakistani worries and fears find expression not only in the controlled press but also in numerous official utterances.

General Zia has kept the UN negotiating process alive, but few informed observers believe that Cardovez will be able to deliver a comprehensive political settlement of the Afghan problem. The fourth round of 'proximity talks' between Pakistan and Afghanistan under the UN negotiation process took place in Geneva in June 1985. Cordovez repeated his shuttle diplomacy between Islamabad and Kabul in May, trying to bring the two sides to a discussion of 'the specific instruments that will contain a settlement'. He asked each side to draw up its own draft of the specific instruments. The exercise stemmed from his belief that when the two sides pored over each other's drafts, they would realize how concretely their respective stands on the vital issues diverged from, or converged with, one another. This was an approach to the deadlock agreed upon by the two sides. Cordovez told reporters in May that the 'current consultations will show if the agreed approach to overcome the problems that have clogged the [negotiation] process since the last two years works'.[14]

In June 1985, an American journalist, Lawrence Lifschultz, came up with a comprehensive account of zigzagging negotiations under the UN auspices.[15] Lifschultz wrote that the main features of an agreement had been worked out nearly two years before, between April and June 1983, when the last substantive negotiations between Pakistan and Afghanistan were held in Geneva under the UN auspices. According to diplomatic sources close to the negotiations, the Soviets indicated through their observer at Geneva, Stanislav Gabrilov, that they were prepared to engage in a phased withdrawal of their forces from Afghanistan if Pakistan were prepared to co-operate in working out the precise modalities of a negotiated settlement. 'At least in 1983 the Soviets appeared to have been serious in seeking a face-saving formula which would permit an exit from their growing military involvement in Afghanistan.'

The 1983 Geneva meetings were held in two phases over the months of April and June. Before the June session began, the Foreign Ministers of Pakistan and Afghanistan provisionally agreed to the protocol of a draft agreement. It was understood that a comprehensive settlement would be based on three preliminary conditions:

1. Soviet forces would be withdrawn in stages from Afghanistan.
2. In a phased manner refugees in Pakistan would be simultaneously repatriated to Afghanistan, and
3. Pakistan would restrain insurgent activity originating within its borders and actively work for an effective ceasefire, so as to allow both the withdrawal of Soviet forces and the repatriation of refugees under as near peaceful conditions as possible.

Movement towards a more comprehensive settlement was to be determined following initial agreement on these points. Lawrence Lifschultz continued:

It was implicitly understood that a political solution based on compromise would have to involve some form of coalition regime emerging in Kabul. The Soviet Union had indicated to a number of non-aligned states including India that it was not averse to such a development. Since Pakistan had been insisting that it would not negotiate directly with Babrak Karmal, it was made known by Soviet representatives that, in the interests of a settlement, Karmal would be prepared to step down and in a transitional arrangement prior to the conclusion of an agreement, he would be replaced as Prime Minister by Sultan Ali Keshtmand.'

Whether the Soviet offer was a purely tactical move or else reflected a changed approach in response to the reality of an escalating stalemate within Afghanistan was never tested.

The exact shape and constituent elements of a future coalition was to be left to a later stage following preliminary agreement on the first steps of the Geneva negotiations and once implementation had been initiated. Nevertheless, Soviet representatives at the time appear to have privately contacted the former King of Afghanistan, Muhammad Zahir Shah, to explore the possibility of establishing at least a transitional national government acceptable to most sides involved in the conflict.

Zahir Shah, self-exiled in Rome since 1973, issued a declaration when the June 1983 negotiating session reopened in Geneva. He asked all Afghan resistance groups to form a unified organization which would speak in the name of the Afghan people. Zahir Shah expressed 'complete solidarity' with the resistance, but said he was doubtful if it were possible to defeat a superpower, given the geopolitical position of Afghanistan. He called for a 'political solution' to this conflict and stressed the roles that a unified resistance organization could play in an active search for a peaceful settlement of the civil war. Zahir Shah told *Le Monde* (22 June 1983), 'One frequently encounters rumours according to which it is said that the Soviet Union will eventually be prepared to enter into discussions with representatives of the Afghan resistance. If this desire is serious, then it is necessary to create a unified organization capable of speaking in the name of the Afghan people.'

The Soviets, for their part, gave the appearance of supporting the plan elaborated by the UN negotiator. On his return to Pakistan following the April 1983 round of Geneva talks, Pakistan's Yakub Khan told reporters that there were 'firm indications' that the Soviet Union would withdraw its forces from Afghanistan under certain agreed conditions. He went on to add, 'I think "indications" would perhaps be an understatement of the affirmations that we have received at the highest level—from no less a person than Mr Andropov himself. I think it would be right to expect that they would adhere to their affirmations'.[16]

However, no promised breakthrough occurred. According to Selig Harrison, Pakistan did not seriously test Soviet terms for a withdrawal of forces in 1983, losing heart for diplomatic brinkmanship at the eleventh hour in the face of American, Saudi and Chinese disapproval.

Islamabad [had] accepted unambiguous language in the UN draft text that would have required a termination of support for the resistance coincident with the start of a Soviet force withdrawal. These Pakistani concessions had produced Soviet assurances in April that Moscow would propose a specific timeframe for the projected withdrawal at the next round. By the time negotiations resumed in June, however, Islamabad had backed off on both key concessions, and Moscow's pledge was never put to the test.[17]

Narrating the conditions and circumstances which created the impasse at Geneva in 1983, Lifschultz wrote:

Following the April 1983 session prior to the reopening of negotiations in June, important events intervened to prevent a settlement being realized. At the end of the April session, two outstanding questions had still to be resolved.

The first pertained to the question of international guarantees, and the second concerned the establishment of a precise timetable for the withdrawal of foreign forces from Afghanistan. The United Nations, in agreement with Kabul and Islamabad, had insisted that before any settlement was made public, the permanent members of the Security Council should indicate their public endorsement of this settlement. This principally concerned the United States, China, and the Soviet Union as those members most directly linked as patrons to the negotiating states.

While Moscow had given the Pakistan Foreign Minister its 'affirmation' on the terms of the draft agreement prepared by the United Nations, it was evident that similar affirmations were necessary from both the Chinese and the Americans if any progress towards a settlement were to advance. In pursuit of this task, the Pakistan Foreign Minister undertook a journey in mid-May 1983 that in one month brought him to Peking, Washington, and Moscow.

He arrived in the Chinese capital on May 15 to discuss with the Chinese the terms of the accord. The Chinese indicated that they had no objections to the draft of the UN agreement, but believed the Soviet Union should publicly indicate that it was prepared to commit itself to a timetable regarding the withdrawal of its forces. Within four days, on May 19, the Soviet Ambassador to Pakistan, Vitaly Smirnov, declared in an interview with *The Muslim* that Afghanistan was prepared to accept the withdrawal of Soviet forces within the framework of firm international guarantees: 'Kabul has expressed its readiness in agreement with the Soviet Union for the withdrawal of the total limited Soviet contingent . . . and even expressed willingness to give a timetable in this regard.' In spite of the use of the standard euphemism of a limited contingent for its nearly 100,000 troops, Smirnov's statement of a mutual Soviet–Afghan willingness to establish a timetable for withdrawal of forces was of key significance, in that it represented the first public reference to what had remained as an important obstacle during the previous negotiating sessions at Geneva.

On May 25, the Pakistan Foreign MInister was in Washington to obtain from the United States its concurrence with the principal outlines of the settlement. He received a cool reception. It was a powerful episode that in itself illustrates the tragic external dimension which prevails over the Afghan civil war. While the Americans were unwilling to formally say 'no', they were not prepared to say 'yes'. Instead, on the eve of the foreign minister's arrival, the Reagan administration revealed for the first time the magnitude of its secret military aid to Afghan resistance groups based in Pakistan. The principal aspects of US covert assistance were already well known, and it came as no surprise when administration sources confirmed that the Central Intelligence Agency had been directed to funnel a variety of light weapons to the rebels. However, what distressed 'those involved in the Geneva talks', wrote Ted Morello, the *Far Eastern Economic Review*'s UN correspondent (9 June 1983) 'was the timing of Washington's disclosures. It was interpreted as a deliberate effort to torpedo the UN peace initiative just when Cordovez had jockeyed the Afghan negotiations to the brink of a breakthrough . . ... Few diplomats place any credence in the Reagan administration's subsequent out-pouring of assurances voiced by everybody from the President himself to US Secretary of State George Shultz and UN Ambassador Jeanne Kirkpatrick that the US supports an Afghan settlement through peaceful negotiations'.

It is known that there is an element within the Reagan administration that advocates US backing for a negotiated settlement. But there is also a hard-line faction that prefers the status quo in Afghanistan as it does in Cambodia as a means of bleeding Moscow's resources and embarrassing it internationally as an aggressor, directly in the first instance, and by proxy in the second. The presumption is that the bleeders, as they are called, prevailed and persuaded the president to send the unmistakable signal that, professions of support for the Cordovez mission notwithstanding, the USA is not ready for a political settlement that would free Moscow of its Afghan albatross.

When the Pakistani Foreign Minister met the American Secretary of State on 25 May, Shultz let it be understood that the United States considered the UN agreement inadequate without the prior replace-ment of the existing regime in Kabul by a more representative govern-ment, Lifschultz continued.

This position effectively destroyed the possibility of an advance at a crucial and delicate stage of the negotiations. Until then it had been clearly under-stood and implicitly accepted during the entire process by all parties involved that the recomposition of the regime in Kabul would occur in parallel with the phased withdrawal of Soviet forces, as had occurred during the precedent of Porkkala in Finland.

During the hearings before the Foreign Relations Committee of the US House of Representatives in July 1983, Selig Harrison declared that

the USA appears to share some of the responsibility for the present slowdown in the negotiations. By all indications, the Reagan administration is not prepared to accept the type of settlement now being negotiated under UN auspices. The underlying assumption of the UN scenario is that a face-saving agreement in Afghanistan cannot directly address the replacement or modification of the Kabul regime as a precondition for Soviet disengagement but must leave this to paralleled processes of political accommodation before, during and after the disengagement period.[18]

From Washington the Pakistani Foreign Minister journeyed to Moscow where on 9 June he met his Soviet counterpart, Andrei Gromyko. Two outstanding questions required further negotiation to achieve greater precision: the withdrawal period for Soviet forces and Islamabad's commitment to support the clause of mutual non-interference. In the agreed framework, Islamabad would commit itself not to provide assistance to the Afghan groups based in Pakistan, or to permit other agencies to use Pakistan as a conduit.

According to Lifschultz, the Soviets had made it known that they would not make any commitment with regard to a precise timetable unless it was clear that their withdrawal would not risk an escalation in covert operations on the part of Pakistan and its American allies.

This formal position on the part of the Soviet Union did not take into account the fact that the greater part of the resistance is internally based within the country. However, they seemed to have believed that once a practical agreement was actually in the process of being implemented, local ceasefire agreements could be negotiated with various internal fronts as had been achieved at various stages, such as in Panjshir. All parties seemed to have been clearly aware that the ultimate achievement of a negotiated settlement would neither be neat nor simple, and would require a determined commitment to the process at all stages.

In Moscow, the Yakub Khan–Gromyko meeting ran into an impasse. Explanations from the Pakistani–American side predictably differed widely from those of Soviet spokesmen. The Islamabad–Washington version is that Yakub Khan found Gromyko unwilling to commit Moscow to a time-frame for the withdrawal of Soviet forces. The Soviets assert that Yakub Khan went back on his earlier commitment that there would be no formal linkage between political change in Kabul and withdrawal of Soviet troops. Yakub Khan told the author in the winter of 1984 that Pakistan remained firmly committed to the Cordovez plan, but the Soviets were not ready to bind themselves to any rigid time-frame; the Soviet position, Yakub said, was that the internal affairs of Afghanistan had to be settled directly and bilaterally between Kabul and Moscow. The Soviet position, as explained to the author by a ranking Indian diplomat as well as by Soviet officials, was that Yakub had succumbed to American pressure and told Gromyko that the 'creation of a stable regime in Kabul' was essential to enable the refugees to return; in other words, Pakistan now insisted that Afghanistan's internal affairs be included in the agenda of negotiation.

Were the Soviets serious in 1983 in their quest for a political settlement? Would they have withdrawn their troops from Afghanistan if Pakistan had concluded the negotiated agreements with Kabul? The Americans have expressed scepticism, but in Pakistan there was certainly an air of expectancy in early 1983, to which the present author was witness. The Soviet readiness to accept a political settlement can be explained by the fact that Yuri Andropov had succeeded Brezhnev as leader of the CPSU. It is quite probable that Andropov wanted to get the Soviet troops out of Afghanistan after he had been elected General Secretary of the CPSU, if an honourable exit could be arranged. His position became stronger on the death of Suslov in 1982 and with the setbacks the Soviet–Afghan forces suffered in Afghanistan. A Third World diplomat who met Andropov in the spring of 1983, six months after the latter had taken over as CPSU General Secretary, claimed in an interview with Lifschultz:

The discussion with Andropov was concerned almost exclusively with Afghanistan. I received two clear impressions: that he was very interested in finding a diplomatic formula through negotiations which would lead to the withdrawal of Soviet forces, and although he did not say so directly, it was my distinct impression that he personally had not supported the decision to invade. He seemed very much the man who wanted to undo what had occurred in this instance. He ended the conversation by lifting his hand, and pulling his fingers down one by one as he enumerated the reasons why a solution had to be found to the Afghanistan issue. He said the situation was harmful not only to relations with the West but with socialist and Third World states. Lastly, he said, pointing downwards, it was harmful for future developments with the Soviet Union.

The Soviet attitude hardened after the passing of Andropov. Not because of his death, perhaps, but because of a realization that Pakistan was not a free agent when it came to Afghanistan, and that the Reagan administration was not willing to permit Pakistan to conclude an agreement which would in reality legitimize the Marxist regime. The Soviet coldness towards Pakistan was demonstrated to the world at the funeral of Andropov. General Zia-ul Haq was probably the first head of state outside the Soviet bloc to announce that he would represent Pakistan at the funeral, accompanied by his Foreign Minister. The author, who was present in Islamabad at the time, witnessed hectic activity in the Pakistan foreign office and the secretariat of the Martial Law Administrator in preparation for General Zia's Moscow trip. Signals were sent to the Kremlin suggesting that Chernenko or at least Gromkyo should receive the Pakistani mourners. But neither the President of Pakistan nor his Foreign Minister was received by Chernenko or any other member of the CPSU Politburo.

In 1983-4 the Soviets escalated their military operations against the Afghan rebels and terminated more than one local ceasefire agreement. The Soviet hardline was confirmed in icy language by Moscow's ambassador to Pakistan who took the unusual step of writing a signed letter to the editor of *The Muslim*, of Islamabad, early in 1985, stating the Soviet position on Afghanistan. Refuting several points made in a number of articles published in the newspaper, ambassador Smirnov reduced the Afghanistan issue to four 'basic realities'. First, the Afghanistan problem was created by the 'hostile action' of several countries against the Marxist regime in Kabul; second, the Soviet troops were in Afghanistan at the invitation of the Afghan Government, fulfilling Moscow's treaty-bound obligations to a friendly regime; third, if Pakistan or any other party wished to conduct negotiations, they must negotiate with Kabul and not with the Soviet Union; and, fourth, the political future of Afghanistan was not negotiable. 'On its part, the Democratic Republic of Afghanistan . . . is ready for political negotiations with the parties concerned with the purpose of settling the situation *around* Afghanistan.'[19] While at the UN and elsewhere, in 1984, Pakistani spokesmen repeated old rhetorics on the Soviet military presence in Afghanistan with diminishing self-confidence, and Foreign Minister Yakub Khan claimed that Soviet refusal to fix a time-limit for the withdrawal of troops was the main obstacle to a political settlement, in reality Moscow had notified Islamabad that it must negotiate a settlement directly and bilaterally with Kabul and that what was negotiable was not political change in Afghanistan but the conditions to be created for the return of the refugees and the future relationship between Afghanistan and Pakistan.

Behind the Smirnov letter was a little-known fact connected with the UN negotiations. Before the third Geneva round in September 1984, Cordovez, in a long private session with General Zia, told the Pakistani leader that Moscow would terminate the negotiations if Islamabad stuck to its stand not to talk directly to Kabul. Unwilling to burn his bridges to the Kremlin, General Zia made a 'visible' concession—he allowed the third round of talks to be held in 'proximity'—Pakistani and Afghan delegates sitting at a room's distance from one another, and Cordovez shuttling between them on foot. General Zia also allowed the concept of two treaties to be born in Geneva, a bilateral treaty between Islamabad and Kabul on the cessation of foreign intervention in Afghanistan and the return of the Afghan refugees, and a second bilateral treaty between Kabul and Moscow providing for the withdrawal of Soviet troops. The timeframe of the withdrawal, the number of residual military advisers to remain in Afghanistan and other related matters were to be determined bilaterally between the Soviet Union and Afghanistan.[20]

While the Government of Pakistan seemed to be bereft of new ideas and initiatives for settling the Afghan issue, its former foreign minister, Agha Shahi, suggested a quid pro quo between the two superpowers as a means of getting Soviet troops out of Afghanistan. Speaking at an international seminar at Villanova University in the United States in December 1984, Shahi said that strict non-alignment of the countries spanning the Persian Gulf and South Asian regions, together with American willingness to give the Soviet Union a role in a comprehensive Middle East settlement, might create a situation congenial to the withdrawal of Soviet forces from Afghanistan. According to a Pakistani newspaper report, Shahi

appeared to be suggesting that once the neutrality of the area was ensured by the regional states pursuing a policy of strict non-alignment, the superpowers could perhaps be persuaded to work towards some sort of mutual accommodation, such as the Soviet Union pulling out of Afghanistan in deference to American wishes, in return for the US responding to Soviet desire to be involved in a Middle East settlement.[21]

With the advent of 1985, the Soviets appeared to be poised at a cross-roads. A commentary in *Pravda* reviewed disclosures that secret assistance by the CIA to the Afghan rebels had become the largest American operation since the Vietnam war. The *Pravda* commentary warned that such escalation would be more than matched by the Soviet side. Since January 1985 a dangerous see-saw escalation had indeed taken place. Soviet armed forces in Afghanistan were estimated to have increased by at least a quarter. As we have seen, they were operating in much greater numbers and much closer to the Pakistan frontier than before. However, *Pravda* did not close the door on a negotiated political settlement. It stressed that the Soviet Union would still 'be ready to withdraw its troops by agreement', and ended its commentary by stating that 'All questions relating to Afghanistan can be solved only by political means. There is no other way.'[22]

In March 1985, Mikhail Gorbachëv became General Secretary of the CPSU, following the death of Chernenko. He received General Zia at Chernenko's funeral, to tell him in the clearest possible terms that the Soviet Union was not prepared to remain engaged in a prolonged stalemate with Pakistan over Afghanistan. While the Soviets apparently affirmed that the terms of the existing draft agreement prepared by the United Nations remained the best option for achieving a withdrawal of Russian troops, the return of the refugees and a ceasefire, Gorbachëv made clear to the Pakistan President that the Soviet Union would be prepared to increase its force five-fold to 500,000 men if diplomatic progress remained frozen and a significant increase in the Pakistan-based cover operations, as reported in the Western press, were to develop.[23] A senior Soviet specialist on Afghanistan, when interviewed by Lawrence Lifschultz concerning the possibility of a negotiated settlement and withdrawal of Soviet forces, stated: 'The option of Finlandization is still possible. It is to be preferred. But if the Geneva negotiations are obstructed, then Soviet policy will be one of Mongolisation.'

Meanwhile, the political mood in Pakistan began to change after the party-less election to the National Assembly in February 1985. The election set in motion a political process in which martial law would have to be lifted within months, the press would win back some freedom, the lifting of censorship could not be delayed too long, and even the political parties stood a chance of being legitimized in 1986.[24] The political elements had become unusually vocal since the election and their views were freely published in the newspaper. It was around the spring of 1985 that all political parties in Pakistan, except the conservative Jamaat-i-Islami, favoured direct negotiation with Afghanistan to resolve the Afghan crisis. Prime Minister Junezo still rejected the concept, but reports indicated that a majority of the members of the National Assembly preferred a direct dialogue with Afghanistan.[25] A remark by the American ambassador to Pakistan, Dean Hinton, on 1 April, that he was 'baffled by the thought process' of those opposition parties that advocated direct talks with Kabul, raised volleys of protest in the Pakistani press, which were echoed several times in the National Assembly. Several members of the National Assembly asked for a debate on the Afghan issue. The Government demurred, but the Speaker announced that he would allow a debate, whereupon the Land Minister came up with a statement that the Foreign Minister would 'take the members of the National Assembly' into his confidence on the delicate nature of the UN-launched negotiations, but that this as well as the debate would better be held in closed session.[26]

In May, General Zia, with startling candour, conceded in an interview with the London-based *Middle East International* that twelve out of the fourteen major political parties in Pakistan were opposed to his Afghan policy and were expected to voice their opposition both within and outside the National Assembly. He identified two different schools of thought which had developed in Pakistan over the last five years regarding Afghanistan. While one set of people, comprising some generals of the Pakistan Army, the Afghan refugees and a section of the Pakistani public, were of the view that Pakistan should continue to play its role as a frontline state in the face of Soviet aggression and should generously help the three million Afghan refugees, the other group, consisting of some generals, most of the politicians and a major section of the Pakistani people, felt that Pakistan had become subservient to the United States as a result of this war. The opposition also alleged, he added, that the United States did not want to end this war and that the deadlock at the Geneva talks on Afghanistan in March/April 1982 had been caused by the United States.[27]

The fourth round of Geneva talks ended without any breakthrough to a political settlement in Afghanistan. Cordovez told reporters that the talks had reached a stage when 'crucial, hard political decisions' were needed,[28] and he did not sound very hopeful that hard decisions would be taken before August, when the talks were to be resumed. The Pakistani Foreign Minister, Yakub Khan, however, told the author in New Delhi early in July that his Government had been doing some 'hard thinking' on Afghanistan; a long stalemate was fraught with dangers for Pakistan. Meanwhile, the Pakistan National Asembly adjourned its budget session without hearing Yakub Khan's promised 'confidential' statement. Members realized that the Afghanistan issue had reached a very delicate stage. The Government was grappling with some very hard questions, and members of the assembly decided that they would rather not needle it at this time.[29]

The Pakistanis were in two minds about the Afghan issue being 'settled' between the two superpowers. Since 1982, government spokesmen had been articulating their apprehensions that a 'second Yalta' could some day leave Pakistan in the cold. Yakub Khan, in his interview, did not expect the Reagan administration to settle the Afghanistan question with the Kremlin over the head, and to the detriment of the interests, of Pakistan. Other Pakistanis were not so certain. The Soviets knew that overt Soviet attempts to bring Pakistan under its influence would further worsen Moscow–Washington relations. They appear to have three alternatives:

(1) seek an understanding with the United States, in which case the consent of Pakistan to that understanding would be relatively easy to obtain;
(2) reach an understanding with Pakistan, thereby creating opportunities for detaching Pakistan from the American global-regional strategy to contain Soviet influence and risking a further downslide in relations with the United States, and
(3) seeking an understanding to which both the United States and Pakistan can be willing subscribers.

Whichever option or options the Soviets may pursue on the diplomatic front, their first priority will continue to be to smash the Afghan resistance. In carrying out their offensive, anti-resistance strategy, they would probably put increasing military pressure on Pakistan in order to make the Pakistani authorities bend to the hard political decisions that they would in fact like to avoid as long as they can. The Soviets probably believe that if Pakistan decides to seek a political understanding with Moscow, the United States will go along with that decision rather than risk an open break with their ally.

In mid-1985 few Americans and fewer Pakistanis are confident that the Afghan resistance can win the war against the Soviet and the PDPA regime. The Americans are generally reluctant to concede the resistance's defeat. Most Americans would prefer to wrest the maximum possible advantage from the Soviet predicament in Afghanistan, to make the Soviets bleed as much and as long as possible, and to make the price of Afghanistan so heavy that the Kremlin will not repeat the adventure in another piece of Third World real estate. A strong minority, however, plead for a political settlement that would turn Afghanistan, hopefully, into a Finland rather than a Mongolia. After the June visit of the Indian Prime Minister, Rajiv Gandhi, to Washington, the Indian press reported that the Reagan administration was finally coming round to an acceptance of the concept of the 'Finlandization' of Afghanistan.[30] If this is correct, the Americans are likely to be disappointed. Afghanistan cannot be a Finland; there is no reason why the Soviets should have a Finland across its southern border in the mid-1980s, when they can have a fully-fledged pro-Soviet Marxist-ruled state with considerable future political and strategic implications for the sensitive regions of the Persian Gulf and South Asia.

Whether the Afghanistan issue is finally settled on the rubblized mountain terrain of the Hindu Kush in more blood, sweat, agony and suffering, or through a negotiated political settlement, it is going to be a long haul. However, eventually, the Saur revolution will be saved, and it will have to address itself to the Herculean task of rebuilding and remoulding the ravaged and devastated Afghanistan. The Afghan revolution is still a tentative revolution. Time, however, is on its side. We now take a look at its future, and its long-term impact on the region.

11 The Future of the Afghan Revolution

In the diverse world of some thirty Marxist regimes, Afghanistan has a number of distinctions all its own. The most profound—in many eyes also highly dubious—distinction is that it is the only Marxist revolution in the Third World which the Soviet Union has had to defend with military force in a protracted civil war. International aid to the resistance in Afghanistan did not make it unique. There have been hardly any Marxist–Leninist revolutions, beginning with the Bolshevik revolution in 1917, which did not immediately provoke international intervention of one kind or another. However, the exodus of three and a half million refugees to two neighbouring countries, and the conversion of the North-West Frontier Province of Pakistan into a huge camp of armed guerrillas, lent the Afghan revolution a dimension not seen in most other Third World Marxist revolutions. Indeed, the metamorphosis of the Afghan revolution differs from the other Marxist revolutions in the Third World since World War II.

In the first place, it was a revolution against neither an imperialist-colonial Western regime nor a reactionary domestic regime planted by a departing colonial power. This very fact puts the Afghan revolution outside the majority of Third World Marxist revolutions (see Szajkowski, 1982). Afghanistan had been a sovereign country since 1920, though never exactly outside the British sphere of influence. From the 1950s right up to the year of the revolution, it was in the Soviet sphere of influence. The Soviet Union contributed much more than any other external power towards the limited modernization of Afghan society and to the emergence of an urban educated middle class.

The Afghan revolution is the second Marxist–Leninist revolution to occur in the Islamic world, but it has practically no similarity with the revolution in South Yemen except that both societies are largely tribal. The Afghan communists did not build or spearhead a national liberation movement against imperialism and colonialism. Unlike South Yemen, no National Liberation Front (NLF) was set up in Afghanistan to struggle for national independence. Unlike Cuba, Chile and Nicaragua, the pre-revolutionary regime in Kabul could not be described as a puppet or even an ally of the United States. The South Yemeni revolution was not pitted against Islam, despite the fact that its chief enemy was Saudi Arabia. The Afghan revolution is the first Marxist revolution in the world to become a target of Islamic fundamentalism.

Afghanistan is not the only Third World country where a numerically small communist party has carried out a successful revolution. The Parti Congolais du Travail or the Congolese Labour Party (PCT) of the People's Republic of Congo has never had a membership of more than 2,000![1] It is somewhat surprising, however, that over twenty years of Soviet influence did not produce a more viable communist party than the PDPA was in 1978. In fact, the Soviets did not wish to help the PDPA enlarge its political base beyond that of a respectable pressure group, and were apparently taken by surprise when the Afghan party captured power. Another factor that distinguishes the Afghan revolution from several other Third World Marxist revolutions is that it was not presided over by the army. It was designed and executed by leaders of the PDPA with the help of its dedicated members in the army. The existence of the PDPA since 1965 and its political functioning for twelve years, never as an open party but as very much a part of the political process, especially in the Daoud republic, is a key point in the Afghan revolution. In a number of Third World countries, a successful revolution has later declared itself to be Marxist-Leninist: Cuba leads this group, but now has Ethiopia, Somalia (during its Marxist incarnation) and Zimbabwe as its members. Afghanistan, on the other hand, had a twelve-year-old communist party, complete with its own left- and right-wing factions. Participating in elections to the national assembly Afghan communists, especially those belonging to the Parcham faction, had become part of the power elite.

The PDPA was responsible for the weakness of the Saur revolution. If the Saur revolution had originated in the army rather than in a twelve-year-old, city-based communist party of urban elites, its course would have been entirely different. It would have commanded the disciplined loyalty of sizeable numbers of officers and larger numbers of soldiers, and since the soldiers were drawn from the tribes—a majority from the Pushtuns—the revolution would probably have provoked less hostility in the rural areas.

Of all the Marxist revolutions in the Third World, the Afghan revolution has come most conspicuously from above. The Chinese revolution actually set the pattern for subsequent revolutions in the Third World: protracted peasant revolutions in the countryside, the establishment of a revolutionary government in liberated areas, and then advancing from the rural areas to the urban centres of power. Within this broad shared frame, each revolution has earned its own distinct quality in the context of the powers that were pitted against it. Some of the revolutionary movements fought and overpowered effete West European colonial powers: Portugal after the passing of Salazar; others—in South Yemen and Zimbabwe—came to a political settlement with retreating British power. Still others fought against the intervening military power of the United States backing local right-wing regimes: Vietnam, Laos and Kampuchea. A fourth category of revolutions—Cuba, Ethiopia, Nicaragua—fought and overpowered local reactionary oppressive regimes.

The Saur revolution broke out in Kabul. Its struggle for power began and ended in Kabul. Superficially, it remotely resembled the Bolshevik revolution. But the PDPA was nowhere near the party of Lenin in leadership quality, organization, ideology, and disciplined cadres. Nor was the Afghan state in an advanced stage of decay and disintegration, like the Tsarist state in Russia. There was no insurrection in Kabul; only a takeover, in which the people had no part to play, acting as mere observers. For the first six months, the distant villages nestling between the rugged fingers of the Hindu Kush did not even feel the impact of the seminal political change that had occurred in Kabul. Only when the PDPA took the revolution to the countryside, with the Decrees on radical land and other reforms, did the people become aware of what it actually meant to live in a state ruled by communists. The Saur revolution had no rural base, no rural following, and yet it proceeded to change rural life by fiat and coercion. It met with immediate, widespread resistance.

Not only was the Afghan revolution *not* an anti-imperialist national-liberation revolution, but it occurred at a time when the anti-imperialist struggles of the Islamic countries of the Middle East had faded into history, and the socio-political forces had broadly realigned in favour of the conservative, pro-American elements. The National Liberation Front in South Yemen rode the crest of the anti-imperialist wave released by Nasserism, and was, in fact, able to count almost automatically on the powerful help of Nasser.[2] As Fred Halliday wrote in a book analysing the dynamics of the South Yemeni revolution,

The revolutionary movements in the Arabian peninsula have grown out of, and in conflict with, the policies of Nasserism. Their theories are formulated in universal categories which are then applied to the specific conditions of the Arab world. They insist on the need for a proletarian leadership in the liberation struggle and suggest a critique of the class character of the pre-existing 'Arab socialist' governments. They have mainly used not the military coup but protracted people's war.[3]

Most of the Arab nationalist movements, including the one led by Nasser, lacked proletarian leadership. It was only in South Yemen that Marxists were able to capture the leadership of a nationalist struggle, and Yemeni Marxism grew out of the protracted war that the NLF had to fight, first against the British, and later against the forces of indigenous conservatism strongly backed by Saudi Arabia, leader of conservative, anti-revolutionary forces in Arabia.

The political ambience of 1978 was very different from that of the late sixties and early seventies. Nasserism had died with Nasser. The emergence of oil power radically altered power alignments in the Middle East and the Persian Gulf. The Soviet Union had suffered a severe setback in Egypt. Sadat had signed a separate peace treaty with Israel. The conservative forces—Egypt, Saudi Arabia, Jordan and Iran—backed by the United States, dominated the politics of the Middle East and the Gulf region. The Shah of Iran was using oil money and newly acquired military power to reduce the influence of the Soviet Union in the Gulf area, as well as South Asia. The Shah wanted the two regions to be less polarized between the United States and the Soviet Union, and Afghanistan, with its surfeit of Soviet influence, was one of the targets of his foreign policy.

The political influence of the Soviet Union had diminished in the Gulf and the Middle East—and even in India to some extent, following the installation of the Janata party government in Delhi, with its declared commitment to 'genuine non-alignment'. At the same time, the Soviet Union had emerged unmistakably as a global military power capable of intervening, and willing to intervene, in national liberation struggles on behalf of its friends and allies. In the early 1970s, the Soviets were supplying crucial military help to three Third World areas at the same time: to the North Vietnamese in South-east Asia, to the Indians in South Asia (during the Bangladesh war), and to the Egyptians in the Middle East. In the mid-seventies, Soviet military help proved a decisive factor in the Vietnam war, and the triumph of communist revolutions in the three Indo-China states; Cuban troops, airlifted in Soviet transport planes with heavy war equipment, determined the fate of the revolutions in Angola and Mozambique. This introduced an entirely new phenomenon in world politics. Hitherto, the United States alone could decisively intervene in internal war in the Third World to restore conservative anti-communist regimes to power. In 1973, the Soviet Union did not come to the help of Salvador Allende in Chile[4] as it did to the leftist regime in Nicaragua in the 1980s. Whatever the state of Soviet political fortunes in specific Third World regions at specific periods of time, the fact that the Soviet Union was capable of intervening with arms on behalf of revolutionary movements and had the will to intervene, given a decisively favourable balance of forces, undoubtedly made a vital difference to Third World conflicts after 1975.

From the 1970s onwards, most successful Marxist-led national liberation movements owed their victories to Soviet military assistance. Indeed, the Soviets had been helping these movements since the sixties; the existence of a socialist bloc of nations led by the USSR as a superpower made a vital difference to several of these movements. Amilcar Cabral, charismatic leader of the Marxist-led national liberation movement in the former Portuguese colony of Guinea, now the Republic of Guinea-Bissau and Cape Verde, wrote, as far back as 1965:

It is our duty to state . . . loud and clear that we have firm allies in the socialist countries . . . since the socialist revolution and the events of the second world war, the face of the world has been definitely changed. A socialist camp has arisen in the world. This has radically changed the balance of power, and this socialist camp is today showing itself fully conscious of its duties . . .. I have the honour of telling you openly . . . that we are receiving substantial and effective aid from these countries.[5]

The Afghan revolution is, however, the only Marxist revolution which the Soviets have had to defend with an impressive use of military power. The reason why the Soviets intervened in Afghanistan with 100,000 troops will always remain a matter of controversy. The fact of the intervention, however, will remain undisputed. Having taken over the responsibility of defending the Saur revolution, the Soviets have also assumed the responsibility for it to succeed. The success of the Afghan revolution, however, will mean one thing for the Kremlin, another for Afghans. Bogdan Szajkowski has correctly pointed out that a Marxist revolution in the developing world is primarily an alternative, tested model of development. The mainstream of twentieth-century revolutions is a combination of national liberation *and* national development.[6] These revolutions have not occurred in the developed capitalist countries of Europe, as Marx had predicted would happen. The revolutions of the twentieth century began with the Bolshevik revolution in semi-industrialized Russia; Lenin and, even more conspicuously, Stalin perceived the revolution to be an alternative model of development, with rapid industrialization, collectivization of agriculture, central planning, and forced public participation in the development process. The dictatorship of the proletariat, one-party rule, rigid command and control of the life of the population, even the use of coercion and terror were justified by the *necessity* for rapid and radical remoulding of largely or almost entirely agricultural societies into fully industrialized ones, accomplishing in decades what the capitalist industrialized countries had done over centuries. The development ethos of the Marxist revolution was manifested in the Chinese slogan 'red and expert', as much as in the concept of a non-capitalist road so elaborately sketched in the development literature that has grown up in the Soviet Union since the late 1950s.

For the Afghans, development alone will not be sufficient recompense for the revolution if it is bereft of the conscious identity of an independent, sovereign people. The Afghans may reconcile themselves to the fact of Marxist rule, but they will not identify themselves with the Marxist state until they are convinced that it is a sovereign and independent state controlled by themselves, and not directed from Moscow. The compelling circumstances of a satellite revolution that existed in Eastern Europe do not exist in Afghanistan. Afghanistan, in April 1978, was not threatened by an external power. The United States had only a skeletal presence in the country; the influence of the Shah of Iran on Mohammed

Daoud perturbed neither the Kremlin nor the Afghan nationalists. Indeed, the Soviet intervention was seen as a foreign invasion by the vast masses of the Afghan people, and if an anti-communist rebellion in any country acquired aspects of a national liberation movement, it was in Afghanistan. It was unfortunate that the Afghan resistance was adopted by the United States, Saudi Arabia and Pakistan, and became a huge nest of social and political reaction and militant Islamic fundamentalism. The Saur revolution derived its resilience from three main sources: Soviet military might and generous resource commitment; the adoption of the resistance by the leading imperialist power, the United States, and its reactionary allies, Pakistan and Saudi Arabia; and the hopeless heterogeneity of the resistance groups, with no ideological and political cement that could glue them together into a national liberation movement.

The Afghan revolution, however, lacked the patriotic fire of the other Third World Marxist-led revolutions. Each or most of them were genuine national liberation movements, whether they were aimed at foreign imperialist powers or, as in Cuba and Nicaragua, domestic reaction backed by foreign imperialism. This is not to suggest that Karmal and members of the PDPA are not patriotic Afghans. As Selig Harrison found for himself (and so did the author), the Afghan communists do possess patriotic fervour and are dedicated to the cause of the revolution, which is, in their view, genuine sovereignty *and* rapid radical modernization and development. But they are, in 1985, a very small minority in Afghanistan, even if one accepts the PDPA membership figures given out by Karmal, and, on Karmal's own admission, the vast mass of Afghans remain deeply alienated from the revolution even when they reconcile themselves to the regime and lend it the semblance of formal co-operation.

As external military aid to the Afghan insurgents was stepped up in 1982-3, the PDPA tried to persuade the Afghans that their motherland was facing an imperialist onslaught, and that patriotism demanded that they rally to the revolution. From 1983 onwards, PDPA propaganda has sought to portray the Saur revolution as a defender of Afghanistan's sovereignty and independence as well as its traditional non-alignment. However, with 100,000 Soviet troops engaging the insurgents all over the country, the propaganda sounded hollow to Afghan ears and failed to win them over to the side of the revolution.

Mass alienation from the revolution will not disappear in the near future, even as the PDPA regime continues to gain political ground. The Soviets will, therefore, be constrained to keep the Saur revolution under the protection of their arms much longer than they would have liked to. They, as well as the PDPA leaders, are pinning their hopes on the building up of a committed, disciplined Afghan army in the next five to ten years. Thousands of young officers have been and are being trained in the Soviet Union, and, as Karmal has disclosed, 60 per cent of the party members are fighting the resistance as part of the army. Together with building a new Afghan army with Soviet-trained officers and carefully recruited soldiers, the Soviets are also training thousands of PDPA cadres and many thousand more young Afghans. It is, then, easy to visualize that both the PDPA and the CPSU leaderships expect the party and the army to develop as the twin pillars of the Afghan revolution. This is true to the model of all Marxist revolutions in the Third World. In the specific context of Afghanistan's fragmented, tribalized culture, cohesion and co-operation between the party and the army will not be easy to achieve. True, Babrak Karmal has achieved a certain measure of unity and cohesion in the party; since 1983, there have not been any important purges. At the same time, lack of party unity, factionalism and ennui have been the recurrent themes of Karmal's, and before him, Taraki's and Amin's, reports to the fifteen plenums of the PDPA central committee held since 1978. Since 1983 Karmal has been more positive about unity and cohesion in the army than in the party. But it will be foolhardy to expect the PDPA and the Afghan army, even in their Sovietized incarnations, to be free of factionalism, which may explode into violent factional in-fighting, leading to *coups* and counter-*coups* in a communist state.[7]

The diverse world of Marxist–Leninism is peopled with diverse models of development in a bewildering mix of Western and non-Western cultures. No two communisms are the same, and Afghan communism, as and when it develops its own identity will not only remain Afghan, but will increasingly rediscover its Afghan-ness. Even in the midst of the civil war, when economic development has been largely a Soviet portfolio, Babrak Karmal has had to remind the Afghan communists that the Soviets could not resolve Afghanistan's economic and social problems; this must be done by Afghans themselves. The daunting task of applying the Marxist–Leninist concepts and theories of development to concrete tribal-feudal and Islamic realities of Afghanistan will challenge the PDPA leaders for many decades to come. The task will have to be accomplished within the specific tribal, linguistic, cultural and ethnic complexities of Afghan society and the centrality of Islam in the Afghan social fabric.

Paradoxically, the great intensity of the civil war may make the task easier for the PDPA when Afghanistan settles down to face its terrible devastation. The revolution and the civil war will have been great levellers. They have smashed the barriers of ethnicity, tribalism, language and physical distance. They have brought diverse Afghans together on both sides as never before in their history. The populations of Kabul and the other big cities have swelled beyond imagination, and people have learned to fight together, work together, suffer together. Strong motivation has been created on both sides. How the ravaged Afghan society will get back its cultural moorings, what specific types of tribal coalitions and rivalries will take shape and how they will impact on the political process are areas of speculation which angels would fear to tread. The nationalities policy of the PDPA regime, if thoroughly implemented, will probably help it to remould Afghan society on a new model, and if this happens, its impact may be felt on both neighbouring Pakistan and Iran. A gnawing question is whether the Afghans will continue to be as violent and gun-happy in a Marxist state as they have been for hundreds of years. The civil war has militarized the population, especially the youth. The PDPA itself is now a party of armed Afghans fighting the resistance. Militias have been formed by both contending sides in the border areas, especially the areas along the Pakistani border inhabited by different Pushtun tribes. Pockets of armed resistance to the revolution will continue for years after any political settlement, as and when this comes about. If the PDPA finally wins the civil war with the help of Soviet arms, and resistance groups are eventually abandoned by their present patrons, pacification will be a much more formidable and protracted business than if the civil war ends in a negotiated political settlement. Even in the latter case, will it be possible for the regime to disarm the Afghans and persuade or force them to beat their swords into ploughshares? Or will the Afghan revolution be plagued by endemic violence for a long period of time? Will there be a tendency to violence among the leaders of the PDPA burnt by competing and clashing aspirations for power?

The question of armed violence is as relevant to the *mujahidin* based on Pakistani territory as it is to the population of Marxist-ruled Afghanistan. Among the unique qualities of the Afghan revolution is the huge exodus of refugees, estimated at three and a half million, into Pakistan and Iran, the great bulk of them—three million—in Pakistan. Soldiers of national liberation movements in the Third World have as a rule *not* fled their countries and taken shelter in adjoining states. Members of the FLN in Algeria did not escape to Morocco and Tunisia; the Yemenis stuck to their home ground; the Vietnamese, Laotians and Kampucheans did not seek shelter outside the borders of their respective countries. There was of course free movement of the Vietcong and North Vietnamese communists across the borders of the North and the South, and some movement of people from one Indo-China state to the other. The pattern changes when resistance develops against communist regimes. Afghanistan has become an extreme case in the reverse direction. The openness of the border with Pakistan as well as the tribal affinities between the Pathans inhabiting the North-West Frontier Province of Pakistan and the adjoining Pushtun-inhabited areas of Afghanistan acted as a strong incentive for vast numbers of Afghans to flee to Pakistan to escape the rigours of the Saur revolution, as well as to fight back as mujahidins. However, this exceptional flight of people could not have happened if the authorities in Pakistan had not offered the Afghans political asylum and facilities to wage civil war against the revolutionary regime in Afghanistan.

Louis Dupree has noted a significant result of the refugee movement out of Afghanistan, which, he believes, is loaded with political implications. Among the Pushtun refugees who have assembled on Pakistani territory are many who had been compelled to move from the southern to the northern provinces of Afghanistan in the nineteenth-century reign of Amir Abdur Rahman Khan (1880–1901). Since the Soviet military intervention, large numbers of northern-based Pushtuns have taken their families to the security of refugee camps in Pakistan and then returned to their 'zones of origin' to fight with their 'distant cousins'. This, Dupree notes, was a 'process of re-emigration'. Several of these northern Pushtun refugees with whom Dupree talked told him that 'after the first Russo–Afghan war ended, they would remain in their traditional homelands and not return to the north.' Basing his work on this and other evidence, Dupree wrote in 1985, 'The redistribution of ethnic groups might make it easier for Afghanistan to reconstitute itself as a federation of regions based on ethno-linguistic units—when and if the Soviets ever leave Afghanistan to come face-to-face with its own destiny.'[8] The redistribution of ethnic groups as a result of internal and external refugee movements will also make it relatively easier for the PDPA to design the DRA regime on a sounder basis of international and inter-ethnic relationships. A group of Soviet and Afghan scholars is working on a new nationalities design for Afghanistan at the PDPA's Institute of Social Sciences in Kabul.[9]

The levelling of ethnic and tribal barriers among the three million Afghan refugees encamped in Pakistan is of greater consequence for Pakistan's political and social stability. Dupree reports that the refugee camps have 'learned to tolerate each other, and actually show signs of cohesive action plan when pitted against or challenged by local Pakistanis.' These cross-ethnic cohesive attitudes, Dupree visualizes, 'will be indispensable in an independent, multi-linguistic, Soviet-free Afghanistan.'[10] In the short and medium term, however, this attitudinal and behavioural cohesiveness may present the regime in Pakistan with a formidable challenge if the refugees cannot be sent back to an Afghanistan ruled by a government of their choice or at least one agreeable to them.

As of February 1985, three million Afghan refugees were located in 235 Refugee Tented Villages (RTV) in the NWFP, sixty-one in Baluchistan and ten in the Punjab.[11] In every respect, it is a diversified mass of uprooted people. About three-quarters of the refugees are women and children, and the children have lost their chance of education and may well have to grow up in an alien country if they cannot return to Afghanistan in the near future. Among the refugees are members of the former royal family, of the bureaucracy, highly educated people who had jobs in the university or colleges or worked as journalists and writers, technocrats, disenchanted Marxists belonging to the Khalq and Parcham factions of the PDPA, displaced students, military officers, nomad and gipsy groups, semi-nomadic and semi-stationary groups and migrant labourers. They came into Pakistan in three large waves, though the movement has hardly stopped at any time since April 1978. The great bulk of the refugees are illiterate. About a quarter of a million are said to be armed, constituting a salient element of the resistance inside Afghanistan. Most of the resistance groups operating in Afghanistan have their headquarters and their leaders encamped in Peshawar.

The Pakistan Government has fed the refugees on promises that they will be able to return to an Afghanistan liberated from the Soviet invaders and from Marxism. This promise has been reiterated by numerous government leaders—of the United States, China, Egypt, Saudi Arabia, France, Japan and several other countries—who have visited the refugee camps since January 1980. International contributions to the maintenance of the Afghan refugees have been adequate so far: about half the cost is said to be borne by Pakistan. In the five and a half years of civil war in Afghanistan, the tides of fortune have flowed unevenly, sometimes in favour of the resistance, at times of the Soviet-Afghan troops. Since 1983, however, the Soviets have escalated the attacks on resistance groups, and in mid-1985 they seem to have scored significant successes in the provinces where the guerrillas were controlling large rural areas. Destruction of vast areas of the countryside has deprived the resistance of their essential supplies of food and water. Since 1981 the Karmal regime has been conducting a loud campaign urging the refugees to return to their homes. It declared a general amnesty and promised rehabilitation with honour and dignity. Since 1981 Kabul Radio has been reporting the return of relatively small batches of refugees and the Afghan media have been playing up their rehabilitation. In the spring and summer of 1985, the Pakistan press reported the return to Afghanistan of the leader of a resistance group as well as a religious leader with 'millions of followers in Pakistan as well as Afghanistan'. However, the total number of refugees who have returned to Afghanistan has made no significant difference to the Afghan refugee situation. Next to the Bangladesh liberation war which drove more than seven million refugees into the adjacent states of India, the civil war in Afghanistan has led to the largest refugee exodus in history. The vital differences between the two refugee situations is that, in the case of Bangladesh, the then Indian Prime Minister, Indira Gandhi, was able to create a political situation in Bangladesh for the return of the refugees.

Pakistan cannot create a similar situation in Afghanistan, nor can the United States, nor the Afghan refugees or the resistance within Afghanistan.

The Afghan refugees cannot be separated from the Afghan revolution. Their continued presence in Pakistan, with diminishing chances of their return to Afghanistan, has begun to create social, economic and political problems of tremendous consequence for Pakistan, and, to a much lesser extent, Iran. Dupree has sketched some of these long-term problems:

If—and when—after 'X' number of years, the refugees become convinced that they cannot go home again, what will they do? Become good Pakistani (or Iranian) citizens? Could the refugees be integrated into Pakistani and Iranian socio-political and economic bodies? Or are they already being integrated? If so, will it be possible to transplant large numbers outside the North-West Frontier and Baluchistan province? Those few refugees sent to the Punjab Province since 1982, on the edge of NWFP, have been most unhappy and may leave for the hills during the hot season.

Or, alternatively, will the Afghan Pushtun refugees join their Pakistani Pushtun cousins to oppose the central government of Pakistan, and possibly, violently or non-violently, try to create an independent 'Pushtunistan'? Or does 'Pushtunistan' already exist? Peshawar, for the first time in its history, has become an Afghan (Pushtun) city because of the massive flow of refugees.

And will the Baluch refugees join Pakistani *and* Iranian Baluch to create an independent 'Baluchistan?' The 'Balkanization' of Pakistan and Iran could possibly trigger off similar patterns from India back through West Asia—and elsewhere.[12]

In the long run, perhaps in ten years from now, the political impact of Marxist-ruled Afghanistan will be quite strong on Pakistan. If the PDPA can stabilize its national democracy in Afghanistan, with support from democratic non-Marxist elements, its political and economic experiments will be most closely watched by the elites of Pakistan. A successful remoulding of the relationships among the Afghan national groups would have a strong impact on Pakistan. If the Pushtuns dominate political and economic life in Afghanistan, the Punjabis do the same in Pakistan. If the DRA can build a new model of the Pushtuns' relationship with the smaller and weaker national groups, the model's attraction for

Pakistanis, especially the elite of the three minority provinces, is likely to be strong.

The strategic impact of a Marxist-ruled Afghanistan, closely tied up with the Soviet Union, on Pakistan will be felt sooner and more profoundly. Pakistan cannot afford to live in hostility or even unfriendliness with the Soviet Union and India for any period of time—a reality which Pakistani strategic thinkers have recognized since 1982. From Afghanistan, the Soviets will be in a much better position to influence Pakistan's internal politics, as well as the imagination and thinking of the Pakistani elites.

Sections of the opposition political elite in Pakistan have kept in close touch with the PDPA regime in Afghanistan ever since the Saur revolution. Khan Wali Khan, the National Awami Party leader of the NWFP, has been a regular visitor to Kabul; his aged father, Khan Abdul Gaffar Khan, still a respected figure in the Frontier Province, has lived the greater part of the last five years in the Afghan capital. Leaders of the 'defunct' political parties in Pakistan, with the exception of the Jamaat-i-Ulema and the Pir Pagara faction of the Muslim League, have consistently stood for friendly relations with an Afghanistan ruled by the PDPA. The banned Pakistan People's Party (PPP), which is still the most popular political faction in the country, has never shared the military's perception of the Marxist take-over in Kabul. Its two foremost leaders, Begum Nusrat Bhutto and Benazir Bhutto, the wife and daugher, respectively, of the hanged Zulfikar Ali Bhutto, interviewed by *The Guardian*, of London, in 1980, rejected the military regime's policy on Afghanistan. Begum Bhutto said that what was happening in Afghanistan was an internal affair of that country; Pakistan had no right to interfere. If the PPP were in power, she said, it would not allow the Afghan refugees to wage a war of resistance from Pakistani territory. The Soviets had no quarrel with Pakistan. General Zia had 'blown up' the Afghan situation to 'attract attention'. The Begum added,

We should never forget that whenever we have had wars with India, the Afghans have never made use of that excuse to attack us from their side. We should not pay them back by allowing these people who call themselves *mujahidin* to use our territory to attack them . . .. If the Soviets came to Pakistan in hot pursuit, it will be the fault of the government here.[13]

Speaking in the same vein, Benazir Bhutto said that Pakistan should have tried other means of resolving the crisis and should not have rushed to the United States, accusing the Soviet Union, whom she described as 'a superpower and the fifth largest Muslim nation in the world'. Miss Bhutto added, 'We don't want to become pawns in anybody's hands. Our country must think for itself. The question is: how do you make these Soviet troops go back? You don't do it by closing all doors. You don't get results by cold war. You get results through *détente*.'[14]

These remarks, made in April 1980, have become more relevant in the latter half of 1985 when sizeable sections of the public in Pakistan, even outside the banned portals of the defunct political parties, are asking the Government to negotiate directly with Kabul and Moscow. In the Pakistan National Assembly in May and June 1985, several members criticized the Government for 'toeing the American line', compelling Government spokesmen to assert that Pakistan was following its own policy and not a policy 'dictated by America'.[15] General Zia himself admitted that public opinion in Pakistan was divided down the middle on whether Pakistan's Afghan policy served its own national interests or those of the United States.

The Soviets will continue to use their carrot-and-stick policy for Pakistan in the next few years, perhaps brandishing the stick more than the carrot, which will be kept dangling all the time to offer the Pakistani elite the image of an alternative external source of aid and patronage. Neither the Afghan revolution nor the PDPA regime in Afghanistan can be seen separately from Soviet power and influence in the strategic regions of Arabia and South Asia. The Soviets will not destabilize Pakistan overtly; their interest lies not in the balkanization of Pakistan but in the establishment of good-neighbourly relations with a united, integrated sovereign Pakistan, uncoupled from the strategic postures of American foreign policy. With Afghanistan as an outpost of Soviet influence, Moscow will find it easier to operate its Pakistan policy and with greater chances of success.

The rulers of Pakistan have kept their country behind a barrier of anti-Sovietism for the nearly four decades of its existence. Pakistan's founder and first Governor-General, M. A. Jinnah, and its first Prime Minister, Liaquat Ali Khan, deliberately sought and obtained political, economic and strategic linkages with the United States in the very first years of the country's existence. At the height of the cold war, Pakistan forged an alliance with the United States, thereby provoking Soviet displeasure. The link with the United States became stronger and assumed a sharper anti-Soviet edge after the emergence of Indo–Soviet friendship in the 1950s. However, throughout the history of an unfriendly relationship that is four decades old, the Soviets have not completely abandoned their hope of better relations with Pakistan and Pakistan has not totally buried the prospect of friendly relations with its superpower neighbour in the north either. In 1968 the Soviets went to the extent of offering military aid to Pakistan, but drew back when they came up against obdurate objection and a sense of disappointment from India. Since 1971 India has remained the kingpin of Moscow's South Asian policy. However, consistent with its India-centred policy in South Asia, the Soviets have persevered in building a co-operative relationship with Pakistan.

They have behaved to Pakistan with considerable sophistication during the Afghan crisis. Despite Pakistan's choice of the role of a front-line state in the United States strategy to contain Soviet influence, despite Pakistan allowing its territory to be used by the Afghan mujahidin, and despite Pakistan administering the CIA-financed programme of military supplies to the resistance within Afghanistan, the Soviets have continued to build large development projects in that country, and, indeed, in 1983, handed over to the Pakistan Government the Karachi steel plant, the first steel plant in the country. The Soviets have offered Pakistan a large portfolio of development projects, including nuclear power plants and assistance to explore and develop its oil deposits. The Pakistanis, for their part, have taken care not to burn all of their bridges to the Soviet Union.

As noted, a significant Soviet constituency has grown up in Pakistan for the first time in the 1980s. Also, for the first time, Pakistan has had a very visible Soviet ambassador in the person of Anatoly Smirnov, who, between 1983 and 1985, addressed no less than twenty-four seminars, student audiences, chambers of commerce and press club meetings in Islamabad, Lahore and Karachi.[16] The Soviets offered Pakistan stable and enduring friendship, but, as Agha Shahi, then Foreign Minister, disclosed in 1980, the Soviets made it 'conditional on the nature of Pakistan's relations with its two neighbours, India and Afghanistan'.[17]

Yet, when Shahi announced Pakistan's rejection of the Carter administration's 'peanut' offer of $400 m. in aid, he did look to the Soviet Union as an alternative source of help. 'We shall remain persistent in our search for a relationship of trust and confidence with that great power and we do not view the future with pessimism', declared Shahi in concluding his announcement.

In 1985 the Soviets do not view their future in South Asia with pessimism either. The friendship with India has not only survived their military move into Afghanistan, but also the assassination of Indira Gandhi; it is likely to grow stronger still under the prime ministership of Rajiv Gandhi.[18] The Soviets hope that, as the Afghan revolution settles down, and as Afghanistan is moulded towards the Marxist–Leninist model of non-capitalist development, Moscow would be able to bring Afghanistan, Pakistan and India together in a network of friendly, good-neighbourly relationships.

The Afghan revolution and the Marxist regime in Kabul are of considerable importance to the Soviets in the context of contemporary manifestations of Islamic fundamentalism. Nothing perturbed the CPSU leaders more than Amin's grotesque mishandling of Islam after the establishment of the PDPA regime. The Soviets could hardly afford to see the Afghan masses waging a successful *jihad* against the revolutionary Marxist regime set up in Kabul. They were afraid not only of the repercussions of such a disaster on the Soviet Union's Central Asian republics, but also on the Marxist state of South Yemen, and on progressive secular movements on a wide front in the Middle East, the Persian Gulf, and the Indian Ocean littoral. The CPSU leaders were under a compulsion to prove that there was no fundamental contradiction between Marxism and Islam.

The Soviets face two different manifestations of Islamic fundamentalism in the 'situation around Afghanistan': the radical fundamentalism of the Aytollah Khomeini in Iran, and the conservative fundamentalism of Pakistan. Both varieties are hostile to the Marxist regime of Afghanistan, but they are unable to unite on a common political platform, and are indeed fighting each other in some resistance-held areas of Afghanistan. The Soviets, of course, regard Iranian fundamentalism as more dangerous than Pakistan's. The majority of the Islamic people of Afghanistan belong to the Sunni sect, as do the majority of the people of Pakistan. The Soviets' perception of Iranian fundamentalism has changed in the last few years from positive-negative to entirely negative. In an authoritative analysis of Iranian fundamentalism in May 1985, Academician R. Ulyanovskiy, a noted CPSU theoretician, drew the grim conclusion that the Iranian revolution which, in 1978-9, was a 'genuine all-people's festive event', was captured by the clergy in 1980 in collusion with 'bourgeois business and large landowners'. In 1981 the clergy 'completely exhausted its progressive potential' and 'turned into a counterrevolutionary force'. In 1982-3, the clergy came down heavily on the progressive and left-wing elements, particularly the Tudeh party. 'Tens of thousands of the best sons of the people were executed or imprisoned.'

The conservative clergy has succeeded in stopping the social revolution and in tearing it away from the overthrow of the monarchical power and the elimination of American domination, that is, from political revolution. Herein lies the profound and perfidious plan of the clergy that is closely connected with bourgeois business and large landlords.[19]

The war with Iraq did not permit Tehran to play a major role in inflaming Afghans' Islamic passions against the Marxist regime. Indeed, for the Iranian fundamentalists, it has been as important to fight Marxism as the conservative Islamic fundamentalism of Saudi Arabia and Pakistan, to which the vast majority of Afghans have inclined. To be sure, this has helped the Afghan communists as well as the Soviets. But it has also heightened the imperative to demonstrate that Marxism can work in a deeply Islamic Afghanistan. The contemporary Soviet perception of Islam has focused on two major contradictions. One is the urge to break out of the binds of native reaction befriended by foreign imperialism. The other is the defensive-offensive imperatives of the forces of reaction and the status quo. These two contradictions of Islamic fundamentalism are heightened by the general disarray of the Islamic powers, their lack of unity and cohesion, and their failure to satisfy the political aspirations of the Muslim masses.

The conservative Islamic fundamentalist elements see the United States as their great patron and ally. The radical Islamic fundamentalists are anti-American as well as anti-Soviet; in the Soviet perception— basically more anti-communist than anti-capitalist. Islam is a neighbour of the Soviet Union which is itself the homeland of fifty million Muslims. The Soviets therefore need a battle plan to meet the challenge of Islamic fundamentalism. The battle plan that has been forged in Moscow since the 1970s has three main planks. The first is the Soviet Union's friendly relations with a number of Muslim nations—Syria, Algeria, Libya; to a lesser extent, Kuwait and Jordan. Linked to Soviet friendship with these countries is the Kremlin's hostility towards Israel and its support for Arab demands against the Jewish state. The second plank is the Marxist–Muslim identity of the Soviet Union. The Soviets are projecting more vigorously than before to the Islamic peoples not only the modernized and developed Central Asian republics of the Soviet Union but also a Muslim shade of Soviet communism. The Soviet ambassador to Kabul is a Muslim; a Muslim led the Soviet delegation to the celebration of the twentieth anniversary of the founding of the PDPA. The ambassador who has replaced Smirnov in Islamabad is also a Muslim.

The third plank of the Soviet battle plan is Marxist revolution in Islamic nations. The Soviets seem to believe that as the fundamentalist tide ebbs, South Yemen and Afghanistan will draw the minds and ears of the Muslims of Arabia, the Middle East and South Asia as attractive models of development and modernization. Iran and Pakistan will be special targets of the Soviet battle plan against Islamic fundamentalism. Marxist-ruled Afghanistan and the Soviet presence in the Hindu Kush are expected to play a major part in determining the political shape and conduct of Iran in the turmoil that most people expect to break out when the Ayatollah Khomeini is no more. Moscow will not spoil for another adventure in Iran or Pakistan. It will not provoke the United States to another cold war-like confrontation in the Persian Gulf or South Asia. But if it is convinced that its vital security and political interests are seriously threatened, it will not hesitate to intervene merely because intervention may provoke the United States to impose economic 'sanctions' or turn its back on arms control and limitation agreements. There are no ground rules for Soviet–American competition for power and influence in the Third World. The Soviets will not buy *détente* at the price of what Americans mean by 'restraint' in the Third World. They intervened in Afghanistan at a time when the correlation of forces in Arabia and South Asia was not exactly in Moscow's favour.

Notes

Chapter 1

1. Hamidullah Amin, 'The Human and Physical Aspects of Afghan Regionalism', paper read at a conference on Rural Life in Afghanistan held at the University of Nebraska, Omaha, 23–25 September, 1976. See also Graham Kerr, 'Strategies in Identifying and Collecting Data', presented at the same conference.
2. For a detailed account of regionalism in Afghanistan, see Amin and G. Schilz, *A Geography of Afghanistan*, University of Nebraska, Omaha, Center for Afghanistan Studies, 1976.
3. Amin, op. cit.
4. Quoted in C. Colin Davies, *The Problem of the North-West Frontier 1890–1908*, Cambridge, 1932, p. 153.
5. Asghar H. Bilgrami, *Afghanistan and British India 1793-1907, A Study in Foreign Relations*, Sterling Publishers, New Delhi, 1972, pp. 276-8. The buffer concept was rejected by Afghanistan also.
6. The Russian Consul-General in Calcutta, Nabokov, in his reports to the Foreign Affairs ministry of the Imperial Government, regularly covered British-Afghan relations. A recurrent theme in his dispatches was that Russia should fully co-operate with Britain so that the British would take care of Russian interests in Afghanistan.

   Once we have accepted the British in principle as solicitors with the Amir till our political interests in Middle Asia do not clash with those of the British, the stronger is the authority of the Government of India in Kabul the easier it would be for us to achieve the safety of our interests and fulfilment of our demands. [Subhas Chacravorty (ed.), *Anatomy of the Raj: Russian Consular Reports*, New Delhi, People's Publishing House, 1981, p. 291.]

   Nabokov's reports show how great was Russian concern about Islamic fundamentalism spreading from Afghanistan to Turkey.
7. Bisheshwar Prasad, *The Foundations of India's Foreign Policy: 1882-1914*, Calcutta, Naya Prokash, 1979, pp. 304-6.
8. Cited in Fred Halliday, 'Revolution in Afghanistan', *New Left Review*, London, November–December 1978.

9. For details, see Thomas T. Hammond, *Red Flag Over Afghanistan: The Communist Coup, the Soviet Invasion and the Consequences*, Boulder, Colorado, Westview Press, 1984, pp. 12–16. Hammond relies heavily on George (Grigori) Agabekov's *OGPU: The Russian Secret Terror*, New York, Brentano's, 1931. Agabekov worked for OGPU in Afghanistan from 1924 to 1926. Agabekov's book shows how zealously the Soviets were protecting the Soviet state in the 1920s, especially its Central Asian republics, from the ruling classes and religious elements in Turkey, Iran and Afghanistan.

10. When Amanullah was in trouble, Ghulam Nabi, described as his frontman, was said to have raised an army of Soviet Central Asian Muslims to come to his help. As Nabi and his men were marching down towards Kabul, word was received that Amanullah had abdicated and fled to India. Most of the soldiers recruited by Nabi deserted. See Agabekov op. cit., and Alexander Barmine, *One Who Survived: The Life of a Russian Under the Soviets*, New York, Putnam, 1945. Barmine was a Soviet diplomat who defected to the United States.

11. V. Gregorian, *The Emergence of Modern Afghanistan*, Palo Alto, Stanford University Press, 1969, p. 377.

12. This periodization of Afghanistan's foreign policy is adopted from Alfred L. Monks, *The Soviet Intervention in Afghanistan*, Washington DC, American Enterprise Institute for Public Policy Research, 1981, pp. 11–13.

13. Cited in *Hidden War: The Struggle for Afghanistan*, a staff report prepared for the Committee on Foreign Relations, United States Senate, April 1984, Washington DC, US Government Printing Office, p. 6.

14. Ibid., p. 5.

15. Richard S. Newell, *The Politics of Afghanistan*, Ithaca, Cornell University Press, 1972, pp. 122–3.

16. *Hidden War . . .*, op. cit., n. 9, p. 5.

17. Ibid.

18. Nikita Khrushchev, *Khrushchev Remembers*, Boston, Little Brown, 1970, pp. 507–9.

19. Cited in Gunther Nollan and Hans Jurgen Wiche, *Russia's Southern Flank*, New York, Praeger, 1962, p. 136.

20. Louis Dupree, 'Afghanistan Under the Khalq', *Problems of Communism*, July–August 1979.

21. Hammond, op. cit., n. 8, p. 29.

22. Karmal's address to a function celebrating the 20th anniversary of the founding of the People's Democratic Party of Afghanistan (PDPA), *Kabul New Times*, 21 January 1985.

23. Dupree, op. cit., n. 19.
24. This was done by invoking Article 1 of the Press Law; paragraph 3 of Article 1 stipulated that 'The goals which the law aims to secure consist of safeguarding the fundamentals of Islam, constitutional monarchy, and other values enshrined in the constitution.' Dupree, op. cit.
25. Robert Hennman, 'Afghanistan under the Red Flag', *International Journal of Middle Eastern Studies*, **9**, 3, May 1978.
26. Cited in Hammond, op. cit., n. 8.
27. Aerogramme No. A-7 from the American embassy in Kabul to the State Department dated 26 June 1971, containing the Policy Review. Hammond, op. cit., p. 28 (Note 8) says, 'This is one of many classified State Department documents obtained (by him) under the Freedom of Information Act.' He lists nine other documents containing policy assessments by the American ambassador in Kabul.

Chapter 2

1. Dupree, op. cit., Ch. 1, n. 8.
2. 'United States mission in Afghanistan 1972 Policy Review', contained in aerogramme No. A-66 from Kabul to the State Department, dated 5 June 1972, cited in Hammond, op. cit., Ch. 1, n. 8.
3. Hasan Kakar, 'The Fall of the Afghan Monarchy', *International Journal of Middle Eastern Studies*, **9**, 2, May 1978; Shaheen F. Dil, 'The Cabal in Kabul: Great Power Interaction in Afghanistan', *American Political Science Review*, **71**, 2, June 1977.
4. Dupree, op. cit.
5. Ibid.
6. Secret aerogramme No. A-20 from Kabul to the State Department, dated 30 April 1975, cited in Hammond, op. cit., p. 43.
7. Ibid.
8. *Wall Street Journal*, 20 September 1977.
9. Hammond, op. cit., p. 41.
10. *Pravda*, 6 April 1977.
11. Amir Tahiri, 'The Persian Gulf: The Non-Arab Littoral', paper presented at conference on The Persian Gulf and the Indian Ocean in International Politics, Tehran, 25–27 March 1975. Tahiri's paper was subsequently published in a revised form with the title 'Policies of Iran in the Persian Gulf Region' in Abbas Ameiri (ed.), *The Persian Gulf and the Indian Ocean in*

International Politics, Tehran, Institution for International Political and Economic Studies, 1975, pp. 259–77. In the revised version Tahiri said that Iran had agreed to give Afghanistan 'access to Bandar Abbas through a new rail link starting in Kandahar'. He praised Daoud for 'maintaining a balance between the two superpowers'. Iran, he said, had welcomed Daoud's regime 'after some initial misgivings'. And Daoud had dissolved all the crypto-communist groups regardless of their pro-Peking or pro-Moscow leanings, had purged Soviet-trained technicians from the leadership of government-backed enterprises in Afghanistan and replaced them with personnel trained in the West, and, at the same time, had reasserted the predominant position of the Mohammadzai clan in the Afghan political and administrative set-up. Tahiri also claimed that the Shah had succeeded in persuading Daoud to mute his support for Pushtunistan. Iran, he added, had been 'extremely cautious all along' not to adopt 'a high-profile posture in Afghanistan'. The Shah's long-term expectation was that Afghanistan, with its higher level of development, would serve 'as an additional link' in the 'long chain of stability' that was being 'patiently created in this region'. Pp. 271–2. Tahiri was close to the Iranian Foreign Office. He told the author that his paper 'broadly reflected the thinking of the Shah'.

12. Cited in Hammond, op. cit., pp. 38–9. Selig Harrison wrote in the *Washington Post* of 13 May 1979, 'It was the Shah of Iran, not Leonid Brezhnev, who triggered the chain of events culminating in the overthrow of the Mohammed Daoud regime.'

13. Louis Dupree, *Afghanistan 1977: Does Trade plus Aid Guarantee Development?*, Hanover, N.H., American Universities Field Staff Report, South Asia Series, **21**, 3, August 1977, p. 4.

14. Bhabani Sen Gupta, 'Communism in India: A New Context', *Problems of Communism*, July–August 1981.

15. Dupree, 'Afghanistan Under the Khalq', op. cit.

16. Ibid.

17. Nancy P. Newell and Richard S. Newell, *The Struggle for Afghanistan*, Ithaca, Cornell University Press, 1981, Ch. 4. The details of the communist coup that follow are largely taken from the Newells' book.

18. Professor Malcolm Yapp, of the University of London, believes that the coup was 'planned and executed on the spur of the moment by frightened officers'. Cited in Hammond, op. cit., p. 31.

19. Dupree, 'Afghanistan Under the Khalq', op. cit.

20. *The Struggle for Afghanistan*, op. cit., pp. 68–9.

21. News Conference on 6 May 1978, cited in Hammond, op. cit., p. 50.

22. Cyrus Vance, *Hard Choice: Critical Years in America's Foreign Policy*, New York, Simon & Schuster, 1983, p. 384.
23. Hammond, op. cit., p. 54.
24. Amin's orders were made public in Kabul in 1980. See *Democratic Republic of Afghanistan Annual*, Kabul, Government Printing Press, 1980, pp. 44–8. Also, Dupree, *Red Flag Over the Hindu Kush*, *Part II, The Accidental Coup or Taraki in Blunderland*, Hanover, N.H., American Universities Field Staff Report, South Asia Series, 45, 1979, pp. 15–16.
25. Author's interviews with PDPA officials in Kabul.

Chapter 3

1. Roderick Aya, 'Theories of Revolution Reconsidered', *Theory and Society*, **8**, 1, pp. 39–99.
2. *Afghanistan: Multifaceted Revolutionary Problems*, Kabul, Government Printing Press, 1982, pp. 1–3.
3. A. S. Grachev (ed.), *The Undeclared War: Imperialism vs. Afghanistan*, Moscow, Progress Publishers, 1980, pp. 24–5.
4. Ghulam Muradov, 'The Democratic Republic of Afghanistan: Second Stage of the April Revolution', *Social Sciences Today*, Moscow, 1981, pp. 179–80.
5. D. Kesavkia, 'Protecting the Gains of the April Revolution', *Asia and Africa Today*, Moscow, 3, 1980.
6. S. Golyakov, *New Times*, 20, 1980.
7. S. Golyakov, *New Times*, 34, 1982.
8. M. Nazif Shahrani, 'Marxist "Revolution" and Islamic Resistance', in M. Nazif Shahrani and Robert L. Canfield (eds), *Revolutions and Rebellions in Afghanistan*, Berkeley, Institute of International Studies, California University Press, 1983, p. 7.
9. Ibid., p. 34.
10. Ibid., p. 37.
11. Ibid., p. 35.
12. Thomas J. Barfield, 'Structural Weaknesses in Provincial Administration', ibid., p. 180.
13. David J. Katz, 'Central Authority and the Vaygal Valley Kalasha', ibid., p. 112.
14. R. Lincoln Keiser, 'The Rebellion in Darra-i-Noor', ibid., p. 126.
15. 'Structural Weaknesses in Provincial Administration', op. cit., pp. 172–4.

16. 'Marxist Revolution and Islamic Resistance', op. cit., p. 18.
17. Hugh Beattie, 'Effects of the Saur Revolution in Nahrain' in *Revolutions and Rebellions in Afghanistan*, op. cit., p. 188.
18. Ibid.

Chapter 4

1. Louis Dupree, 'Afghanistan Under the Khalq', op. cit.
2. Ibid.
3. From all available accounts, except for Soviet-Afghan sources after 27 December 1979, Hafizullah Amin was the moving spirit in the founding of the PDPA. However, in the 1980s, Amin became a 'CIA agent', and was rejected to the dustbin of history. Babrak Karmal is now the official founder of the ruling party, and he staked his claim publicly at the party meeting held in April 1985 to celebrate the 20th anniversary of its establishment. See Ch. 1, n. 21.
4. One estimate is that about one-third of the officers of the Afghan Army and Air Force were supporters of the PDPA at the time of the revolution. Author's interviews with PDPA officials.
5. In the first struggle for power within the Marxist regime, the Soviets did not back Karmal. They advised a broad national democratic strategy, but stood quite firmly behind the dominant Khalq faction. Interviews in Kabul.
6. See report of Taraki's press conference of 6 May 1978 in *FBIS*, 9 May, 1978, pp. S 1–2.
7. The formation of the Revolutionary Council was announced by Kabul Radio as Decree No. 1 of the Marxist regime on 30 April 1978. The names of its members were not given.
8. Karmal had practically no following among the military officers. Abdul Qader, however, joined Karmal's Cabinet formed after the coup of 27 December 1979.
9. The text of the constitution can be seen as an appendix to Hammond, *Red Flag Over Afghanistan*, op. cit., pp. 229–40, with an interesting introductory note.
10. *Pravda*, 19 May 1978.
11. *New York Times*, 16 June 1978.
12. *FBIS*, 9 June 1978, pp. S–3.

13. *Times of India*, 18 September 1978.
14. Robert Neumann, 'Afghanistan Under the Red Flag', in Z. Michael Zsaz, *The Impact of the Iranian Events Upon the Persian Gulf and U.S. Security*, Washington DC, American Foreign Policy Institute, 1979, p. 138; see also Dupree, 'Afghanistan Under the Khalq', op. cit. The purge affected hundreds of trained civil servants and a number of ranking military officers. General Abdul Qader, Defence Minister, was charged with conspiracy and thrown into prison—an indication of the insecurity of Amin and of his suspicious nature.
15. A few months later, they were ordered back to Kabul. None of them went.
16. Dupree, 'Afghanistan Under the Khalq', op. cit.
17. M. Nazif Shahrani, 'Marxist Revolution and Islamic Resistance' in Shahrani and Canfield (eds), *Revolutions and Rebellions in Afghanistan*, op. cit., pp. 12–17.
18. Nancy Dupree, 'The Rights of Afghan Women', *Christian Science Monitor*, 25 June 1980. Others believe that the Marxist regime was the first to confer equality of status on women. 'For long centuries most (of the women in Afghanistan) were treated like slaves . . . sold into marriage and denied the right to participate in social and economic life . . .. Equality for women was proclaimed immediately after the April revolution.' M. Bechtel, 'Afghanistan: The Proud Revolution', *New World Review*, **49**, 1, 1981, p. 11.
19. Vladimir Glukhoded, 'Economy of Independent Afghanistan', *Social Sciences Today*, 1981, pp. 222–45. Glukhoded's figures are controversial. Sadhan Mukherjee, of the Communist Party of India (CPI) estimated the total peasant debt in Afghanistan at 722 m. afghanis, covering 4.3 million peasants. *What Is Happening in Afghanistan*, New Delhi, CPI Publications, 9, July 1981, p. 16.
20. *Kabul New Times*, 16 June 1978.
21. Ibid. Also, *Indian Express*, Delhi, 18 June 1978.
22. Nancy Dupree, 'Revolutionary Rhetoric and Afghan Women' in *Revolutions and Rebellions in Afghanistan*, op. cit., pp. 312–13; also her 'Behind the Veil in Afghanistan', *Asia*, **1**, 2, August 1978, pp. 10–15; *Progress Report 1977*, Kabul, Ministry of Information and Culture (MIC); and Dr Anihita Ratibzad's interview with *Soviet Women*, 5, February 1980.
23. 'Revolutionary Rhetoric and Afghan Women', op. cit., p. 311.
24. *Kabul New Times*, 23 August 1978. Also see editorial in *Kabul New Times* dated 28 May 1978.
25. *Kabul New Times*, 9 September 1978.

26. Hugh Beattie, 'Effects of the Saur Revolution in Nahrin Area of Northern Afghanistan', in *Revolutions and Rebellions in Afghanistan*, pp. 189–91.

27. Nancy Tapper, 'Causes and Consequences of Abolition of Brideprice', in *Revolutions and Rebellions in Afghanistan*, op. cit., pp. 291–305.

28. Leon B. Poullada, *Reform and Rebellion in Afghanistan 1919–1929: King Amanullah's Failure to Modernize a Tribal Society*, Ithaca, Cornell University Press, 1973, p. 135.

29. There is considerable controversy about Afghanistan's pre-revolutionary agrarian structure. One view, held by D. Wilber (*Afghanistan: Its People, Its Society, Its Culture*, New Haven, Human Relations Area Files Press, 1962, p. 226) is that Afghanistan is predominantly a country of small owner-operated farms. Dupree's estimate is that 60 per cent of the holdings were of this type ('USAID and Social Scientists Discuss Afghanistan's Development Prospects', *AUFS Field Reports*, South Asia Series, **21**, 2, p. 5). A third view is that about 40 to 50 per cent of the rural population was landless. Fred Halliday, 'Revolution in Afghanistan', *New Left Review*, **112**, November–December 1978. Evidently there were large local variations and no scientific nation-wide agrarian survey had been undertaken.

30. Hugh Beattie, 'Effects of the Saur Revolution in Nahrin in Northern Afghanistan', op. cit., p. 192.

Daoud's land reforms permitted landowners to retain 100 jiribs of double-cropped irrigated or orchard land, 150 jiribs of single-cropped irrigated land, or 200 jiribs of dry farming land. These reforms were akin to those promulgated in Pakistan by Field-Marshal Ayub Khan in the sixties.

Kabul New Times reported on 18 June 1979, with a flourish of revolutionary hyperbole, that 85 per cent of the land reforms had been completed in the summer of that year, and that 233,000 families had received 2,700,000 jiribs of land. In 1980, land reforms were virtually halted in most of Afghanistan.

31. *Afghanistan: The Target of Imperialism*, Kabul, DPDA Printing Press, 1983, pp. 10–11.

Chapter 5

1. Mikhail Ilyinsky, 'Afghanistan: The Irreversible Tide', *Asia and Africa Today*, 2, 1982.

It may be noted that, when the Saur revolution took place, there was nothing like the Iranian-type radical Islam as a fundamentalist religious movement. The Afghan revolution had to contend with Islamic fundamentalism as a formidable opponent only in 1979. Amin was tempted to overpower Islamic fundamentalism with revolutionary reforms and ruthless suppression of opposition.

2. L. R. Polonskaya, 'Religion in the Life of Developing Countries in Asia and Africa', in Bhabani Sen Gupta (ed.), *Soviet Perspectives of Contemporary Asia*, New Delhi, South Asia Publications, 1974, pp. 85–93.

3. Clifford Geertz, *The Interpretation of Cultures*, New York, Basic Books, 1973, p. 168; Leon B. Poullada, *Reform and Rebellion in Afghanistan 1919–1922*, op. cit., pp. 94–8, 169–70, 208.

4. M. Nazif Shahrani, 'Marxist "Revolution" and Islamic Resistance' in *Revolutions and Rebellions in Afghanistan*, op. cit., p. 35.

5. L. Lincoln Keiser, 'The Rebellion in Derra-i-Nur' in ibid., p. 126; Oliver Roy, 'Neither Bled to Death nor Deserted', *Guardian Weekly*, London, 14 December 1983.

6. Nancy P. Newell and Richard S. Newell, *The Struggle for Afghanistan*, op. cit., 1981, pp. 93–4.

7. 'Marxist Revolution and Islamic Resistance', op. cit., p. 46.

8. David J. Katz, 'Central Authority and the Vaygal Valley Kalasha', in *Revolutions and Rebellions in Afghanistan*, op. cit., pp. 114–15.

9. Cited in N. Newell and R. Newell, *The Struggle for Afghanistan*, op. cit., p. 104.

10. Cited in 'Marxist Revolution and Islamic Resistance', op. cit., p. 47.

11. Ibid.

12. *New York Times*, 13 January 1980. Harrison reported that there were between 40 and 160 different armed rebel groups in Afghanistan. 'Too many rebel leaders envisioned themselves as Afghanistan's emerging Ayatollah and they have been unwilling to allow the practical benefits of coordination to cloud their views.' Later, in 1983, battlefield co-ordination was achieved by several rebel groups, although political differences persist. Biographical details about rebel leaders have been taken from 'Marxist "Revolution" and Islamic Resistance', op. cit.

For one of the best accounts of the Afghan resistance, see Anthony Hyman, *Afghanistan under Soviet Domination*, London, Macmillan, 1982, Ch. 7. For perhaps the best journalistic field report, see Gerard Ghaliand, *Report from Afghanistan*, New York, Viking Press, Penguin, 1981.

13. Fred Halliday, 'War and Revolution in Afghanistan', *New Left Review*, **119**, January–February 1980, pp. 20–41.

Chapter 6

1. Thomas Hammond, in *Red Flag Over Afghanistan*, op. cit., gives a well-documented account of the pre-Soviet intervention perceptions of the April revolution by American foreign policy-makers, including President Carter, Secretary of State, Cyrus Vance and National Security Adviser, Zbigniew Brzezinski. See Chs. 7 and 10.

2. M. Nazif Shahrani, 'Causes and Context of Responses to the Saur Revolution in Badakshan', in *Revolutions and Rebellions in Afghanistan*, op. cit., pp. 159–60.

3. Halliday, 'War and Revolution in Afghanistan', op. cit.

4. There are contrary views regarding the legendary arms-carrying Afghan villager. Shahrani observes that 'The assumption that everyone in the countryside is armed is not accurate. Only small segments of rural Pushtun have been allowed to carry arms; with minor exceptions, in the towns and villages they never did.' 'Marxist "Revolutions" and Islamic Resistance', p. 7. R. Lincoln Keiser, on the other hand, notes that 'much of the population of Darra-i-Nur was armed'. 'The Rebellion in Darra-i-Nur', op. cit., p. 124.

5. Halliday, 'War and Revolution in Afghanistan'. Also, Halliday, 'A Revolution Consumes Itself', *The Nation*, 229, 17 November 1979.

6. Louis Dupree, *The Democratic Republic of Afghanistan, 1979*, Hanover, N.H., American Universities Field Staff Reports (AUFSA), 32, Asia, 1979.

7. Halliday, 'Revolution in Afghanistan', op. cit.

8. Ibid.

9. See the papers by these scholars in *Revolutions and Rebellions in Afghanistan*, op. cit.

10. Richard F. Strand, 'The Evolution of Anti-Communist Resistance in Eastern Nuristan', ibid., pp. 77–93.

11. Strand, op. cit., pp. 91–3.

12. 'Central Authority and the Vaygal Valley Kalasha', op. cit., pp. 111, 117.

13. Ibid., p. 115.

14. Ibid., pp. 17–18.

15. 'The Rebellion in Darra-i-Nur', op. cit., pp. 123–6.

16. 'Causes and Context of Responses to the Saur Revolution in Badakhshan', op. cit., p. 139.

17. Ibid., pp. 160–1.

18. Ibid., p. 163.

19. Thomas J. Barfield, 'Weak Links on a Rusty Chain: Structural Weaknesses

in Afghanistan's Provincial Administration', in *Revolutions and Rebellions in Afghanistan*, op. cit., pp. 170–83.

20. Ibid., p. 182.
21. Hugh Beattie, 'Effects of the Saur Revolution in the Nahrin Area of Northern Afghanistan', in *Revolutions and Rebellions in Afghanistan*, pp. 184–208.
22. Ibid., p. 203.
23. Fred Halliday is about the only neo-Marxist scholar to have critically examined the Afghan revolution and the Soviet role in it: see Halliday 'Revolution in Afghanistan', (1978) op. cit.
24. Halliday, 'War and Revolution in Afghanistan', (1980), op. cit.
25. Halliday, 'Afghanistan: A Revolution Consumes Itself', (1979), op. cit.
26. Ibid.
27. Ibid.
28. Ibid.
29. Ibid.
30. Ibid.
31. *Far Eastern Economic Review*, 5 October 1979; *Kabul New Times*, 15 September 1979.
32. *Kabul New Times*, 16 September 1979. About this time, the Foreign Minister, Shah Wali, was reportedly given refuge in the Soviet Embassy. Major Taroon was described by the American embassy in Kabul as a 'brutal, psychopathic killer', second 'only to Amin in the amount of blood on his hands'. Hammond, *Red Flag Over Afghanistan*, op. cit., p. 92.
33. FBIS, 10 October 1979; Halliday, 'Revolution in Afghanistan', op. cit.
34. For instance, Prime Minister Kosygin did not stop in Kabul while flying back to Moscow from New Delhi, nor send the customary message of greetings while flying over Afghanistan. The Soviet ambassador Puzanov did not attend a ceremonial opening of a PDPA training centre and arrived very late at a meeting marking the opening of the constitutional convention. Amin's Foreign Minister, Shah Wali, who had reputedly sought refuge in the Soviet embassy, openly accused that embassy of plotting to kill Amin, and demanded the recall of Puzanov. None of these developments came to light at the time, and in public Amin behaved as if his relations with Moscow were excellent. See Hammond, op. cit., pp. 85–6.
35. Hammond, op. cit., pp. 88–90. *Kabul New Times*, 27 October and 15 November 1979. Amin also promised his countrymen a new constitution and released hundreds of political prisoners, but he arrested and imprisoned an almost equal number of other Afghans.

36. United States embassy cable to State Department, cited in Hammond, op. cit., p. 90.
37. *FBIS*, 16 October 1979 and 11 December 1969. United States embassy cable to State Department. See Hammond, op. cit., p. 94.
38. Author's interviews with DRA officials in Kabul. Zia-ul Haq had a different version. Early in December, he received an SOS from Amin requesting an immediate meeting. He could not go 'for obvious reasons', but sent his Foreign Minister, Shahi. But the day Shahi was to go to Kabul, the Russians arrived. It was 'too late', said Zia, meaning that no meeting took place between Amin and Shahi. *The Washington Post*, 14 February 1980.

Chapter 7

1. Information received by author from scholars at the Institute of Oriental Studies, Academy of Sciences, Moscow, in June 1982.
2. Halliday, 'Revolution in Afghanistan', op. cit.
3. Academician Evgenii Primakov cited five US 'provocations' which built up the 'atmosphere' for the Soviet action. These were Presidential Directive No. 18 of August 1977, calling for the creation of the Rapid Deployment Force (RDF); the pledge by the NATO countries in May 1978 to increase their military spending; the NATO decision to deploy medium-range missiles in Western Europe; the United States freezing 'in practice' of the signing of the SALT II agreement; and 'the flirtations which the United States is carrying on with China'. *FBIS*, Soviet series, 22 January 1981, p. A5.
4. *FBIS*, Soviet series, 22 January 1981, p. A5.
5. Henry Trofimenko, 'The Third World and US–Soviet Cooperation; A Soviet View', *Foreign Affairs*, **59**, summer, 1981.
6. This interpretation was given to the author by a senior Soviet journalist in New York in the autumn of 1982. He cannot be identified.
7. Cyrus Vance, *Hard Choices: Critical Years in America's Foreign Policy*, New York, Simon and Schuster, 1983, pp. 385–95.
8. *Defense/Space Daily*, 12 February 1980.
9. *Pravda*, 23 February 1980.
10. *FBIS*, Soviet series, 22 January 1981, p. A5.
11. The text of the message can be found in the *New York Times*, 22 January 1980. 'It was the hard, anti-Soviet address that largely reflected Brzezinski's

views rather than [those] of Vance. Said a senior State Department official, "Brzezinski has finally got his cold war".' *Time* magazine, 4 February 1980.

12. *New York Times*, 5 January 1980.

13. For Indian and South Asian perceptions of the Soviet intervention as well as South Asian diplomacies for coping with it, see Bhabani Sen Gupta, *The Afghan Syndrome: How to Live with Soviet Power*, Delhi, Vikas, 1982; and K. P. Mishra (ed.), *The Soviet Intervention in Afghanistan*, Delhi, Vikas, 1982.

Chapter 8

1. Karl von Clausewitz, *On War*, Anatol Rapoport edn, Baltimore, Maryland, Penguin Press, 1968, p. 121.

2. *Pravda*, 23 January 1980.

3. Amin did ask several times for Soviet military help in suppressing the resistance. Obviously he did not request intervention for his own ouster. The Soviet media maintained that the Soviets had nothing to do with the coup against Amin, his arrest and execution. 'That was the doing of the Afghans themselves', observed *New Times*, No. 17, 1980.

   Kabul Radio did appear to have broadcast in Dari at 22.40 hours GMT, on 27 December 1979, an Afghan 'demand' for Soviet military assistance in the critical situation in Afghanistan. The appeal was broadcast *after* the arrest of Amin and the end of his rule. Its exact words were:

   Because of the continuation and expansion of aggression, intervention and provocations by the foreign enemies of Afghanistan and for the purpose of defending the gains of the Saur revolution, territorial integrity, national independence and the preservation of peace and security, and on the basis of the treaty of friendship, good-neighbourliness and cooperation dated 5 December 1978, the Democratic Republic of Afghanistan earnestly demands that the USSR render urgent political, moral, and economic assistance, including military aid, to Afghanistan. FBIS, 28 December 1979, p. S2.

4. *The Statesman*, New Delhi, 26 January 1980.

5. *The Guardian*, 29 January 1980.

6. *Pravda*, 10 May 1980.

7. *Pakistan Times*, 7 March 1980.

8. See *The Afghan Syndrome: How to Live with Soviet Power*, op. cit., Ch. 6, for an analytical interpretation of Indian diplomacy in response to the Soviet intervention.

9. *Times of India*, 17 October 1981.

10. Richard P. Cronin, *Afghanistan: Soviet Invasion and US Response*, Library of Congress, Congressional Research Service, Issue Brief No. 1180006, March 1981, pp. 8–9, mimeo.

11. *Pravda*, 3 August 1982.

12. The Panjsher Valley fighting has been widely reported in the international press. Several Western reporters have been able to visit the valley with the resistance leader, Masud, who has become a hero of the legend of the Afghan resistance. Gerald Ghaliand's *Report from Afghanistan* (n. 13, to Ch. 5) is mostly about the Panjsher Valley fighting. There is an element of irony that Afghanistan's most fundamentalist Islamic rebel leader, who swears by the Iranian revolution, should become a focus for the Western legend of the resistance. The Soviets have mobilized a formidable array of military force and have engaged in flexible tactics to overpower Masud's guerrilla forces. For the 1984 fighting, see *Newsweek*, 11 June 1984, and Afghan Information Centre Monthly *Bulletin*, April 1984.

13. Selig S. Harrison, 'Afghanistan: Self-Determination and a Soviet Force Withdrawal', *Parameters* (journal of the United States Army War College), winter, 1984.

14. Joseph J. Collins, 'The Soviet Military Experience in Afghanistan', paper read at International Conference on Afghanistan, sponsored by the Institute of International Studies, University of North Carolina, at Columbia, February 8–9, 1984. The papers are shortly to be published in a book.

15. Ibid.

16. Ibid.

17. Collins, ibid., came to these figures from various official American sources, especially the Department of State, *Afghanistan: Four Years of Occupation*, special report No. 112, December 1983 and background briefing by Department of State officials in December 1983.

    Individual Americans have claimed that Afghanistan has been costing the USSR 1 per cent of its annual revenue. Jeri Laber, 'Disaster for the Afghans', *The New York Times*, 26 November 1984.

18. BBC World News Service, 21 December 1984.

19. Selig S. Harrison, 'Afghanistan', op. cit.

20. Richard P. Cronin, *Afghanistan after Five Years: Status of the Conflict, the Afghan Resistance, and the US Role*, Congressional Research Service, Library of Congress, January 1985.

21. *New York Times*, 16 July 1984.

22. Zalmay Khalizad, *The United States and the War in Afghanistan*, paper read at the International Conference on Afghanistan, n. 14.

23. *The Muslim*, Islamabad, 28 March 1985.
24. *The Muslim*, 13 June 1985.

Chapter 9

1. *FBIS*, 17 November 1980, p. C3.
2. *Kabul New Times*, 1 January 1980. (*Kabul Times* was changed to *Kabul New Times* on this day.)
3. *FBIS*, 31 December 1979; *Kabul New Times*, 1 January 1980.
4. Thomas T. Hammond, *Red Flag Over Afghanistan*, op. cit., pp. 150–1; *New York Times*, 5 August 1980; Eliza Van Holland, *Afghanistan: A Year of Deception*, Washington DC, Department of State, special report No. 79, pp. 3–5.
5. *New Times*, Moscow, No. 18, May 1980; *Indian Express*, Delhi, 16 April 1980.
6. Ibid.
7. For a first-hand account, see Kuldip Nayar's report in *Indian Express*, 26 February 1980.
8. *New Times*, No. 17, 1982.
9. *Kabul New Times*, 11 June 1981. Implementation of land reforms was slow, it was now officially admitted. Karmal said early in 1982, '12 provinces have refused to accept the operational groups or have not given positive answers to the demands of the ministry of agriculture and land reforms.' *Kabul New Times*, 27 February 1982.

   A twelve-point action programme to implement land and water reforms more vigorously was adopted in February 1982 on the basis of a resolution adopted by the joint DPDA–Government commission on land and water reforms. *Kabul New Times*, 25 February 1982.
10. *Kabul New Times*, 15–16 March 1982.
11. *Kabul New Times*, 16–20 March 1982.
12. Ibid.
13. The text of the action programme can be read in *Kabul New Times*, 28–29 April, and 2–4 May 1982.
14. *Kabul New Times*, 1 April 1982.
15. *Kabul New Times*, 2–15 August 1982.
16. *Kabul New Times*, 29 December 1982.
17. *Kabul New Times*, 2–8 February 1983. Cessation of fighting was made a precondition for talks with tribal chiefs based in Pakistan. The statement claimed that 'a large number of the armed groups' had surrendered to the

government; 'others too are coming and joining with us. . . . We invite our brothers, we would talk with them, hold jirghas with them. We are ready to console our aggrieved brothers, dress the wounds of the wounded brothers and wipe the tears of our displaced mothers and sisters.' This appeal was beamed to the members of the resistance and the refugees in Pakistan in the name of Karmal for days and months.

For offers to talk to Pakistan and Iran, see Bakhtar news agency release of 16 February 1983.

18. *Kabul New Times*, 13 February 1983.
19. *Kabul New Times*, 9 March 1983.
20. *Kabul New Times*, 21 August 1983.
21. *Kabul New Times*, 19 March 1983.
22. *Kabul New Times*, 16 May 1983.
23. For Karmal's speech, see *Kabul New Times*, 24–28 March, 1983.
24. *Kabul New Times*, 25–26 May, 1983. Foreign trade turnover in 1982–83 was higher by 4 per cent than the figures of 1981–82. *Kabul New Times*, 24 August, 1983.
25. *Kabul New Times*, 13 November 1983.
26. *Kabul New Times*, 28 December 1983.
27. *Kabul New Times*, 2 January 1984.
28. *Kabul New Times*, 27 January 1984.
29. *Kabul New Times*, 12 February 1984.
30. *Kabul New Times*, 15 March 1984.
31. *Kabul New Times*, 25 August and 1, 8 September 1984.
32. *Kabul New Times*, 26 June 1984.
33. *Kabul New Times*, 4–5 March 1984.
34. *Kabul New Times*, 1–3 October 1984.
35. *Kabul New Times*, 13 January 1985.
36. *Kabul New Times*, 24 February 1985.
37. *Kabul New Times*, 14 February 1985.
38. *Kabul New Times*, 23 March 1985.
39. *Kabul New Times*, 28, 30 March 1985.
40. *The Muslim*, Islamabad, 9 June 1985, quoting a BBC report.
41. *The Muslim*, 2 June 1984.
42. *The Muslim*, 9 June 1985.

Chapter 10

1. The Soviet Union does not expect the resistance to die out completely in the near future. Soviet leaders have been telling Indian diplomats since 1983 that if the supply of weapons from outside stopped, the Afghan Government would cope with the residual rebellion with relative ease. It took the Soviets about fifteen years to extinguish anti-Bolshevik resistance in the Central Asian republics of the Soviet Union.

2. Statement of 22 January 1980.

3. Since 1981, the resolutions have been calling for the cessation of *all* foreign intervention as well as the withdrawal of Soviet troops.

4. From the beginning, the CPSU leaders have perceived the Afghan resistance and the external help received by it as a threat to the integrity and security of the southern flank of the Soviet Union. The patriotic aspect of the Soviet intervention has been and continues to be vigorously projected to the Soviet people. This writer's personal experience is that this aspect of the official line commands considerable public credibility.

5. *Izvestia*, 4 December 1984.

6. *New York Times*, 3 December 1984.

7. *New York Times*, 5 January 1980.

8. *New York Times*, 28 November 1984. The allocation for 1985 was double that of 1983. In 1983 Saudi Arabia chipped in with $100m.

9. *New York Times*, 28 November 1984.

10. Ibid.

11. Ibid.

12. For details, see Bhabani Sen Gupta, 'United States: Afghan Obsession', *India Today*, New Delhi, 31 January 1984.

13. For insights into Pakistan's long-term security strategic thinking, explained to the author by ranking Pakistani officials, see the author's 'Pakistan: Thinking Anew', *India Today*, 30 June 1983.

14. *The Muslim*, 12 May 1985.

15. Lawrence Lifschultz's long article has been widely published in India and Pakistan. *The Muslim* serialized it on 12–13 June 1985, the *Times of India* on 20–25 June.

    See also, for a fuller and to a large extent corroborated overview of the UN negotiation process, Selig S. Harrison, 'Rough Plan Emerging for Afghan Peace', *New York Times*, 12 July 1982, and 'A Breakthrough in Afghanistan?', *Foreign Policy*, **51**, summer, 1983; and Bhabani Sen Gupta, 'A Regional Approach to a Political Settlement in Afghanistan', paper read at International Conference on Afghanistan, Ch. 8, n. 14.

16. Cited in Lifschultz.

17. Ibid. This view is corroborated by Harrison. See his 'Are We Fighting to the Last Afghan?', *Washington Post*, 27 December 1984, and his essay, 'The Soviet Union in Afghanistan: Retrospect and Prospect', in *International Security in Southwest Asia*, New York, Praeger, 1984.

18. The testimony was given on 28 July 1983. American government spokesmen strongly denied allegations that the United States was obstructing the UN effort, and the Pakistan Foreign Minister has on several occasions denied that he had been facing American objections to his efforts to work out a settlement. Personal discussions with Yakub Khan in 1983, 1984, 1985.

19. *The Muslim*, 6 January 1985.

20. Disclosed to the author by a high Pakistani source.

21. A brief report of Shahi's presentation, carried by the Pakistan Press Agency, appeared in *The Muslim* of 10 December 1984.

22. *Pravda*, 14 February 1985.

23. The Tass version of Gorbachëv's tough talk with General Zia-ul Haq omitted all reference to a larger Soviet force, but left no doubt that the Soviet leader had administered a stern warning to the Pakistani President; *News from the Soviet Union* (daily bulletin issued by the Soviet embassy in New Delhi), 15 March 1985. General Zia at first tried to convince his countrymen that he had had a cordial meeting with Gorbachëv. Later, he admitted that the meeting was chilly.

24. Censorship was somewhat relaxed after the election; the press took advantage of the change in the political climate. Speeches made in the National Assembly and the provincial assemblies were often highly political, and these were freely reported in the press.

25. The writer found, during a visit to Pakistan, that with the sole exception of the pro-military and conservative Jamaat-i-Islami, which lost heavily in the election, every political group was in favour of direct negotiation with either Moscow or Kabul, or both.

26. The debate was not held during that session.

27. *The Daily Jang* (Urdu), Lahore and Karachi, 19 May 1985.

28. *The Muslim*, 10 June 1985.

29. That is how Yakub Khan explained to the author the reason why the debate did not take place.

30. *The Hindu*, 21 June 1985. In fact, the term 'finlandization' has always been very loosely used with regard to Afghanistan. If it is taken to mean 'non-aligned' or 'neutral', Afghanistan will be as much so as, say, Ethiopia or the People's Democratic Republic of Yemen. It is idle to expect that Marxist

rule will vanish from Kabul. Afghanistan will not join the Warsaw Pact, but will have a bilateral security-orientated treaty with the USSR—which the 1978 treaty is in fact. The Soviets, however, would be willing to include in the DRA Cabinet one or more representatives of non-communist parties, even Afghan refugee organizations on the condition that they pledge their loyalty to the Democratic Republic of Afghanistan.

Chapter 11

1. Samuel Decalo, 'People's Republic of Congo', in Bodgan Szajkowski, *Marxist Governments: A World Survey*, Vol. I, London, Macmillan, 1981, pp. 218–19.
2. Fred Halliday, *Arabia Without Sultans*, London, Pelican Books, 1974.
3. Ibid., p. 25.
4. Moscow did not extend significant economic help, and rendered only token military assistance to the Marxist Government of Chile headed by Allende. Until 1972, Soviet economic aid totalled $400m. and was fully tied to projects and imports. During his visit to Moscow in December 1972, Allende had hoped to secure Soviet credits of $500m., part of it in hard currency. He returned to Santiago with much less. The exact amount of credit pledged by Moscow was not disclosed, but it was nowhere near $500m., though a small part of it was in hard currency. The Soviets also extended $50m. worth of military supplies, but Allende did not make use of it as he knew that the army officers would oppose the introduction of Soviet weapons into Chile's predominantly American arsenal. See Robert Moss, *Chile's Marxist Experiment*, New York, Wiley, 1973, pp. 202–4.
5. Amilcar Cabral, *Revolution in Guinea: An African People's Struggle*, London, Stage I, undated, p. 67.
6. Bodgan Szajkowski (ed.), *Marxist Governments: a World Survey*, Vol. II, op. cit., p. 10.
7. There have been coups in the Marxist regimes of Yemen and Congo; the Marxist regime in the tiny Grenada collapsed to internal feuds before it was extinguished by the American invasion of 1983. Struggles for power in the large and grass-roots revolutionary regimes, often stemming from the clash of differing political views, are to be distinguished from lethal rivalries within narrow-based cabals in several Marxist-ruled countries. Very few academic studies have been made so far of the typologies of intra-regime conflicts in Marxist regimes and of the dynamics of these conflicts.

8. Louis Dupree, 'Afghan Refugees and the Short and Long-term Social Implications of the War in Afghanistan', paper read at International Conference on Afghanistan at Columbia, North Carolina, op. cit.

9. Author's interviews with Afghan scholars.

10. Dupree, op. cit., n. 8.

11. Ibid.

12. Ibid.

13. *Indian Express*, 14 April 1980.

14. *Indian Express*, 18 April 1980.

15. *The Muslim*, 29 May 1985.

16. Smirnov was invited to speak, among others, by the Pakistan Institute of Strategic Studies, the Islamabad University, the Press Club of Karachi, the High Court Bar Association at Lahore, and the Pakistan Chamber of Commerce at Karachi. He made himself unusually visible for a Soviet ambassador in any Third World country, and was extensively interviewed and photographed prior to his transfer from Islamabad in the summer of 1985.

17. *Pakistan Times*, 7 March 1980.

18. This is exactly what happened. See Bhabani Sen Gupta, 'A Tale of Two Visits', *Illustrated Weekly of India*, Bombay, 4 July 1985.

19. R. Ulyanovskiy, 'The Fate of the Iranian Revolution', *Kommunist*, in Russian, No. 8, signed to press 23 May 1985, *FBIS*, Soviet Union, 19 June 1985, **III**, 118, Annexe No. 054, pp. 1–8.

A Very Select Personal Bibliography

The literature on Afghanistan is vast, mainly because of the strategic position occupied by the country between the British–Indian empire and the Russian empire. The great bulk of the literature is British or Russian. There are about a dozen histories of Afghanistan, of the British–Indian period, by Indian historians. American scholarly interest in Afghanistan is of relatively recent vintage, beginning in the 1950s and steadily, though slowly, gathering momentum through the 1970s. The Saur revolution of April 1978 was not intellectually provocative. However, millions of words have been written in more than a dozen languages on Afghanistan since the Soviet military intervention of December 1979. The great bulk of this literature is propaganda from one or the other of the several perspectives on the Afghan revolution and the second cold war generated by the Soviet intervention. The bibliographical note that follows is intended to be the author's personal guide to a very select portion of the literature on Afghanistan, meant for those non–specialists who may like to understand the issues pertaining to the Afghan revolution with greater clarity and in greater depth.

For an overview of Afghan history since the last decades of the nineteenth century until the withering of the British empire in the subcontinent, the reader may pick up Vartan Gregorian, *The Emergence of Modern Afghanistan: Politics of Reform and Modernization*, Stanford, Stanford University Press, 1974 edn, and supplement it profitably with Leon B. Poullada, *Reform and Rebellion in Afghanistan 1919–1929: King Amanullah's Failure to Modernize a Tribal Society*, Ithaca, Cornell University Press, 1973. Also recommended is Richard S. Newell, *The Politics of Afghanistan*, Ithaca, Cornell University Press, 1972.

British interactions with Afghanistan are of considerable interest and importance. Indeed, the British imperialist strategic perception of Afghanistan as a buffer between Russia (later the USSR) and British India (later, Pakistan and India or the subcontinent) has surprisingly survived many technological and power-political changes in the world since World War II. Olaf Caroe's *The Pathans: 550 BC–1957*, London, Macmillan, 1965, is still regarded as the most authentic British study of the Pathan–Afghan problem as seen by a seasoned imperialist. Also recommended are two books by Indian historians and two by a Pakistani historian: Asghar H. Bilgrami, *Afghanistan and British India: 1793–1907, A Study in Foreign Relations*, New Delhi, Sterling Publishers, 1972; Bisheshwar

Prasad, *The Foundations of India's Foreign Policy: Imperial Era 1882–1912*, Calcutta, Naya Prokash, 1979, and M. Hasan Lawun Kakar, *Afghanistan: A Study in Internal Development 1880–1901*, Lahore, Punjab University Press, 1971, and his *Government and Society in Afghanistan: The Reign of Amir 'Abd al-Rahman Khan*, Austin, University of Texas Press, 1979.

On Afghanistan itself, D. N. Wilbur's *Afghanistan: Its People, Its Society, Its Culture*, New Haven, HRAF Press, 1962 is a good, reliable introductory volume. Richard Tapper's edited volume, *The Conflict of Tribe and State in Iran and Afghanistan*, London, Croom Helm, 1983; Ashraf Ghani, 'Islam and State-Building in a Tribal Society: Afghanistan: 1880–1801', in *Modern Asian Studies*, **12**, 2, 1978, pp. 269–84; and Louis Dupree, *Afghanistan*, Princeton, Princeton University Press, 1973, together with M. Zazif Shahrani and Robert L. Canfield (eds), *Revolutions and Rebellions in Afghanistan*, Berkeley, California University Press, 1983, are among the best one can read to get a fuller understanding of the complexities of Afghan society, politics and government.

The mass circulation Soviet journals—*New Times*, *International Affairs*, and *Asia and Africa Today*—have published a great number of reports, articles and polemics on the Afghan crisis since January 1980. However, there has also been a good deal of serious Soviet writing on Afghanistan since April 1978. The non-expert reader interested in Soviet perspectives on Afghanistan may usefully read the 1981 issue of *Social Sciences Today*, for a number of in-depth studies of Afghanistan's social, economic and political problems by a group of Soviet specialists. The special issue's subtitle is *Afghanistan: Past and Present*.

The Afghan revolution and the Soviet military intervention to defend it from collapse are also to be seen in the context of ethnic and Islamic aspects of the Central Asian republics of the USSR. Recommended reading are: E. Allworth (ed.), *Central Asia: A Century of Russian Rule*, New York, Columbia University Press, 1967; Bohdan Bociurkiw and J. W. Strong (eds), *Religion and Atheism in the USSR and Eastern Europe*, London, Macmillan, 1975; Bohdan Bociurkiw, 'Changing Soviet Image of Islam: Domestic Scene', *Journal, Institute of Muslim Minority Affairs*, **2**, 2–3, 1980–81, pp. 9–25; Henry Bradsher, *Afghanistan and the Soviet Union*, Durham, Duke University Press, Policy Studies, 1983; William O. McGagg, jun. and Brian Silver (eds), *Soviet Asian Ethnic Frontiers*, New York, Pergamon Press, 1979; and Bhabani Sen Gupta (ed.), *Soviet Perspectives on Contemporary Asia*, New Delhi, South Asia Publishers, 1984.

For insights into the new phenomenon of Islamic fundamentalism, useful readings include Cyriak K. Pullapilly (ed.), *Islam in the Contemporary World*, Notre Dame, Ind., Cross Roads Books, 1980; Rudoph Peters, *Islam and*

Colonialism: The Doctrine of Jihad in Contemporary History, The Hague, Mouton, 1979; Michael Gilsenan, *Recognizing Islam*, London, Croom Helm, 1982; Fred Halliday, *Arabia Without Sultans*, London, Pelican Books, 1974;

It is necessary to see the Afghan revolution and the Marxist regime in Afghanistan in the context of contemporary national liberation movements in the Third World and the Marxist regimes born out of some of these struggles. The literature is huge, both from the Western and Soviet sides as well as from Third World authors. An interesting, short reading list: Norman Miller and Roderick Aya (eds), *National Liberation: Revolution in the Third World*, New York, Free Press, 1971; John Girling, *Revolution and Intervention*, Sydney, Australian National University Press, 1982; John W. Lewis, *Peasant Rebellions and Communist Revolutions in Asia*, Stanford, Stanford University Press, 1974; Roderick Aya, 'Theories of Revolution Reconsidered', *Theory and Practice*, **8**, 1, 1979, pp. 39–99; Barrington Moore jun., *Social Origins of Dictatorship and Democracy, Lord and Peasant in the Making of the Modern World*, Boston, Beacon Press, 1966; Amilcar Cabral, *Revolution in Guinea: A People's Struggle*, London, Stage I, undated; Robert Moss, *China's Marxist Experiment*, New York, Wiley, 1973; and Fred Halliday, *Arabia Without Sultans*. The three volumes of *Marxist Governments: A World View*, edited by Bodgan Szajkowski, General Editor of the series in which the present book is published, are most useful reading in comparative communism.

The reader will find in the Notes to the chapters of this volume references to most of the significant publications on Afghanistan since the Saur revolution and the Soviet intervention. While reading through this enormous volume of material, it is good to caution oneself that hardly anyone is or can be without bias or partisanship in a crisis of this magnitude. The reader's attention should be drawn specifically to the publications of Dupree, Newells, Halliday, Harrison and Hammond. Hammond's *Red Flag Over Afghanistan*, a very highly partisan book, has a wealth of 'secret' official documents he obtained from the State Department by invoking the Fifth Amendment.

Harrison's *In Afghanistan's Shadow: Baluch Nationalism and Soviet Temptation*, New York, Carnegie Endowment for International Peace, 1981, is relevant to the long-term consequences of the Afghan revolution in the area around Afghanistan. For the Carter administration's responses to and perceptions of the Afghan revolution and the Soviet intervention, three indispensable volumes are: Jimmy Carter, *Keeping Faith*, New York, Bantam Books 1982; Zbigniew Brzezinski, *Power and Principle: Memoirs of the National Security Adviser*, New York, Farrar, Straus, Giroux, 1983; and Cyrus Vance, *Hard Choices: Critical Years in America's Foreign Policy*, New York, Simon and Schuster, 1983. At least two useful publications have emerged from Congressional concern over

Afghanistan: *East–West Relations in the Aftermath of Soviet Invasion of Afghanistan*, Washington DC, Government Printing Office, 10 January 1980; and *An Assessment of the Afghanistan Sanctions: Implications for Trade and Diplomacy in the 1980s*, report prepared by Dr John P. Hardt, Congressional Research Service, Washington DC, Government Printing Office, April 1981. The State Department has been issuing annual and overall surveys of the Afghan situation as special reports (example: *Soviet Dilemmas in Afghanistan*, special report No. 72, June 1980). Amnesty International and Helsinki Watch have been issuing reports on human rights violations in Afghanistan.

Soviet publications have been much fewer in number than American and West European put together. The interested reader may like to look into *The Truth about Afghanistan: Documents, Facts, Eye-witness Reports*, Moscow, Novosti, 1980; Mikhail Ilynisky, *Afghanistan: Onward March of the Revolution*, New Delhi, Sterling, 1982; Boris Petkov, *Afghanistan Today: Impressions of a Journalist*, New Delhi, Sterling, 1983.

For South Asian perceptions of the Soviet intervention in Afghanistan, see Bhabani Sen Gupta, *The Afghan Syndrome: How to Live with Soviet Power*, New Delhi, Vikas Publishing House, 1982; K. P. Mishra (ed.), *Afghanistan in Crisis*, New Delhi, Vikas, 1981; G. S. Bhargava, *South Asian Security after Afghanistan*, Lexington, Mass., D.C. Heath, 1983; *Pakistan Progressive*, New York, **3**, 2, 1980, pp. 22–47; Fath-ur Rahman and A. Qureshi, *Afghans Meet Soviet Challenge*, Peshawar, Institute of Regional Studies, 1, 1981.

The Yearbook of International Communism 1985 carries an excellent survey of the affairs of the People's Democratic Party of Afghanistan in 1984 by Richard Cronon (Stanford, Hoover Institute Press, 1985). Anthony Arnold's *Afghanistan's Two Party Communism*, Stanford, Hoover Institute, 1981, is informative, but dated; as are Dupree's several papers mentioned in the Notes to the text of this volume. For the PDPA's own authentic reports, etc., the best sources are *Kabul New Times* and *Public Opinion Trends* (POT), *Afghanistan* series, New Delhi.

Finally, the reader may like to see the Soviet intervention in Afghanistan in the larger context of Soviet foreign policy and Moscow's involvement with Third World revolutions and conflicts. Recommended books are: Bhabani Sen Gupta: *Soviet–Asian Relations in the Seventies and Beyond: An Interperceptional Study*, New York, Praeger, 1976; Hedrick Smith, 'Russia's Power Strategy', *New York Times Magazine*, 27 January 1980; Roger E. Kanet (ed.), *Soviet Foreign Policy in the 1980s*, New York, Praeger, 1982; Robert H. Donaldson (ed.), *The Soviet Union and the Third World*, London, Croom Helm, 1981; E. J. Feuchtwangar and Peter Nailor (eds), *The Soviet Union and the Third World*, London, Macmillan, 1981; Rashid Khalidi, *The Soviet Union in the Middle East in the 1980s*, Beirut,

Institute of Palestine Studies, 1980; Aryeh Yodfat, *The Soviet Union and the Arabian Peninsula: Soviet Policy toward the Persian Gulf and Arabia*, London, Macmillan, 1983; Aryeh Yodfat, *The Soviet Union and Revolutionary Iran*, London, Croom Helm, 1984; J. Gregory Oswald and Anthony J. Strong, *The Soviet Union and Latin America*, New York, Praeger, 1970; and Martin McCaulay (ed.), *The Soviet Union After Brezhnev*, New York, Holmes and Meier, 1983.

Index